What People Are Saying About
Chicken Soup for the Pet Lover's Soul . . .

". . . If you liked James Herriot's books, you'll love *Chicken Soup for the Pet Lover's Soul.*"

James Wight
veterinarian and son of James Herriot

"The stories in *Chicken Soup for the Pet Lover's Soul* are powerful, heartwarming and full of life. Every story speaks to me of the special love we share with our pets. My dog Sheldon and I especially enjoyed this book."

Stephen R. Covey
author, *The Seven Habits of Highly Effective People*

"In our relationship to the world, the profoundest mystery of all is the power of love. *Chicken Soup for the Pet Lover's Soul* is about this mystery. It comes from and reveals the deepest recesses of the heart. This book is a joyful experience."

Roger A. Caras
author and president, ASPCA

"Thanks for honoring some of our most important friends on earth—our pets. *Chicken Soup for the Pet Lover's Soul* vividly illustrates how they enrich our lives in so many ways. I couldn't put the book down. You will love it!"

Monty Roberts
author, *The Man Who Listens to Horses*

"As a pet owner and lover, I know how important animals are to our sense of well-being and how deeply we love them. *Chicken Soup for the Pet Lover's Soul* is a perfect tribute to our special relationship with our pets."

Leeza Gibbons
executive producer and host, *Leeza*

". . . Three things have sustained me through the worst and best of times: dogs, cats and chicken soup. Now all three of those life-saving ingredients are combined in this collection of moving stories about the unique role that our beloved animals play in our lives. Keep the tissues handy. You'll need them."

Mordecai Siegal
author, *The Davis Book of Dogs,*
president, Dog Writer's Association of America, Inc.

"*Chicken Soup for the Pet Lover's Soul* is a happy lick and a friendly meow in your future—great reading for you and your pet in your 'Cocoon'!"

Faith Popcorn
consumer trend forecaster and founder, BrainReserve

"Simply the best feel-good collection of true stories from people who have loved and been loved by an animal companion."

Phyllis Levy
books editor, *Good Housekeeping* magazine

"*Chicken Soup for the Pet Lover's Soul* will help you heal, be happy and inspired and even save the world in the only way these miracles are possible: by sharing the spirit of hope and love that passes through all living things."

Michael Capuzzo
coauthor, *Cat Caught My Heart* and syndicated columnist, *Newsday*

"Finally a book I can read to my dogs! Seriously, *Chicken Soup for the Pet Lover's Soul* is a wonderful book—every story is a gem!"

Mathilde de Cagney
trainer of "Eddie" on *Frasier*

"These stories capture the true essence of the wonderful bond that exists between pets and their people. Every pet lover should have this book!"

Jeff Werber, D.V.M.
host of *Petcetera* on the Animal Planet Channel

"In a lifetime of loving animals, I have rarely come across anything as special as the stories in this book. If you've ever known the generous love of a companion animal, you'll cherish these stories."

Gina Spadafori
editorial director, Pet Care Forum on America Online,
author, *Dogs for Dummies,* coauthor, *Cats for Dummies*

"Take two stories and you'll feel better in the morning. Your spirits will be lifted by these true-life tales!"

Steve Dale
syndicated columnist, "My Pet World" and *PetLife* magazine
and host, WGN Radio's "Pet Central"

"Bravo! *Chicken Soup for the Pet Lover's Soul* is comforting and delicious."

Bea Arthur
actress

CHICKEN SOUP FOR THE PET LOVER'S SOUL

Stories About Pets as Teachers, Healers, Heroes and Friends

Jack Canfield
Mark Victor Hansen
Marty Becker, D.V.M.
Carol Kline

Health Communications, Inc.
Deerfield Beach, Florida

www.hci-online.com

We would like to acknowledge the following publishers and individuals for permission to reprint the following material. (Note: The stories that were penned anonymously, that are public domain, or that were written by Jack Canfield, Mark Victor Hansen, Marty Becker or Carol Kline are not included in this listing.)

After an exhaustive search, we were unable to find the authors or copyright holders of the following stories, which we have included in the book:

Things We Can Learn from a Dog by Author Unknown

The Rainbow Bridge by Author Unknown

If you are, or if you know, the authors or copyright holders, please contact us and we will properly credit you and reimburse you for your contribution.

(Continued on page 398)

Library of Congress Cataloging-in-Publication Data

Chicken soup for the pet lover's soul: stories about pets as teachers, healers, heroes and friends / [edited by] Jack Canfield . . . [et al.].

p. cm.

ISBN 1-55874-572-6 (hardcover) — ISBN 1-55874-571-8 (paperback)

1. Pets—Anecdotes. 2. Pet owners—Anecdotes. 3. Human-animal relationships—Anecdotes. I. Canfield, Jack

SF416.C48 1998 97-50409

818'.540308036—dc21 CIP

ISBN 1-55874-571-8 (trade paper) — ISBN 1-55874-572-6 (hardcover)

Publisher: Health Communications, Inc.
3201 S.W. 15th Street
Deerfield Beach, FL 33442-8190

Cover illustration by Jan Bryan-Hunt, courtesy of Hallmark Licensing Inc., Kansas City, Missouri, ©1998.

This book is dedicated with love to:
the millions of devoted and caring pet lovers of the world, and to *all* the animals who share the earth with us, especially the world's pets, who show us what it means to love fully and unconditionally.

We also dedicate this book to all veterinarians and their team members, whose big hearts and dedicated, compassionate service make us proud beyond measure to honor and support them.

To our hero, James Herriot, the Yorkshire veterinarian who has touched the lives of millions of people and forever changed the way we view the special connection between mankind and the rest of the animal kingdom.
May his star always shine brightly!

And finally, to God, from whom all blessings flow, whose loving hand daily manifests itself through our pets—who are our angels, friends, teachers and healers.

Chicken Soup for the pet Lover's Soul
ROSANDICH

Contents

1. ON LOVE

2. PETS AS TEACHERS

3. PETS AS HEALERS

4. CELEBRATING THE BOND

5. AMAZING ANIMALS

6. ON COMPANIONSHIP

7. SAYING GOOD-BYE

Acknowledgments

This book took the dedicated and passionate help of family, friends, staff, business partners, celebrities and some hometown heroes to make it happen!

First, a huge thank you to our families!

To Jack's wife, Georgia, and his son, Christopher, who in the midst of the pressure-filled weeks it takes to finish a book like this, constantly reminded him to slow down, smell the roses, play fetch with Daisy, feed the fish and "purr the cats." To Jack's mother, Ellen, who instilled in him a love for all creatures big and small, and whose stepfather, Fred, worked so hard to purchase, house and feed them—from the purebreds to the numerous strays that inevitably appeared on their doorstep.

To Mark's wife, Patty, who has the biggest heart for animals of almost anyone we know in the whole world; and to his daughter, Elisabeth, who often declares that she is going to become an animal chiropractor, and to his daughter, Melanie, who has decided that one of her chief missions in life is to help save the elephants on the planet.

To Marty's beloved wife, Teresa, and his precious children, Mikkel and Lex, without whose abundant love, laughter and vitality this book would not have been possible, nor worth the journey. To Virginia Becker and the late Bob Becker, who taught Marty to love, honor and serve all of God's creatures, visibly and fully. To Valdie, Jim and Rockey Burkholder, whose goodness, serenity and support have allowed Marty to marinate in a hometown oasis of beauty, simplicity and goodness.

To Carol's husband, Larry, for his deep and enduring love and his support on all levels. And to her stepchildren, Lorin and McKenna, for pitching in and doing whatever had to be done at home to help this book come together. You guys are the best! Your love and support are inexpressibly dear to us. And your patience and inexhaustible enthusiasm are deeply appreciated.

Special and heartfelt thanks to Marci Shimoff, for her incredible support and generous encouragement during all stages of putting this book together. Your friendship is a gift. We love you, Marci.

Grateful thanks go to Heather McNamara, our senior editor, who worked so hard to make this book happen and was instrumental at every stage.

Thanks to Nancy Mitchell, for her incredible effectiveness in getting all the permissions we needed and keeping all of the simultaneous "book action" straight.

Thanks to Patty Aubery, who oversaw every aspect of the production with warmth, humor and skill. You are amazing.

Kimberly Kirberger, our managing editor, who read and commented on the manuscript during its various incarnations; and Ro Miller, for handling correspondence and phone communications with our many contributors (and for sharing her story about the wild birthday parties she'd throw for her dog, Clay-boy).

Veronica Romero, Leslie Forbes, Lisa Williams, Laurie Hartman and Teresa Esparza, for holding down the fort while the rest of us wrote and edited.

Linn Thomas, Carole Kasel, Bonnie Dodge and J. J.

Aanest, for helping Marty solicit, collect and acknowledge thousands of phone calls, letters, faxes and e-mail messages.

Judy Palma, a real pet lover, for reading every story and giving her feedback so lovingly.

David Sykes, director of the Noah's Ark Foundation, for his compassionate and tireless dedication to rescuing animals and his sincere support of this project.

Jennifer Read Hawthorne, for her comfort and advice at several crucial moments. It meant a lot to us.

Fred C. Angelis, Jack's stepfather, who read and commented on every story in the book. Your feedback was invaluable.

Tami Wells, D.V.M., for her help as a field consultant.

Sharon Linnea and Ann Reeves, for their excellent and timely help with editing.

Some key industry partners, Bayer Animal Health and Iams Pet Nutrition, for supporting this book—first as pet lovers, and second as companies that have devoted incredible resources, both personal and professional, over many years to helping pets live happier, healthier, fuller lives. We would like to single out John Payne from Bayer, and John Talmadge, D.V.M., and Rich Kocon from The Iams Company for special recognition. They are special friends, good stewards of the resources at their disposal and special shepherds of the family-pet bond.

The people who wholeheartedly supported our efforts to get word out about submitting stories for our book. We want to thank *Dog Fancy, Veterinary Economics,* and *PetLife* magazines. Special thanks to Lucille Deview from the *Orange County Register,* who knows how important pets are to the elderly and featured a request for submissions in her syndicated column.

Thanks to all of the people who agreed to dedicate a few weeks to evaluating, commenting upon and improving the stories you see in this book. We could never have created such a high-quality book without them. The panel of readers included: Judy Palma, Fred C. Angelis, Virginia Becker, Elizabeth Brown, Patty Burlingame, Valdie Burkholder, Diana Chapman, Joanne Clevenger, Robin Downing, D.V.M., Lisa Drucker, Pam Finger, Mary Gagnon, Saly Gavre, Karyn Gavzer, Suzanne Giraudeau, Nancy Richard Guilford, Elinor Hall, Allison Janse, Rita M. Kline, Robin Kotok, Hale and Dolores Kuhlman, Roger Kuhn, D.V.M., Nancy Leahy, M. B. Leininger, D.V.M., Wendy S. Myers, Holly Moore, Ann Reeves, Karen Robert, Maida Rogerson, Marci Shimoff, Annie Slawik, Laura May Story, C.V.T., Carolyn Teale, Anne Tremblay, Susan B. Tyler, Hilda Villaverde, Elizabeth Walker, Celeste Wallace, Patricia Wallis, Dottie Walters, Wendy Warburton, Luree Welch, Diana and Ted Wentworth, Terry Wilson and Rachel Zurer.

All the people at our publisher, Health Communications, Inc.—especially Peter Vegso and Gary Seidler—for believing in this book from the moment it was proposed, and for getting it into the hands of millions of readers.

Christine Belleris, Matthew Diener, Allison Janse and Lisa Drucker, our editors at Health Communications, and Randee Goldsmith, our *Chicken Soup for the Soul* product manager. They were always there to support us and give us words of encouragement along the way.

Our incredibly creative and effective publicists Kim Weiss and Ronni O'Brien.

Claude Choquette, who manages year after year to get each of our books translated into over twenty languages around the world.

Anna Kanson at *Guideposts* and Taryn Phillips at *Woman's World.* Thanks for your continued support on all our projects.

All of Marty's veterinary colleagues from around the world who have helped shine energizing light on the sanctity and precious nature of the family-pet bond: R. K. Anderson, Scott Campbell, Rich Ford, Ray Glick, Bob Kibble, Mary Beth Leineinger, Brad Swift, Chuck Wayner and James Wight, to name a few.

We want to give special recognition to the father of the human-animal bond, Leo Bustad, who gave Marty and many others a guiding light to follow in their careers as they pursued what mattered most.

Other, nonveterinary colleagues who have inspired us or touched our lives in some special way that contributed directly and significantly to the success of this book and the causes it promotes: Ron Butler, Ben Coe, Don Dooley, Bill Mason, Clay and Mary Mathile, Susan Morgenthaler, Jana Murphy, Anne Sellaro, Gina Spadafori, Becky Turner-Chapman and many more.

We also wish to thank the more than 3,000 people who took the time to submit stories, poems and other pieces for consideration. While all of the stories we received were special, sadly, the book could only be so long and most could not be included.

Because of the enormity of this project, we may have left out names of some people who helped us along the way. If so, we are sorry. Please know that we really do appreciate all of you.

We are truly grateful for the many hands and hearts that have made this book possible.

We love and appreciate you all!

Introduction

We are delighted to share with you a special gift: *Chicken Soup for the Pet Lover's Soul.* These stories were selected to give you a deeper, richer appreciation of the entire animal kingdom, as well as of the pets who share our lives.

Each of the thousands of stories we received for possible inclusion in our book was a gift. The selection process was difficult, but the stories that were chosen for *Chicken Soup for the Pet Lover's Soul* all vividly illustrate how a loving, interdependent relationship with a pet is life-enhancing.

We were touched by the many stories illustrating the tremendous love that flows so abundantly between pets and their owners. In return for our care, precious pets provide unconditional love, seemingly limitless affection and "to-die-for" loyalty. They love us, believe in us, and greet us with unbridled enthusiasm all the time, no matter what.

While reading all these stories, we noticed that some definite themes emerged. The first and strongest: pets today are a part of the family! Most pet owners consider their animal companions to be family members, while many even regard their pets as children. The family-pet bond is truly a powerful one!

It also became clear that pets offer people more than simple companionship. For some individuals, having a pet to care for actually gives meaning to life: a reason to get up in the morning, a reason to want to come home at night. Pets satisfy our timeless and tangible requirement as humans to love and be loved—and to need and be needed.

Many stories we received reflected the positive influence pets have on their owners. Pets draw us out of ourselves and bring out the kindest impulses of humanity. They connect us to nature and the rest of the animal kingdom, making us more conscious of the mysteries of God inherent in all things. Because of our pets, a deeper part of ourselves is unlocked—a part more compassionate, less arrogant, not as hurried; a part of us that is more willing to share our lives fully with other beings. When that happens, we know a truer, fuller, simpler meaning of happiness.

There were also many stories about a pet's power to comfort and even heal. Our pets keep us from getting sick as often, and if we do become sick, we recover faster.

Taken together, the evidence is overwhelming: pets are good for our hearts, bodies and souls.

After reading these stories, you may find yourself basking in the warm memories of a beloved pet. We also hope to give you a new perspective on animal companions that you will put into action—loving them unconditionally and valuing the simple gifts they bring to your life. If you don't have a pet, perhaps these stories will inspire you to enrich your life by going to your local animal shelter and adopting an animal who needs your love and will return it a thousandfold. Or, if you aren't in a position to adopt an animal, you can make life a little brighter for your fellow creatures by volunteering your time—even as little as an hour a week—to walk, feed, groom or just love the homeless animals at your local shelter.

Ultimately, it is our deepest prayer that this book will positively impact the lives of millions of pets and people around the world.

Share with Us

We would love to hear your reactions to the stories in this book. Please let us know what your favorite stories were and how they affected you.

Also, please send us stories you would like to see published in *A 2nd Helping of Chicken Soup for the Pet Lover's Soul.* You can send us stories you have written or ones you have read and liked.

Send your stories to:

Chicken Soup for the Pet Lover's Soul

P.O. Box 30880

Santa Barbara, CA 93130

To e-mail or visit our Web site:

http://www.chickensoup.com

We hope you enjoy reading this book as much as we enjoyed compiling, editing and writing it.

1

ON LOVE

Love is God's creation, the whole
and every grain of sand in it.
Love every leaf, every ray of God's light.
Love the animals, love the plants,
love everything. If you love everything,
you will perceive the divine mystery in things.
Once you perceive it, you will begin to
comprehend it better every day. And you
will come at last to love the whole world
with an all-embracing love.

Fyodor Dostoyevsky

YOU LIKE ME, DON'T YOU, FARLEY. YOU LIKE ME NO MATTER WHAT.

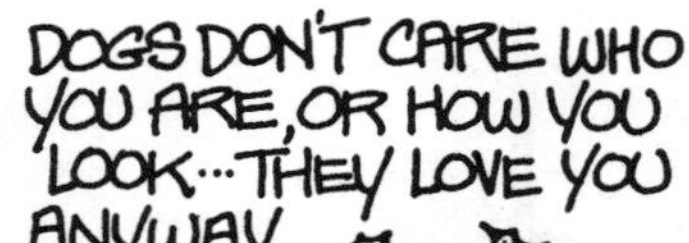
DOGS DON'T CARE WHO YOU ARE, OR HOW YOU LOOK... THEY LOVE YOU ANYWAY.

DOGS WERE MADE TO MAKE YOU HAPPY.

.... I WONDER WHY GOD LET **PEOPLE** RUN THE WORLD.
LYNN

Delayed Delivery

Stella had been prepared for her husband's death. Since the doctor's pronouncement of terminal cancer, they had both faced the inevitable, striving to make the most of their remaining time together. Dave's financial affairs had always been in order. There were no new burdens in her widowed state. It was just the awful aloneness . . . the lack of purpose to her days.

They had been a childless couple by choice. Their lives had been so full and rich. They had been content with busy careers and with each other. They had many friends. Had. That was the operative word these days. It was bad enough losing the one person you loved with all your heart. But over the past few years, she and Dave repeatedly coped with the deaths of their friends and relations. They were all of an age—an age when human bodies began giving up. Dying. Face it—they were old!

And now, approaching the first Christmas without Dave, Stella was all too aware she was on her own.

With shaky fingers, she lowered the volume of her radio so that the Christmas music faded to a muted background. To her surprise, she saw that the mail had arrived.

With the inevitable wince of pain from her arthritis, she bent to retrieve the white envelopes from the floor. She opened them while sitting on the piano bench. They were mostly Christmas cards, and her sad eyes smiled at the familiarity of the traditional scenes and at the loving messages inside. She arranged them among the others on the piano top. In her entire house, they were the only seasonal decoration. The holiday was less than a week away, but she just did not have the heart to put up a silly tree, or even set up the stable that Dave had built with his own hands.

Suddenly engulfed by the loneliness of it all, Stella buried her face in her hands and let the tears come. How would she possibly get through Christmas and the winter beyond it!

The ring of the doorbell was so unexpected that Stella had to stifle a small scream of surprise. Now who could possibly be calling on her? She opened the wooden door and stared through the window of the storm door with consternation. On her front porch stood a strange young man, whose head was barely visible above the large carton in his arms. She peered beyond him to the driveway, but there was nothing about the small car to give a clue as to his identity. Summoning courage, the elderly lady opened the door slightly, and he stepped sideways to speak into the space.

"Mrs. Thornhope?"

She nodded. He continued, "I have a package for you."

Curiosity drove caution from her mind. She pushed the door open, and he entered. Smiling, he placed his burden carefully on the floor and stood to retrieve an envelope that protruded from his pocket. As he handed it to her, a sound came from the box. Stella jumped. The man laughed in apology and bent to straighten up the cardboard flaps, holding them open in an invitation for her to peek inside.

It was a dog! To be more exact, a golden Labrador

retriever puppy. As the young gentleman lifted its squirming body up into his arms, he explained, "This is for you, ma'am." The young pup wiggled in happiness at being released from captivity and thrust ecstatic, wet kisses in the direction of the young man's face. "We were supposed to deliver him on Christmas Eve," he continued with some difficulty, as he strove to rescue his chin from the wet little tongue, "but the staff at the kennels start their holidays tomorrow. Hope you don't mind an early present."

Shock had stolen Stella's ability to think clearly. Unable to form coherent sentences, she stammered, "But . . . I don't . . . I mean . . . who . . .?"

The young fellow set the animal down on the doormat between them and then reached out a finger to tap the envelope she was still holding.

"There's a letter in there that explains everything, pretty much. The dog was bought while her mother was still pregnant. It was meant to be a Christmas gift."

The stranger turned to go. Desperation forced the words from her lips. "But who . . . who bought it?"

Pausing in the open doorway, he replied, "Your husband, ma'am." And then he was gone.

It was all in the letter. Forgetting the puppy entirely at the sight of the familiar handwriting, Stella walked like a sleepwalker to her chair by the window. She forced her tear-filled eyes to read her husband's words. He had written the letter three weeks before his death and had left it with the kennel owners, to be delivered along with the puppy as his last Christmas gift to her. It was full of love and encouragement and admonishments to be strong. He vowed that he was waiting for the day when she would join him. And he had sent her this young animal to keep her company until then.

Remembering the little creature for the first time, she

was surprised to find him quietly looking up at her, his small panting mouth resembling a comic smile. Stella put the pages aside and reached for the bundle of golden fur. She thought that he would be heavier, but he was only the size and weight of a sofa pillow. And so soft and warm. She cradled him in her arms and he licked her jawbone, then cuddled into the hollow of her neck. The tears began anew at this exchange of affection and the dog endured her crying without moving.

Finally, Stella lowered him to her lap, where she regarded him solemnly. She wiped vaguely at her wet cheeks, then somehow mustered a smile.

"Well, little guy, I guess it's you and me." His pink tongue panted in agreement. Stella's smile strengthened, and her gaze shifted sideways to the window. Dusk had fallen. Through fluffy flakes that were now drifting down, she saw the cheery Christmas lights edging the roof lines of her neighbors' homes. The strains of "Joy to the World" floated in from the kitchen.

Suddenly Stella felt the most amazing sensation of peace and benediction wash over her. It was like being enfolded in a loving embrace. Her heart beat painfully, but it was with joy and wonder, not grief or loneliness. She need never feel alone again.

Returning her attention to the dog, she spoke to him. "You know, fella, I have a box in the basement that I think you'd like. There's a tree in it and some decorations and lights that will impress you like crazy! And I think I can find that old stable down there, too. What d'ya say we go hunt it up?"

The puppy barked happily in agreement, as if he understood every word. Stella got up, placed the puppy on the floor and together they went down to the basement, ready to make a Christmas together.

Cathy Miller

Reprinted by permission of George B. Abbott.

Frisk

Sometimes, when our dog and cat patients died, the owners brought them in for us to dispose of them. It was always a sad occasion and I had a sense of foreboding when I saw old Dick Fawcett's face.

He put the improvised cat box on the surgery table and looked at me with unhappy eyes.

"It's Frisk," he said. His lips trembled as though he was unable to say more.

I didn't ask any questions, but began to undo the strings on the cardboard container. Dick couldn't afford a proper cat box, but he had used this one before, a home-made affair with holes punched in the sides.

I untied the last knot and looked inside at the motionless body. Frisk. The glossy black, playful little creature I knew so well, always purring and affectionate and Dick's companion and friend.

"When did he die, Dick?" I asked gently. He passed a hand over his haggard face and through the straggling grey hairs. "Well, I just found 'im stretched out by my bed this morning. But . . . I don't rightly know if he's dead yet, Mr. Herriot."

I looked again inside the box. There was no sign of breathing. I lifted the limp form on to the table and touched the cornea of the unseeing eye. No reflex. I reached for my stethoscope and placed it over the chest.

"The heart's still going, Dick, but it's a very faint beat."

"Might stop any time, you mean?"

I hesitated. "Well, that's the way it sounds, I'm afraid."

As I spoke, the little cat's rib cage lifted slightly, then subsided.

"He's still breathing," I said, "but only just." I examined the cat thoroughly and found nothing unusual. The conjunctiva of the eye was a good colour. In fact, there was no abnormality.

I passed a hand over the sleek little body. "This is a puzzler, Dick. He's always been so lively—lived up to his name, in fact, yet here he is, flat out, and I can't find any reason for it."

"Could he have 'ad a stroke or summat?"

"I suppose it's just possible, but I wouldn't expect him to be totally unconscious. I'm wondering if he might have had a blow on the head."

"I don't think so. He was as right as rain when I went to bed, and he was never out during t'night." The old man shrugged his shoulders. "Any road, it's a poor look-out for 'im?"

"Afraid so, Dick. He's only just alive. But I'll give him a stimulant injection and then you must take him home and keep him warm. If he's still around tomorrow morning, bring him in and I'll see how he's going on."

I was trying to strike an optimistic note, but I was pretty sure that I would never see Frisk again and I knew the old man felt the same.

His hands shook as he tied up the box and he didn't speak until we reached the front door. He turned briefly to me and nodded. "Thank ye, Mr. Herriot."

I watched him as he walked with shuffling steps down the street. He was going back to an empty little house with his dying pet. He had lost his wife many years ago—I had never known a Mrs. Fawcett—and he lived alone on his old age pension. It wasn't much of a life. He was a quiet, kindly man who didn't go out much and seemed to have few friends, but he had Frisk. The little cat had walked in on him six years ago and had transformed his life, bringing a boisterous, happy presence into the silent house, making the old man laugh with his tricks and playfulness, following him around, rubbing against his legs. Dick wasn't lonely any more, and I had watched a warm bond of friendship growing stronger over the years. In fact, it was something more—the old man seemed to depend on Frisk. And now this.

Well, I thought, as I walked back down the passage, it was the sort of thing that happened in veterinary practice. Pets didn't live long enough. But I felt worse this time because I had no idea what ailed my patient. I was in a total fog.

On the following morning I was surprised to see Dick Fawcett sitting in the waiting room, the cardboard box on his knee.

I stared at him. "What's happened?"

He didn't answer and his face was inscrutable as we went through to the consulting room and he undid the knots. When he opened the box I prepared for the worst, but to my astonishment the little cat leaped out onto the table and rubbed his face against my hand, purring like a motorcycle. The old man laughed, his thin face transfigured. "Well, what d'ye think of that?"

"I don't know what to think, Dick." I examined the little animal carefully. He was completely normal. "All I know is that I'm delighted. It's like a miracle."

"No, it isn't," he said. "It was that injection you gave 'im. It's worked wonders. I'm right grateful."

Well, it was kind of him, but it wasn't as simple as that. There was something here I didn't understand, but never mind. Thank heaven it had ended happily.

The incident had receded into a comfortable memory when, three days later, Dick Fawcett reappeared at the surgery with his box. Inside was Frisk, motionless, unconscious, just as before.

Totally bewildered, I repeated the examination and then the injection and on the following day the cat was normal. From then on, I was in the situation which every veterinary surgeon knows so well—being involved in a baffling case and waiting with a feeling of impending doom for something tragic to happen.

Nothing did happen for nearly a week, then Mrs. Duggan, Dick's neighbour, telephoned.

"I'm ringin' on behalf of Mr. Fawcett. His cat's ill."

"In what way?"

"Oh, just lyin' stretched out, unconscious-like."

I suppressed a scream. "When did this happen?"

"Just found 'im this morning. And Mr. Fawcett can't bring him to you—he's poorly himself. He's in bed."

"I'm sorry to hear that. I'll come round straight away."

And it was just the same as before. An almost lifeless little creature lying prone on Dick's bed. Dick himself looked terrible—ghastly white and thinner than ever—but he still managed a smile.

"Looks like 'e needs another of your magic injections, Mr. Herriot."

As I filled my syringe, my mind seethed with the thought that there was indeed some kind of magic at work here, but it wasn't my injection.

"I'll drop in tomorrow, Dick," I said. "And I hope you'll be feeling better yourself."

"Oh, I'll be awright as long as t'little feller's better." The old man stretched out a hand and stroked the cat's shining fur. The arm was emaciated and the eyes in the skull-like face were desperately worried.

I looked around the comfortless little room and hoped for another miracle.

I wasn't really surprised when I came back the next morning and saw Frisk darting about on the bed, pawing at a piece of string which the old man was holding up for him. The relief was great but I felt enveloped more suffocatingly than ever in my fog of ignorance. *What the hell was it?* The whole thing didn't make sense. There was no known disease with symptoms like these. I had a strong conviction that reading a whole library of veterinary books wouldn't help me.

Anyway, the sight of the little cat arching and purring round my hand was reward enough, and for Dick it was everything. He was relaxed and smiling.

"You keep gettin' him right, Mr. Herriot. I can't thank you enough." Then the worry flickered again in his eyes. "But is he goin' to keep doin' it? I'm frightened he won't come round one of these times."

Well, that was the question. I was frightened too, but I had to try to be cheerful. "Maybe it's just a passing phase, Dick. I hope we'll have no more trouble now." But I couldn't promise anything and the frail man in the bed knew it.

Mrs. Duggan was showing me out when I saw the district nurse getting out of her car at the front door.

"Hello, Nurse," I said. "You've come to have a look at Mr. Fawcett! I'm sorry he's ill."

She nodded. "Yes, poor old chap. It's a great shame."

"What do you mean! Is it something serious?"

"Afraid so." Her mouth tightened and she looked away from me. "He's dying. It's cancer. Getting rapidly worse."

"My God! Poor Dick. And a few days ago he was bringing his cat to my surgery. He never said a word. Does he know?"

"Oh yes, he knows, but that's him all over, Mr. Herriot. He's as game as a pebble. He shouldn't have been out, really."

"Is he . . . is he . . . suffering?"

She shrugged. "Getting a bit of pain now, but we're keeping him as comfortable as we can with medication. I give him a shot when necessary and he has some stuff he can take himself if I'm not around. He's very shaky and can't pour from the bottle into the spoon. Mrs. Duggan would gladly do it for him, but he's so independent." She smiled for a moment. "He pours the mixture into a saucer and spoons it up that way."

"A saucer . . . ?" Somewhere in the fog a little light glimmered. "What's in the mixture?"

"Oh, heroin and pethidene. It's the usual thing Dr. Allinson prescribes."

I seized her arm. "I'm coming back in with you, Nurse."

The old man was surprised when I reappeared. "What's the matter, Mr. Herriot? Have you left summat?"

"No, Dick, I want to ask you something. Is your medicine pleasant-tasting?"

"Aye, it's nice and sweet. It isn't bad to take at all."

"And you put it in a saucer?"

"That's right. Me hand's a bit dothery."

"And when you take it last thing at night there's sometimes a bit left in the saucer?"

"Aye, there is, why?"

"Because you leave that saucer by your bedside, don't you, and Frisk sleeps on your bed . . ."

The old man lay very still as he stared at me. "You mean the little beggar licks it out?"

"I'll bet my boots he does."

Dick threw back his head and laughed. A long, joyous laugh. "And that sends 'im to sleep! No wonder! It makes me right dozy, too!"

I laughed with him. "Anyway, we know now, Dick. You'll put that saucer in the cupboard when you've taken your dose, won't you?"

"I will that, Mr. Herriot. And Frisk will never pass out like that again?"

"No, never again."

"Eee, that's grand!" He sat up in bed, lifted the little cat and held him against his face. He gave a sigh of utter content and smiled at me.

"Mr. Herriot," he said, "I've got nowt to worry about now."

Out in the street, as I bade Mrs. Duggan good-bye for the second time, I looked back at the little house.

"'Nowt to worry about,' eh? That's rather wonderful, coming from him."

"Oh aye, and he means it, too. He's not bothered about himself."

I didn't see Dick again for two weeks. I was visiting a friend in Darrowby's little cottage hospital when I saw the old man in a bed in a corner of the ward.

I went over and sat down by his side. His face was desperately thin, but serene.

"Hello, Dick," I said.

He looked at me sleepily and spoke in a whisper. "Now then, Mr. Herriot." He closed his eyes for a few moments, then looked up again with the ghost of a smile. "I'm glad we found out what was wrong with t'little cat."

"So am I, Dick."

Again a pause. "Mrs. Duggan's got 'im."

"Yes. I know. He has a good home there."

"Aye . . . aye . . ." The voice was fainter. "But oftens I wish I had 'im here." The bony hand stroked the counterpane and his lips moved again. I bent closer to hear.

"Frisk . . ." he was saying, "Frisk . . ." Then his eyes closed and I saw that he was sleeping.

I heard the next day that Dick Fawcett had died, and it was possible that I was the last person to hear him speak. And it was strange, yet fitting, that those last words were about his cat.

"Frisk . . . Frisk . . ."

James Herriot, D.V.M.

Becky and the Wolf

His name is not wild dog anymore, but the first friend, because he will be our friend for always and always and always.

Rudyard Kipling

With all her big brothers and sisters off to school, our ranch became a lonely place for our three-year-old daughter, Becky. She longed for playmates. Cattle and horses were too big to cuddle and farm machinery dangerous for a child so small. We promised to buy her a puppy but in the meantime, "pretend" puppies popped up nearly every day.

I had just finished washing the lunch dishes when the screen door slammed and Becky rushed in, cheeks flushed with excitement. "Mama!" she cried. "Come see my new doggy! I gave him water two times already. He's so thirsty!"

I sighed. Another of Becky's imaginary dogs.

"Please come, Mama." She tugged at my jeans, her brown eyes pleading. "He's crying—and he can't walk!"

"Can't walk"? Now that was a twist. All her previous

make-believe dogs could do marvelous things. One balanced a ball on the end of its nose. Another dug a hole that went all the way through the earth and fell out on a star on the other side. Still another danced on a tightrope. Why suddenly a dog that couldn't walk?

"All right, honey," I said. By the time I tried to follow her, Becky had already disappeared into the mesquite. "Where are you?" I called.

"Over here by the oak stump. Hurry, Mama!"

I parted the thorny branches and raised my hand against the glare of the Arizona sun. A numbing chill gripped me.

There she was, sitting on her heels, toes dug firmly in the sand, and cradled in her lap was the unmistakable head of a wolf! Beyond its head rose massive black shoulders. The rest of the body lay completely hidden inside the hollow stump of a fallen oak.

"Becky." My mouth felt dry. "Don't move." I stepped closer. Pale-yellow eyes narrowed. Black lips tightened, exposing double sets of two-inch fangs. Suddenly the wolf trembled. Its teeth clacked, and a piteous whine rose from its throat.

"It's all right, boy," Becky crooned. "Don't be afraid. That's my mama, and she loves you, too."

Then the unbelievable happened. As her tiny hands stroked the great shaggy head, I heard the gentle thump, thump, thumping of the wolf's tail from deep inside the stump.

What was wrong with the animal? I wondered. Why couldn't he get up? I couldn't tell. Nor did I dare to step any closer.

I glanced at the empty water bowl. My memory flashed back to the five skunks that last week had torn the burlap from a leaking pipe in a frenzied effort to reach water during the final agonies of rabies. Of course! Rabies! Warning signs had been posted all over the county, and hadn't Becky said, "He's so thirsty"?

I had to get Becky away. "Honey." My throat tightened. "Put his head down and come to Mama. We'll go find help."

Reluctantly, Becky got up and kissed the wolf on the nose before she walked slowly into my outstretched arms. Sad yellow eyes followed her. Then the wolf's head sank to the ground.

With Becky safe in my arms, I ran to the barns where Brian, one of our cowhands, was saddling up to check heifers in the north pasture.

"Brian! Come quickly. Becky found a wolf in the oak stump near the wash! I think it has rabies!"

"I'll be there in a jiffy," he said as I hurried back to the house, anxious to put Becky down for her nap. I didn't want her to see Brian come out of the bunkhouse. I knew he'd have a gun.

"But I want to give my doggy his water," she cried. I kissed her and gave her some stuffed animals to play with. "Honey, let Mom and Brian take care of him for now," I said.

Moments later, I reached the oak stump. Brian stood looking down at the beast. "It's a Mexican *lobo*, all right," he said, "and a big one!" The wolf whined. Then we both caught the smell of gangrene.

"Whew! It's not rabies," Brian said. "But he's sure hurt real bad. Don't you think it's best I put him out of his misery?"

The word "yes" was on my lips, when Becky emerged from the bushes. "Is Brian going to make him well, Mama?" She hauled the animal's head onto her lap once more, and buried her face in the coarse, dark fur. This time I wasn't the only one who heard the thumping of the *lobo*'s tail.

That afternoon my husband, Bill, and our veterinarian came to see the wolf. Observing the trust the animal had in our child, Doc said to me, "Suppose you let Becky and me tend to this fella together." Minutes later, as child and vet reassured the stricken beast, the hypodermic found its mark. The yellow eyes closed.

"He's asleep now," said the vet. "Give me a hand here, Bill." They hauled the massive body out of the stump. The animal must have been over five feet long and well over one-hundred pounds. The hip and leg had been mutilated by bullets. Doc did what he had to in order to clean the wound and then gave the patient a dose of penicillin. Next day he returned and inserted a metal rod to replace the missing bone.

"Well, it looks like you've got yourselves a Mexican *lobo,*" Doc said. "He looks to be about three years old, and even as pups, they don't tame real easy. I'm amazed at the way this big fella took to your little gal. But often there's something that goes on between children and animals that we grownups don't understand."

Becky named the wolf Ralph and carried food and water to the stump every day. Ralph's recovery was not easy. For three months he dragged his injured hindquarters by clawing the earth with his front paws. From the way he lowered his eyelids when we massaged the atrophied limbs, we knew he endured excruciating pain, but not once did he ever try to bite the hands of those who cared for him.

Four months to the day, Ralph finally stood unaided. His huge frame shook as long-unused muscles were activated. Bill and I patted and praised him. But it was Becky to whom he turned for a gentle word, a kiss or a smile. He responded to these gestures of love by swinging his bushy tail like a pendulum.

As his strength grew, Ralph followed Becky all over the

ranch. Together they roamed the desert pastures, the golden-haired child often stooping low, sharing with the great lame wolf whispered secrets of nature's wonders. When evening came, he returned like a silent shadow to his hollow stump that had surely become his special place. As time went on, although he lived primarily in the brush, the habits of this timid creature endeared him more and more to all of us.

His reaction to people other than our family was yet another story. Strangers terrified him, yet his affection for and protectiveness of Becky brought him out of the desert and fields at the sight of every unknown pickup or car. Occasionally he'd approach, lips taut, exposing a nervous smile full of chattering teeth. More often he'd simply pace and finally skulk off to his tree stump, perhaps to worry alone.

Becky's first day of school was sad for Ralph. After the bus left, he refused to return to the yard. Instead, he lay by the side of the road and waited. When Becky returned, he limped and tottered in wild, joyous circles around her. This welcoming ritual persisted throughout her school years.

Although Ralph seemed happy on the ranch, he disappeared into the surrounding deserts and mountains for several weeks during the spring mating season, leaving us to worry about his safety. This was calving season, and fellow ranchers watched for coyotes, cougars, wild dogs and, of course, the lone wolf. But Ralph was lucky.

During Ralph's twelve years on our ranch, his habits remained unchanged. Always keeping his distance, he tolerated other pets and endured the activities of our busy family, but his love for Becky never wavered. Then the spring came when our neighbor told us he'd shot and killed a she-wolf and grazed her mate, who had been running with her. Sure enough, Ralph returned home with another bullet wound.

Becky, nearly fifteen years old now, sat with Ralph's head resting on her lap. He, too, must have been about fifteen and was gray with age. As Bill removed the bullet, my memory raced back through the years. Once again I saw a chubby three-year-old girl stroking the head of a huge black wolf and heard a small voice murmuring, "It's all right, boy. Don't be afraid. That's my mama, and she loves you, too."

Although the wound wasn't serious, this time Ralph didn't get well. Precious pounds fell away. The once luxurious fur turned dull and dry, and his trips to the yard in search of Becky's companionship ceased. All day long he rested quietly.

But when night fell, old and stiff as he was, he disappeared into the desert and surrounding hills. By dawn his food was gone.

The morning came when we found him dead. The yellow eyes were closed. Stretched out in front of the oak stump, he appeared but a shadow of the proud beast he once had been. A lump in my throat choked me as I watched Becky stroke his shaggy neck, tears streaming down her face. "I'll miss him so," she cried.

Then as I covered him with a blanket, we were startled by a strange rustling sound from inside the stump. Becky looked inside. Two tiny yellow eyes peered back and puppy fangs glinted in the semi-darkness. Ralph's pup!

Had a dying instinct told him his motherless offspring would be safe here, as he had been, with those who loved him? Hot tears spilled on baby fur as Becky gathered the trembling bundle in her arms. "It's all right, little . . . Ralphie," she murmured. "Don't be afraid. That's my mom, and she loves you, too."

Penny Porter

Friends

Twenty-one years ago, my husband gave me Sam, an eight-week-old schnauzer, to help ease the loss of our daughter, who was stillborn. Sam and I developed a very special bond over the next fourteen years. It seemed nothing that happened could ever change that.

At one point, my husband and I decided to relocate from our New York apartment to a new home in New Jersey. After we were there awhile, our neighbor, whose cat had recently had kittens, asked us if we would like one. We were a little apprehensive about Sam's jealousy and how he would handle his turf being invaded, but we decided to risk it and agreed to take a kitten.

We picked a little, gray, playful ball of fur. It was like having a road runner in the house. She raced around chasing imaginary mice and squirrels and vaulted from table to chair in the blink of an eye, so we named her Lightning.

At first, Sam and Lightning were very cautious with each other and kept their distance. But slowly, as the days went on, Lightning started following Sam—up the stairs, down the stairs, into the kitchen to watch him eat, into the living room to watch him sleep. As time passed, they became inseparable. When they slept, it was always together; when they ate, it was always next to each other. When I played with one, the other joined in. If Sam barked at something, Lightning ran to see what it was. When I took either one out of the house, the other was always waiting by the door when we returned. That was the way it was for years.

Then, without any warning, Sam began suffering from convulsions and was diagnosed as having a weak heart. I had no other choice but to have him put down. The pain of making that decision, however, was nothing compared with what I experienced when I had to leave Sam at the vet and walk into our house alone. This time, there was no Sam for Lightning to greet and no way to explain why she would never see her friend again.

In the days that followed, Lightning seemed heartbroken. She could not tell me in words that she was suffering, but I could see the pain and disappointment in her eyes whenever anyone opened the front door, or the hope whenever she heard a dog bark.

The weeks wore on and the cat's sorrow seemed to be lifting. One day as I walked into our living room, I happened to glance down on the floor next to our sofa where we had a sculptured replica of Sam that we had bought a few years before. Lying next to the statue, one arm wrapped around the statue's neck, was Lightning, contentedly sleeping with her best friend.

Karen Del Tufo

The Puppy Express

The Topps stood on the shoulder of the road and watched as their truck's engine shuddered and died. Nancy and Joe, their two children, Jodi, twelve, and Matthew, fifteen, and their elderly dog, Snoopy, were 1,500 miles from home, stranded on a highway in Wyoming, with the old truck clearly beyond even Joe's gift for repairs. The little dog, peering around the circle of faces with cataract-dimmed eyes, seemed to reflect their anxiety.

The Topps were on the road because five months before, a nephew had told Joe there was work to be had in the Napa Valley and he and Nancy decided to gamble. Breaking up their home in Fort Wayne, Indiana, they packed up the kids and Snoopy and set out for California. But once there, the warehousing job Joe hoped for didn't materialize, Nancy and the kids were very homesick, and their funds melted away. Now it was January and, the gamble lost, they were on their way back to Fort Wayne.

The truck had taken them as far as Rock Springs, Wyoming, but now there was nothing to do but sell it to a junk dealer for twenty-five dollars and hitch a ride to the bus station. Two pieces of bad news greeted them at the station. Four tickets to Fort Wayne came to much more money than they had, and dogs were not allowed on the bus.

"But we've got to take Snoopy with us." Nancy pleaded with the ticket-seller, tears welling in her eyes.

Joe drew her away from the window. It was no use getting upset about Snoopy, he told her, until they figured how to get themselves on the bus. With no choice but to ask for help, they called Travelers' Aid, and with kind efficiency, the local representative arranged for a motel room for them for the night. There, with their boxes and bags piled around them, they put in a call to relatives back home, who promised to get together money for the fare and wire it the next day.

"But what about Snoopy?" Matthew said as soon as his parents got off the phone.

"We can't go without Snoopy," Jodi stated flatly. At seventeen, Snoopy, a beagle-dachshund mix, had a bit of a heart condition and some kidney problems, and the family worried about her.

Joe picked up the little dog. "Snoopy," he said, tugging her floppy ears in the way she liked. "I think you're going to have to hitchhike."

"Don't tease, Joe," said Nancy shortly.

"I'm not teasing, honey," he assured her, tucking Snoopy into the crook of his arm. "I'm going to try to find an eastbound trucker to take the old girl back for us."

At the local truck stop, Joe sat Snoopy on a stool beside him while he fell into conversation with drivers who stopped to pet her. "Gee, I'd like to help you out," one after another said. "She's awful cute and I wouldn't mind the company, but I'm not going through Fort Wayne this trip." The only driver who could have taken her picked Snoopy up and looked at her closely. "Naw," the man growled, "with an old dog like her, there'd be too many pit stops. I got to make time." Still hopeful, Joe tacked up a sign and gave the motel's phone number.

"Somebody'll call before bus time tomorrow," he predicted to the kids when he and Snoopy got back to the motel.

"But suppose nobody does?" Jodi said.

Joe answered, "Sweetie, we've got to be on that bus. The Travelers' Aid can only pay for us to stay here one night."

The next day Joe went off to collect the wired funds while Nancy and the kids sorted through their possessions, trying to decide what could be crammed into the six pieces of baggage they were allowed on the bus and what had to be left behind. Ordinarily Snoopy would have napped, but now her eyes followed every move of Nancy and the children, and if one of them paused to think, even for a minute, Snoopy nosed at the idle hand, asking to be touched, to be held.

"She knows," Jodi said, cradling her. "She knows something awful is going to happen."

The Travelers' Aid representative arrived to take the belongings they couldn't pack for donation to the local thrift shop. A nice man, he was caught between being sympathetic and being practical when he looked at Snoopy. "Seventeen is really old for a dog," he said gently. "Maybe you just have to figure she's had a long life and a good one." When nobody spoke, he took a deep breath. "If you want, you can leave her with me and I'll have her put to sleep after you've gone."

The children looked at Nancy but said nothing; they understood there wasn't any choice and they didn't want to make it harder on their mother by protesting. Nancy bowed her head. She thought of all the walks, all the romps, all the picnics, all the times she'd gone in to kiss the children goodnight and Snoopy had lifted her head to be kissed too.

"Thank you," she told the man. "It's kind of you to offer. But no. No," she repeated firmly, "Snoopy's part of the family, and families don't give up on each other." She reached for the telephone book, looked up "Kennels" in the Yellow Pages, and began dialing. Scrupulously, she started each call with the explanation that the family was down on their luck. "But," she begged, "if you'll just keep our little dog until we can find a way to get her to Fort Wayne, I give you my word we'll pay. Please trust me. Please."

A veterinary clinic, which also boarded pets, finally agreed, and the Travelers' Aid representative drove them to the place. Nancy was the last to say good-bye. She knelt and took Snoopy's frosted muzzle in her hands. "You know we'd never leave you if we could help it," she whispered, "so don't give up; don't you dare give up. We'll get you back somehow. I promise."

Once back in Fort Wayne, the Topps found a mobile home to rent, one of Joe's brothers gave them his old car, sisters-in-law provided pots and pans and bed linens, the children returned to their old schools, and Nancy and Joe found jobs. Bit by bit the family got itself together. But the circle had a painful gap in it. Snoopy was missing. Every day Nancy telephoned a different moving company, a different trucking company, begging for a ride for Snoopy. Every day Jodi and Matthew came through the door asking if she'd had any luck, and she had to say no.

By March, they'd been back in Fort Wayne six weeks and Nancy was in despair. She dreaded hearing from Wyoming that Snoopy had died out there, never knowing how hard they'd tried to get her back. One day, having tried everything else, she telephoned the Fort Wayne Department of Animal Control and told them the story.

"I don't know what I can do to help," the director, a man named Rod, said when she'd finished. "But I'll tell you this: I'm sure going to try."

A week later, he too had exhausted the obvious approaches. Snoopy was too frail to be shipped in the unheated baggage compartment of a plane. A professional animal transporting company wanted $665 to bring her east. Shipping companies refused to be responsible for her. Rod hung up from his latest call and shook his head. "I wish the old-time Pony Express was still in existence," he remarked to his assistant, Skip. "They'd have brought the dog back."

"They'd have passed her along from one driver to another. It would've been a Puppy Express," Skip joked.

Rod thought for a minute. "By golly, that may be the answer." He got out a map and a list of animal shelters in Wyoming, Nebraska, Iowa, Illinois and Indiana, and began telephoning. Could he enlist enough volunteers to put together a Puppy Express to transport Snoopy by stages across five states? Would enough people believe it mattered so for a little seventeen-year-old dog to be reunited with her family that they'd drive a hundred or so miles west to pick her up and another hundred or so miles east to deliver her to the next driver?

A week later, Rod called the Topps. "The Puppy Express starts tomorrow. Snoopy's coming home!" he told Nancy jubilantly.

The animal control officer in Rock Springs had volunteered to be Snoopy's first driver. When he pulled up outside the clinic, the vet bundled Snoopy in a sweater and carried her to the car. "She's got a cold, " the vet said, "so keep her warm. Medicine and instructions and the special food for her kidney condition are in the shopping bag."

She put the little dog on the seat and held out her hand. Snoopy placed her paw in it. "You're welcome, old girl," the vet said, shaking it. "It's been a pleasure taking care of you. The best of luck. Get home safely!"

They drove the 108 miles to Rawlings, Wyoming. There

they rendezvoused with a woman named Cathy, who'd come 118 miles from Casper to meet them. Cathy laughed when she saw Snoopy. "What a funny-looking little serious creature you are to be traveling in such style," she teased. "Imagine, private chauffeurs across five states." But that evening, when she phoned Rod in Indiana to report that Snoopy had arrived safely in Casper, she called her "a dear old girl," and admitted that, "If she were mine, I'd go to a lot of trouble to get her back, too."

Snoopy went to bed at Cathy's house a nondescript little brown-and-white dog, very long in the tooth, and woke the next morning a celebrity. Word of the seventeen-year-old puppy with a bad cold who was being shuttled across mid-America to rejoin her family had reached the news media. After breakfast, dazed by the camera but, as always, polite, Snoopy sat on a desk at the Casper Humane Society and obligingly cocked her head and showed off the new leash that was a gift from Cathy. And that night, in Fort Wayne, the Topps were caught between laughter and tears as they saw their old girl peer out at them from the television set.

With the interview behind her, Snoopy set out for North Platte, 350 miles away, in the company of a humane society official in Casper who had volunteered for the longest single hop on Snoopy's journey. The two of them stopped overnight and arrived in North Platte at noon the next day. More reporters and cameramen awaited them, but as soon as she'd been interviewed, Snoopy was back on the road for a 138-mile trip to Grand Island.

Twice more that day she was passed along, arriving in Lincoln, Nebraska, after dark and so tired that she curled up in the first doggie bed she saw despite the growls of its rightful owner.

With a gift of a new wicker sleeping basket and a note: "Happy to be part of the chain reuniting Snoopy with her family," Nebraska passed the little dog on to Iowa. After a change of car and driver in Des Moines, Snoopy sped on and by nightfall was in Cedar Rapids.

At nightfall of her fifth day on the road, Snoopy was in Chicago, her next-to-last stop. Whether it was that she was getting close to home or just because her cold had run its course, she was clearly better. Indeed, the vet who examined her told the reporters that, "For an old lady who's been traveling all week and has come more than 1,300 miles, she's in grand shape. She's going to make it home tomorrow just fine." The Topps, watching the nightly update of Snoopy's journey on the Fort Wayne TV station, broke into cheers.

The next day was Saturday, March 17th. In honor of Saint Patrick's Day, the little dog sported a new green coat with a green derby pinned to the collar. The Chicago press did one last interview with her, and then Snoopy had nothing to do but nap until Rod's assistant, Skip, arrived from Fort Wayne to drive her the 160 miles home.

Hours before Snoopy and Skip were expected in Fort Wayne, the Topps were waiting excitedly at the humane shelter. Jodi and Matthew worked on a room-sized banner that, when it was unfurled, read: WELCOME HOME, SNOOPY! FROM ROCK SPRINGS, WYOMING, TO FORT WAYNE, INDIANA, VIA THE PUPPY EXPRESS, with her route outlined across the bottom and their signatures in the corner. Reporters from the Fort Wayne TV stations and newspaper, the Topps, friends and family and the shelter's staff all crowded into the shelter's waiting room.

Somewhere amid the fuss and confusion, Rod found time to draw Nancy aside and give her word that Snoopy would be arriving home with her boarding bill marked "Paid in Full." An anonymous friend of the Humane Society in Casper had taken care of it.

Then the CB radio crackled, and Skip's voice filled the crowded room. "Coming in! The Puppy Express is coming in!"

Nancy and Joe and the children rushed out in the subfreezing air, the reporters on their heels. Around the corner came the pickup truck, lights flashing, siren sounding. "Snoopy's home!" screamed the children. "Snoopy's home!"

And there the little dog was, sitting up on the front seat in her St. Patrick's day outfit, peering nearsightedly out of the window at all the commotion. After two months of separation from her family, after a week on the road, after traveling across five states for 1,500 miles in the company of strangers, Snoopy's odyssey was over.

Nancy got to the truck first. In the instant before she snatched the door open, Snoopy recognized her. Barking wildly, she scrambled across the seat and into Nancy's arms. Then Joe was there, and the children. Laughing, crying, they hugged Snoopy and each other. The family that didn't give up on even its smallest member was back together again.

Jo Coudert

When Snowball Melted

Hope is the thing with feathers
That perches in the soul.
And sings the tune
Without the words,
And never stops at all.

Emily Dickinson

Lovebirds. That's what all our friends called us when we first married.

I guess Don and I deserved it. Money was tight because we were both full-time students, working to pay our way through school. Sometimes we'd have to save up days just for an ice cream cone. Still, our tiny, drab apartment seemed like paradise. Love does that, you know.

Anyway, the more we heard the term "lovebirds," the more we thought about birds. And one day we started saving up for a couple of lovebirds of our own: the feathery kind. We knew we couldn't afford to buy both birds *and* a nice cage, so in his spare moments, Don made the cage himself.

We set our cage in front of a shaded window. Then we waited until the crumpled envelope marked "lovebirds" was full of bills and spare change. At last the day came when we were able to walk down to our local pet store to "adopt" some additions to our little family.

We'd had our hearts set on parakeets. But the minute we heard the canaries singing, we changed our minds. Selecting a lively yellow male and a sweet white female, we named the youngsters Sunshine and Snowball.

Because of our exhausting schedules, we didn't get to spend too much time with our new friends, but we loved having them greet us each evening with bursts of song. And they seemed blissfully happy with each other.

Time passed, and when our young lovebirds finally seemed mature enough to start a family of their own, we went ahead and prepared a nest area and lots of nesting material for them.

Sure enough, one day they began to find the idea very appealing. Snowball was a very exacting supervisor in designing and decorating their nest just so, while Sunshine, his face aglow with love, bent over backward to put everything just where she ordered.

Then one day an egg appeared. How they sang! And a few weeks later when a tiny chick hatched, their happiness seemed to know no bounds. I don't know how it happened genetically, but that baby canary was bright orange. So right off we named him Punkinhead.

The sunny days passed. How proud all of us were when our fledgling tottered out of the nest onto a real grown-up perch!

Then one day, Punkinhead suddenly plunged headlong from his perch to the bottom of the cage. The tiny orange bird just lay there. Both parents and I rushed to his rescue.

But he was dead. Just like that. Whether he'd had a heart attack before he fell or broke his neck in the fall, I'll never know. But Punkinhead was gone.

Though both parents grieved, his little mother was inconsolable. She refused to let either Sunshine or me get near that pitiful little body. Instead of the joyful melodies I usually heard from Snowball, now she gave only the most excruciating cries and moans. Her heart, joy and will seemed completely melted by her sorrow.

Poor Sunshine didn't know what to make of it. He kept trying to push Snowball away from her sad station, but she refused to budge. Instead, over and over she kept trying to revive her adored child.

Finally Sunshine seemed to work out a plan. He convinced her to fly up and eat some seeds every so often, while he stood duty in her place. Then each time she left, he'd quietly place one piece of nesting straw over Punkinhead's body. Just one. But in a few days, piece by piece, it was completely covered over.

At first Snowball seemed disoriented when she looked around, but she didn't try to uncover the chick. Instead, she flew up to her normal perch and stayed there. Then I was able to quietly reach in and remove the little body, straw shroud and all.

After that, Sunshine spent all his time consoling Snowball. Eventually she started making normal sounds, and then one day, her sorrow finally melted and she sang again.

I don't know if Snowball ever realized the quiet labor of love and healing Sunshine had done for her. But they remained joyously devoted for as long as they both lived. Love does that, you know.

Especially to lovebirds.

Bonnie Compton Hanson

An Experiment in Love

A kitten is the rosebud in the garden of the animal kingdom.

Robert Southey

The dog discovered them—four newborn kittens abandoned in tall grass beside the road. When I returned from my walk carrying the tiny creatures in the palm of my hand, my partner, Mike, said firmly, "No more animals." Mike had already been saddled with my dog and three cats, and he wasn't used to a houseful of pets.

"I won't keep them," I promised. "Just till they're old enough to be on their own." Mike looked dubious. "Word of honor," I assured him, never dreaming how much I'd come to regret the easily uttered words.

I made a warm nest for the babies by ripping up an old blue blanket and lining a wicker basket with it. Then I set out for the general store in the village to get advice about feeding them. "You can't raise kittens that young," the storekeeper told me. But he sold me a set of toy nursing bottles and I went home to try. I warmed milk, and after we all got the hang of it, the infants drank avidly.

Two hours later they woke and set up an insistent chorus of soft little screams to be fed again. And every two hours after that. Four times in the night, I crawled out of bed to warm their milk, and in the morning I congratulated myself that they were looking just a little bit stronger, a little bit bigger.

Mike, reporting on their progress to his co-workers, came home one evening with word that his secretary had offered to adopt Peaches, my favorite because of her lovely soft coloring. Now that she soon would be leaving, I found myself picking up Peaches less often. Idly I wondered if no longer being treated as special would affect her personality. Then the thought turned itself around. Suppose I were to give one of the other kittens extra amounts of mothering? Suppose I held and cuddled and talked to him more? Would he grow up to be any different than his siblings? I thought it might be an interesting experiment.

I continued to love all the kittens, but I chose the most unpromising of the kittens as my subject. This was the little black one Mike had named Bat Cat because he was so homely, with his dull fur, squashed porcine face and little folded flaps of skin for ears. The runt of the litter, Bat Cat was always on the bottom of the kitten heap, the last to be picked up, the last to be fed, and so the one who got the least attention. I gave the tiny creature a new name—Boston, short for Boston Blackie—and I repeated it over and over while I held him for his bottle. He would drink until, blissfully full, he fell asleep. Then I tucked him into my sweater so that he slept against my beating heart while I worked at my desk. When he woke, I snuffled his small body with my warm breath and talked to him before putting him back in the basket to play with his siblings.

The effect on the kitten was immediate. His newly opened eyes, vague and unfocused like his siblings, became alert, and he studied my face with interest. Quickly he learned his name and, when I spoke it, he clambered over the folds of the blue blanket as fast as his unsteady little legs could carry him to come to me. Now when he was in the sleeping heap of kittens, he no longer passively accepted the bottom spot; sweetly but determinedly he wriggled out from under and nested himself on top. Was it that, sensing himself valued, Boston began to value himself?

He was the first of the kittens to discover he could purr, the first to make endearingly clumsy attempts to wash himself, the first to undertake the adventure of climbing out of the wicker basket. When the others, exhausted from their tumbling play, fell asleep, he would climb over the side of the basket and search for me. When he found me, he struggled to sit up on his haunches and held out his front paws in a plea to be picked up. Unable to resist, I lifted the tiny body gently, turned him on his back, and nuzzled the star-shaped sprinkling of white hairs on his tummy. After a moment his small paws came up to pat my cheeks and bright eyes searched mine as he listened to the words I murmured.

It is said that when a child is born into this world, the first years of his life are taken up with finding answers to the most basic of questions: Is it a good and benign world? Can the people in it be trusted? Am I loved? If a little kitten can also be curious about such things, then the special love given Boston answered all those questions with a resounding "Yes!"

Even Boston's looks changed. His fur, once rusty and rough, grew sleek and shiny. At first, the luster was just on his head, but gradually the glossiness moved down his entire body until little Boston gleamed from the tip of his nose to the tip of his tail. Though never beautiful, he became so alert and merry, so trusting and affectionate, that the mere sight of him was a delight.

Obviously my experiment in love was an unqualified success. Except for one thing. In the giving and getting of so much love, I had come to adore Boston.

I hoped that Mike would be captured by Boston's charm, too. And while he agreed that the extra attention given Boston had produced a fascinating effect, Mike's interest was mainly academic.

As he grew, Boston became ever more responsive. I never walked in a room without his volunteering a hello. I never said, "How are you, little Boss?" that he did not answer.

After dinner, Boston liked to sit on my shoulder and watch the soap bubbles pop while I washed the dishes. He was in his usual spot one evening when Mike walked in and heard us "talking."

"You're going to miss him when he goes," Mike said.

I wheeled from the sink. "Oh, Mike . . ."

Mike looked steadily back. I saw from his expression that this was a test between us. Would I keep my word to him or did I value a little black kitten more than his wishes? During our relationship, Mike and I had had our troubles learning to trust. I couldn't jeopardize the confidence I had struggled so to gain.

"Yes," I said as evenly as I could. "Yes, I am going to miss him."

Soon all but Boston went to new homes. When Mike came home with word of a church fair that was requesting kittens be donated for sale at a pet table, it was obvious that these were to be my last days with Boston. Now when I cradled him in my arms, it was often tears on my cheeks that he patted. "Oh, little Boss, it's going to be so empty without you," I would tell him, and his eyes would narrow with the effort to understand my distress.

Mike called at noon the day Boston was to go to the fair to remind me that a description of his age, sex and food preferences was to go with him. "I've already typed it up," I said. Mike asked me to read it to him. I had included this final note: "Boston has been handraised with an unusual amount of loving attention, which has made him extraordinarily intelligent and responsive. He is gentle, wise, perfectly behaved, loves all games, likes to ride in the car, has a large vocabulary and is a devoted companion. Please treat him with the great affection he will give you."

Mike was silent for a moment. "You've made him sound like an exceptional creature," he said.

"He is," I said and hung up.

I was in the kitchen getting dinner that night when Mike came home. Boston went to the door to greet him but I couldn't; I was fighting too hard not to cry. It was a long time before Mike joined me. When he did, he was carrying Boston, who had a big red ribbon tied around his neck. Silently, Mike held out an envelope. Inside was a Christmas card and written on it was: "It's only November, but let's give ourselves a Christmas present."

I reached out to hug Mike through my tears.

"If you can be big enough to let him go," he said, "I can be big enough to let him stay."

Jo Coudert

SHE'S LOOKING AT ME. DON'T ACT TOO EXCITED. SHE'LL THINK I'M HIGH-STRUNG.

DON'T ACT TOO CALM. SHE'LL THINK I'M BORING. JUST BE COOL. CONFIDENT, YET CHARMING... COY, YET INTERESTED... JUST BE COOL.. EXUDE COOLNESS...RADIATE COOL...
HUMANE SOCIETY

MAY I SEE THIS ONE ?

WHAT DO YOU THINK ?
I SENSE THAT WE HAVE SOMETHING IN COMMON.
HUMANE

Heartstrings

Dogs have given us their absolute all. We are the center of their universe. We are the focus of their love and faith and trust. They serve us in return for scraps. It is without a doubt the best deal man has ever made.

Roger Caras

People spend their whole lives searching for love. I was no different. Until one day I decided to look in the cages at the local pound. And there was love, waiting for me.

The old dog was considered unadoptable. An underweight beagle-terrier mix, he had been found running along the road on three legs, with a hernia, a damaged ear and BBs imbedded in his hind end.

The people at the humane society kept him his allotted seven days and then some because he was friendly, and they figured if someone had once spent the money to have his leg amputated, maybe that person would be looking for him. But no one came.

I met him on his tenth day. I was dropping off a donation of blankets at the humane society and happened to walk by and see him. Looking down through the wire mesh of his cage, I thought he was an appealing little guy, and my heart went out to him. But I really couldn't take another dog home; I had four already. *There has to be a limit,* I thought, *I can't save them all.*

Driving away from the humane society, I knew the dog would be destroyed if I didn't take him. I felt so helpless. As I passed a church, the sign announcing this week's sermon caught my eye. It was right before Christmas and appropriately it read: "Is There Room at the Inn?"

I knew at that moment there was always room for one more, especially one that needed my love.

As soon as the humane society opened the next morning, their phone rang. "I'm coming for that old beat-up dog. Save him for me," I told them.

I couldn't get there fast enough. And from the moment I claimed him, he gave his heart to me completely.

In my experience, there is nothing like the feeling of rescuing a dog. Dogs are loving creatures already, but add the element of relief and gratitude, and true devotion flows. It is an immensely satisfying bond that I wouldn't trade for all the puppies in the world.

I named the dog Tugs, because he had tugged on my heartstrings, and I did all I could to make his life a happy one. In return, Tugs brought new meaning to the term *adoration*. Wherever I went, he wanted to be there too. He never took his eyes off me and with a simple glance in his direction, his whole body wagged with happiness. Despite his many handicaps and increasingly failing health, his enthusiasm for life was amazing. There was never an evening I came home that Tugs did not meet me at the door, eyes sparkling, his tail wagging excitedly.

We were together for a little over a year. And constantly during that time, I felt a silent current of love from him—strong, steady and deep—unceasingly flowing to me. When it was time for the vet to end his suffering, I held his head in my hands, the tears falling on his old muzzle, and watched as he gently fell asleep. Even in my sadness, I was grateful for the gift of his love.

For someone who has never had this kind of experience with a pet, there are no words to adequately explain it. But if you have loved an animal in this way and been loved so fully in return, nothing more needs to be said. Some people will understand that since Tugs has been gone, my fear of death has lessened—if death means finally joining Tugs, then let it happen when it will.

In the meantime, I continue my work: rescuing abandoned animals and finding them homes where they can taste love and give such happiness in return.

And oftentimes when I look into the sky and see the soft billowy clouds floating there, I find myself sending a little message: *I love you, Tugs.*

Susan Race

A Different Kind of Angel

Foaling season is a time for dreams. We'd just begun breeding Appaloosas on our Arizona ranch, and I was dreaming of blue ribbons and eager buyers. That first year the blazing coats of nine tiny Appaloosas had already transformed our pastures into a landscape of color. Their faces were bright with stars and blazes, their rumps glittering with patches and spots splashed over them like suds.

As we awaited the birth of our tenth foal, I was sure it would be the most colorful of all. Its father was a white stud with chestnut spots over half his body and a multicolored tail that touched the ground. The mother was covered with thousands of penny-size dots. I already had a name for their unborn offspring: Starburst.

"With horses, what you want and what you get are often two different things," my husband, Bill, warned me.

The night of her foaling, I was monitoring the mother on a closed-circuit television Bill had installed in our bedroom. I could see the mare glistening with sweat, her white-rimmed eyes full of anxiety. She was within hours of delivering when I dozed off.

I awoke with a jolt. Three hours had passed! A glance at the monitor revealed the mare was flat-out on her side. The birth was over. But where was the baby?

"Bill! Wake up!" I shook him hard. "Something stole the baby!" Wild dogs, coyotes and other predators invaded my imagination. Moments later we were in the dimly lit corral. "Where's your baby, Mama?" I cried as I got on my knees to stroke the mare's neck.

Suddenly a face popped out of the shadows—thin, dark, ugly. As the creature struggled to stand, I realized why I hadn't seen it on my TV: no colorful spots, no blazing coat. Our foal was brown as dirt.

"I don't believe it!" I said as we crouched for a closer look. "There's not a single white hair on this filly!" We saw more unwanted traits: a bulging forehead, a hideous sloping nose, ears that hung like a jack rabbit's and a nearly hairless bobtail.

"She's a throwback," Bill said. I knew we were both thinking the same thing. *This filly will never sell. Who wants an Appaloosa without color?*

The next morning when our older son Scott arrived for work and saw our newest addition, he minced no words.

"What are we going to do with that ugly thing?" he asked.

By now, the foal's ears stood straight up. "She looks like a mule," Scott said. "Who's gonna want her?"

Our younger girls, Becky and Jaymee, ages fifteen and twelve, had questions too. "How will anyone know she's an Appaloosa?" Becky asked. "Are there spots under the fur?"

"No," I told her, "but she's still an Appy inside."

"That means she's got spots on her heart," said Jaymee. *Who knows,* I wondered. *Maybe she does.*

From the beginning, the homely filly seemed to sense she was different. Visitors rarely looked at her, and if they did, we said, "Oh, we're just boarding the mother." We didn't want anyone to know our beautiful stallion had sired this foal.

Before long, I started noticing that she relished human company. She and her mother were first at the gate at feeding time, and when I scratched her neck, her eyelids closed in contentment. Soon she was nuzzling my jacket, running her lips over my shirt, chewing my buttons off and even opening the gate to follow me so she could rub her head on my hip. This wasn't normal behavior for a filly.

Unfortunately, her appetite was huge. And the bigger she got, the uglier she got. *Where will we ever find a home for her?* I wondered.

One day a man bought one of our best Appaloosas for a circus. Suddenly he spied the brown, bobtailed filly. "That's not an Appaloosa, is it?" he asked. "Looks like a donkey." Since he was after circus horses, I snatched at the opportunity. "You'd be surprised," I said. "That filly knows more tricks than a short-order cook. She can take a handkerchief out of my pocket and roll under fences. She can climb into water troughs. Even turn on spigots!"

"Reg'lar little devil, huh?"

"No," I said quickly, then added on the spur of the moment, "as a matter of fact, I named her Angel!"

He chuckled. "Well, it's eye-catchin' color we need," he told me. "Folks like spotted horses best."

As time passed, Angel—as we now called her—invented new tricks. Her favorite was opening gates to get to food on the opposite side.

"She's a regular Houdini," Bill marveled.

"She's a regular pain," said Scott, who always had to go catch her.

"You've got to give her more attention," I told him. "You spend all your time grooming and training the other yearlings. You never touch Angel except to yell at her."

"Who has time to work with a jughead? Besides, Dad said we're taking her to auction."

"What! Sell her?"

I corralled Bill. "Please give her a chance. Let her grow up on the ranch," I begged. "Then Scott can saddle-break her when she's two. With her sweet nature, she'll be worth something to someone by then."

"I guess one more horse won't hurt for the time being," he said. "We'll put her down on the east pasture. There's not much grazing there, but . . ." Angel was safe for now.

Two weeks later, she was at the front door eating the dry food from our watchdog's bowl. She'd slipped the chain off the pasture gate and let herself out—plus ten other horses as well. By the time Scott and Bill had rounded them up, I could see that Bill's patience was wearing thin.

Over time, her assortment of tricks grew. When Bill or Scott drove to the field, she'd eat the rubber off the windshield wipers. If they left a window open, she'd snatch a rag, glove or notebook off the front seat, then run like the wind.

Surprisingly, Bill began forgiving Angel's pranks. When an Appaloosa buyer would arrive, she'd come running at a gallop, slide to a stop thirty feet away, and back up to have her rump scratched. "We have our own circus right here," Bill told buyers. By now, a small smile was even showing through Scott's thick mustache.

The seasons rolled by. Blazing sun turned to rain—and brought flies by the millions. One day, when Angel was two-and-a-half, I saw Scott leading her to the barn. "She gets no protection at all from that stupid tail," he told me. "I'm gonna make her a new one." That's when I realized Scott's feelings for the horse were starting to change.

The next morning I couldn't help smiling as Scott cut and twisted two dozen strands of bright-yellow baling twine into a long string mop and fastened it with tape around Angel's bandaged tail. "There," he said. "She looks almost like a normal horse."

Scott decided to try to "break" Angel for riding. Bill and I sat on the corral fence as he put the saddle on. Angel humped her back. "We're gonna have a rodeo here!" I whispered. But as Scott tightened the cinch around Angel's plump middle, she didn't buck, as many other young horses would. She simply waited.

When Scott climbed aboard and applied gentle pressure with his knees, the willing heart of the Appaloosa showed. He ordered her forward, and she responded as though she'd been ridden for years. I reached up and scratched the bulging forehead. "Someday she's going to make a terrific trail-riding horse," I said.

"With a temperament like this," Scott replied, "someone could play polo off her. Or she could be a great kid's horse." Even Scott was having a few dreams for our plain brown Appaloosa with the funny-colored tail.

At foaling time, Angel whinnied to the newborns as though each one were her own. "We ought to breed her," I said to Bill. "She's four. With her capacity to love, imagine what a good mother she'd make."

Bill thought this was a good idea. So did Scott. "People often buy bred mares," he said. "Maybe we'd find a home for her." Suddenly I saw an expression on Scott's face I hadn't seen before. *Could he really care?* I wondered.

During the winter months of her pregnancy, Angel seemed to forget about escaping from her corral. Then in early April, as she drew closer to her due date, a heavy rain came and our fields burst to life. We worried Angel would once more start slipping through the gates in her quest for greener pastures.

One morning, I was starting breakfast when Scott came through the kitchen door. His hazel eyes loomed dark beneath his broad-brimmed Stetson. "It's Angel," he said softly. "You better come. She got out of the corral last night."

Trying to hold back my fears, I followed Scott to his pickup. "She's had her foal somewhere," he said, "but Dad and I couldn't find it. She's . . . dying." I heard the catch in his voice. "Looks like she was trying to make it home."

When we got to Angel, Bill was crouched beside her. "There's nothing we can do," he said, pointing to the blue wildflowers in the lush green fields, in easy reach for a hungry horse through the barbed wire. "Loco weed. Some horses love it, but it can be a killer."

I pulled Angel's big head onto my lap and stroked behind her ears. Tears welled in Scott's eyes. "Best mare we ever had," he murmured.

"Angel!" I pleaded. "Please don't go!" Choking back my grief, I ran my hand down her neck and listened to her labored breathing. She shuddered once, and I looked into eyes that could no longer see. Angel was gone.

In a cloud of numbness, I heard Scott call out only a few yards away. "Mom! Dad! Come look at this foal!"

Deep in the sweet-smelling grasses lay a tiny colt. A single spot brightened his face, and stars spangled his back and hips. A pure, radiant Appaloosa, our horse of many colors. "Starburst," I whispered.

But somehow, all that color didn't matter anymore. As his mother had taught us so many times, it's not what's on the outside that counts, but what lies deep inside the heart.

Penny Porter

Home

Eventually you will come to understand that love heals everything, and love is all there is.

Gary Zukav

A freezing downpour washed the black asphalt street in front of the small-town bar. I sat gazing into the watery darkness, alone as usual. Across the rain-drenched roadway was the town park: five acres of grass, giant elm trees and, tonight, an ankle-deep covering of cold water.

I had been in that battered old pub for a half hour, quietly nursing a drink, when my thoughtful stare finally focused on a medium-sized lump in a grassy puddle a hundred feet away. For another ten minutes, I looked out through the tear-streaked windowpane trying to decide if the lump was an animal or just a wet and inanimate something.

The night before, a German shepherd-looking mongrel had come into the bar begging for potato chips. He was mangy and starving and just the size of the lump in question. *Why would a dog lie in a cold puddle in the freezing rain?* I asked myself. The answer was simple: Either it wasn't a dog, or if it was, he was too weak to get up.

The shrapnel wound in my right shoulder ached all the way down to my fingers. I didn't want to go out in that storm. Hey, it wasn't my dog; it wasn't anybody's dog. It was just a stray on a cold night in the rain, a lonely drifter.

So am I, I thought, as I tossed down what was left of my drink and headed out the door.

He was lying in three inches of water. When I touched him, he didn't move. I thought he was dead. I put my hands around his chest and hoisted him to his feet. He stood unsteadily in the puddle, his head hung like a weight at the end of his neck. Half his body was covered with mange. His floppy ears were just hairless pieces of flesh dotted with open sores.

"Come on," I said, hoping I wouldn't have to carry his infected carcass to shelter. His tail wagged once and he plodded weakly after me. I led him to an alcove next to the bar, where he lay on the cold cement and closed his eyes.

A block away I could see the lights of a late-night convenience store. It was still open. I bought three cans of Alpo and stuffed them into my leather coat. I was wet and ugly and the clerk looked relieved as I left. The race-type exhausts on my old Harley-Davidson rattled the windows in the bar as I rode back to the bar.

The barmaid opened the cans for me and said the dog's name was Shep. She told me he was about a year old and that his owner had gone to Germany and left him on the street. He ate all three cans of dog food with an awe-inspiring singleness of purpose. I wanted to pet him, but he smelled like death and looked even worse. "Good luck," I said, then got on my bike and rode away.

The next day I got a job driving a dump truck for a small paving company. As I hauled a load of gravel through the center of town, I saw Shep standing on the sidewalk near the bar. I yelled to him and thought I saw his tail wag. His reaction made me feel good.

After work I bought three more cans of Alpo and a cheeseburger. My new friend and I ate dinner together on the sidewalk. He finished his first.

The next night, when I brought his food, he welcomed me with wild enthusiasm. Now and then, his malnourished legs buckled and he fell to the pavement. Other humans had deserted him and mistreated him, but now he had a friend and his appreciation was more than obvious.

I didn't see him the next day as I hauled load after load up the main street past the bar. I wondered if someone had taken him home.

After work I parked my black Harley on the street and walked down the sidewalk looking for him. I was afraid of what I would find. He was lying on his side in an alley nearby. His tongue hung out in the dirt and only the tip of his tail moved when he saw me.

The local veterinarian was still at his office, so I borrowed a pickup truck from my employer and loaded the limp mongrel into the cab. "Is this your dog?" the vet asked after checking the pitiful specimen that lay helplessly on his examining table.

"No," I said, "he's just a stray."

"He's got the beginnings of distemper," the vet said sadly. "If he doesn't have a home, the kindest thing we can do is put him out of his misery."

I put my hand on the dog's shoulder. His mangy tail thumped weakly against the stainless steel table.

I sighed loudly. "He's got a home," I said.

For the next three nights and two days, the dog—I named him Shep—lay on his side in my apartment. My roommate and I spent hours putting water in his mouth and trying to get him to swallow a few scrambled eggs. He couldn't do it, but whenever I touched him, his tail wagged slightly at the very tip.

At about 10 A.M. on the third day, I went home to open

the apartment for the telephone installer. As I stepped through the door, I was nearly flattened by a jumping, wiggling mass of euphoric mutt. Shep had recovered.

With time, the mangy starving dog that nearly died in my living room grew into an eighty-pound block of solid muscle, with a massive chest and a super-thick coat of shiny black fur. Many times, when loneliness and depression have nearly gotten the best of me, Shep has returned my favor by showering me with his unbridled friendship until I had no choice but to smile and trade my melancholy for a fast game of fetch-the-stick.

When I look back, I can see that Shep and I met at the low point of both of our lives. But we aren't lonely drifters anymore. I'd say we've both come home.

Joe Kirkup

Innocent Homeless

No matter how little money and how few possessions you own, having a dog makes you rich.

Louis Sabin

The hastily scrawled sign on the crumpled cardboard read: BROKE—NEED DOG FOOD. The desperate young man held the sign in one hand and a leash in the other as he paced back and forth on the busy corner in downtown Las Vegas.

Attached to the leash was a husky pup no more than a year old. Not far from them was an older dog of the same breed, chained to a lamppost. He was howling into the brisk chill of the approaching winter evening, with a wail that could be heard for blocks. It was as though he knew his own fate, for the sign that was propped next to him read: FOR SALE.

Forgetting about my own destination, I quickly turned the car around and made a beeline back toward the homeless trio. For years, I've kept dog and cat food in the trunk of my car for stray or hungry animals I often find. It's been a way of helping those I couldn't take in. It's also what

I've used to coax many a scared dog off the road to safety. Helping needy animals has always been an automatic decision for me.

I pulled into the nearest parking lot and grabbed a five-pound bag of dog food, a container of water and a twenty-dollar bill from my purse. I approached the ragged-looking man and his unhappy dogs warily. If this man had somehow hurt these creatures or was using them as come-ons, I knew my anger would quickly take over. The older dog was staring up at the sky, whining pitifully. Just before I reached them, a truck pulled up alongside of them and asked how much the man wanted for the older dog.

"Fifty bucks," the man on the corner replied, then added quickly, "but I really don't want to sell him."

"Is he papered?"

"No."

"Is he fixed?"

"No."

"How old is he?"

"Five. But I really don't want to sell him. I just need some money to feed him."

"If I had fifty bucks, I'd buy him." The light turned green, and the truck sped off.

The man shook his head and continued dejectedly pacing the sidewalk. When he noticed me coming in his direction, he stopped walking and watched me approach. The pup began wagging his tail.

"Hi," I offered, as I drew nearer. The young man's face was gentle and friendly, and I could sense just by looking in his eyes that he was someone in real crisis.

"I have some food here for your dogs," I said. Dumbfounded, he took the bag as I set down the water in front of them.

"You brought water, too?" he asked incredulously. We

both knelt down next to the older dog, and the puppy greeted me enthusiastically.

"That one there is T. C., and this one's Dog. I'm Wayne." The sad, older dog stopped crying long enough to see what was in the container.

"What happened, Wayne?" I asked. I felt a bit intrusive, but he answered me directly and simply. "Well, I just moved out here from Arizona and haven't been able to find work. I'm at the point where I can't even feed the dogs."

"Where are you living?"

"In that truck right there." He pointed to a dilapidated old vehicle that was parked close by. It had an extra long bed with a shell, so at least they had shelter from the elements.

The pup had climbed onto my lap and settled in. I asked Wayne what type of work he did.

"I'm a mechanic and a welder," he said. "But there's nothing out here for either. I've looked and looked. These dogs are my family; I hate to have to sell them, but I just can't afford to feed them."

He kept saying it over and over. He didn't want to sell them, but he couldn't feed them. An awful look came over his face every time he repeated it. It was as if he might have to give up a child.

The time seemed right to casually pass over the twenty-dollar bill, hoping I wouldn't further damage his already shaky pride. "Here. Use this to buy yourself something to eat."

"Well, thanks," he slowly replied, unable to look me in the face. "This could get us a room for the night, too."

"How long have you been out here?"

"All day."

"Hasn't anyone else stopped?"

"No, you're the first." It was late afternoon and quickly

getting dark. Here in the desert, when the sun dropped, the temperature would dip into the thirties.

My mind went into fast-forward as I pictured the three of them going without even a single meal today, perhaps for several days, and spending many long, cold hours cooped up in their inadequate, makeshift shelter.

Seeing people beg for food isn't anything new in this city. But this man stood out because he wasn't asking for food for himself. He was more concerned with keeping his dogs fed than with his own welfare. As a pet-parent of nine well-fed and passionately loved dogs of my own, it hit a deep chord in me.

I don't think I'll ever really know what came over me at that moment, inspiring me to do what I did next, but I just knew it was something I had to do. I asked him if he'd wait there for a few minutes until I returned. He nodded his head and smiled.

My car flew to the nearest grocery store. Bursting with urgency, I raced in and took hold of a cart. I started on the first aisle and didn't quit until I reached the other side of the store. The items couldn't be pulled off the shelves fast enough. *Just the essentials,* I thought. Just food that will last a couple of weeks and sustain their meager existence. Peanut butter and jelly. Bread. Canned food. Juice. Fruit. Vegetables. Dog food. More dog food (forty pounds, to be exact). And chew toys. They should have some treats, too. A few other necessities and the job was done.

"The total comes to $102.91," said the checker. I didn't bat an eye. The pen ran over that blank check faster than I could legibly write. It didn't matter that the mortgage was due soon or that I really didn't have the extra hundred dollars to spend. Nothing mattered besides seeing that this family had some food. I was amazed at my own intensity and the overwhelming motivation that compelled me to spend a hundred dollars on a total stranger. Yet, at the same time, I felt like the luckiest person in the world. To be able to give this man and his beloved companions a tiny bit of something of which I had so much opened the floodgates of gratitude in my own heart.

The icing on the cake was the look on Wayne's face when I returned with all the groceries. "Here are just a few things . . . " I said as the dogs looked on with great anticipation. I wanted to avoid any awkwardness, so I hastily petted the dogs.

"Good luck to you," I said and held out my hand.

"Thank you and God bless you. Now I won't have to sell my dogs." His smile shone brightly in the deepening darkness.

It's true that people are more complicated than animals, but sometimes they can be as easy to read. Wayne was a good person—someone who looked at a dog and saw family. In my book, a man like that deserves to be happy.

Later, on my way home, I purposely drove past that same corner. Wayne and the dogs were gone.

But they have stayed for a long time in my heart and mind. Perhaps I will run into them again someday. I like to think that it all turned out well for them.

Lori S. Mohr

Priorities

I love cats because I enjoy my home; and little by little, they become its visible soul.

Jean Cocteau

The conditions were ideal for a fire.

The parched hillsides that outline the San Francisco Bay area provided the fuel, and the hot gusts of wind would breathe life into the flames. It was a dangerous combination.

On Sunday, July 7, 1985, an arsonist lit the match—the only missing ingredient—and ignited a disaster.

It started as a small fire in the mountains above Los Gatos. Fire crews responded quickly and predicted an easy containment and no property damage. The fire prompted little concern among the residents of this mountainous community as they went about doing what they normally did on a Sunday afternoon. After all, fires, earthquakes and mudslides were part of the way of life in the mountains, the price one paid for seclusion.

Monday morning, as usual, the mountain dwellers descended from their wooded enclaves for jobs in the valley below as the winds picked up and the temperature climbed into the nineties. By the end of the day, the Lexington Hills fire had been upgraded to a major wildfire.

When the residents of the area tried to return to their homes after work, they were stopped. No one could go back. At the roadblock, there were many emotions—fear, anger, despair and panic. Many people were frantic with worry about their pets.

I was one of the volunteers who made up the animal rescue team in our area. As the rescue team made its way to the front of the crowd at the roadblock, we hoped that the police would let us through. When they finally agreed to let us go into the area to look for pets, we set up a table at the Red Cross shelter and began the process of taking descriptions of pets and addresses.

We worked as late as we could that night and returned at daybreak to continue. It was a large area and the fire was spreading—almost faster than we could move to stay ahead of it. But we just kept going. A grueling ten hours had passed since I'd arrived that Tuesday morning. With a few hours of daylight left, and my van empty of rescued animals, I decided to make one last check at the Red Cross shelter. No one had yet told us that we couldn't go back for more animals.

A woman ran up to my van before I'd even parked. She appeared to be in her mid-thirties, with a smooth, blonde pageboy that framed wide, anxious eyes. I knew she was searching for a pet.

She grasped the bottom of my window frame as I stopped the van and blurted out, "Please, miss, can you help me? I gave my address to one of your colleagues yesterday, but I haven't heard from anyone. It's my kitten. She's only eight weeks old. The poor thing must be so . . . frightened." Her voice broke as she spoke.

"Why don't you give me the information again, and I'll

see if I can find your kitten," I told the woman as I pulled a blank piece of paper from my notebook. "Where's your house?"

"Aldercroft Heights. A fireman told me early this morning there were still some houses that hadn't burned."

I could see the hope in her face. But I knew that when the wind changed that afternoon, the fire had headed back in the direction of the Heights—probably to burn what was left.

"My house isn't very big. You could search it in less than five minutes. The kitten likes to lie on the rug in my sewing room, especially when I'm in there working." The recollection brought more tears to the woman's eyes.

Her expression was a mirror image of all of the other displaced people with whom I'd had contact in the past two days. I wanted so much to help them, to ease the anguish and frustration.

"What's the quickest way to your place?" I asked, looking at my map.

The woman used her finger to point out the best route. As she gave me directions, I asked for landmarks. By now a lot of the street signs had melted.

"Okay. I think I have what I need," I said, attaching the paper to my clipboard. "Oh, one last thing. What's your name?"

"April. April Larkin."

I followed April's directions without getting lost. As I got closer to Aldercroft Heights, I could see that the homes I'd passed the day before were now gone. All that remained standing were the chimneys. As I wound up the steep hillside, my gut told me what I'd find. There was no way April's kitten could have survived this inferno.

April had told me her house was exactly one mile up from the horseshoe curve. I watched my odometer. Eight-tenths. Nine-tenths. I was getting close to the devastation.

Too close. What I saw made me want to close my eyes. I stopped the van and covered my mouth with my hands.

The house was gone.

I leaned my head back against the car seat and stared at the ceiling. Tears ran down my cheeks. This was hard . . . really hard. I don't know how long I sat there. But before I left, there was something I knew I had to do. I'd have to look for the kitten. Unfortunately, there wouldn't be a live kitten to place in April's arms. She had told me she'd wait at the Red Cross shelter until I returned. How could I tell her the kitten had died, much less that her whole house was gone?

I knew I didn't want April to see whatever remained of the kitten when she returned. I had to find it and bury it. I got out of the van and forced myself forward.

Through my boots I could feel the heat from the blanket of ash as I wandered through what had once been a home. I used my shovel to poke my way through the rubble. There was so little left, a teacup handle, a twisted metal frame, a chipped ceramic vase—but no kitten. My search seemed futile.

I was on my way back to the van when I heard something. I stopped, but all I recognized was the sound of an approaching helicopter and the persistent wind. After the helicopter passed over, I remained by the van, listening. Hoping. Was it a kitten I'd heard? I suspected not. It had to have been my wish for a miracle that teased my ears.

No! I was wrong. Somewhere nearby there *was* a cat, crying for help.

About then the helicopter was passing overhead on its return trip to scoop more water out of Lexington Reservoir, to douse the southern flank of the fire.

"Get out of here! Move!" I screamed in frustration at the noisy 'copter. "Move!"

It seemed an eternity before it was quiet enough to be able to hear the faint meow again.

"Here, kitty kitty kitty!" I called frantically before the helicopter returned. "Please, where are you?" I moved in no specific direction, hoping to hear again the meow that would lead me to the cat.

There it was . . .

The cry for help was coming from the dried-up creek bed across the road. I dropped my shovel and ran, tripping over blackened bricks and mutilated pieces of metal. At the charred edge of the creek I stood still and listened. My heart was beating fast and my hands were shaking.

"Here, kitty kitty kitty!"

"Meoooow."

Across the creek was the wasted remains of an aluminum ladder, lying almost submerged in ash. The sound had come from there. When I reached the ladder, I gasped. There, huddled next to the first rung, was the tiniest soot-covered kitten I'd ever seen. With the bluest of eyes, it looked up at me and meowed.

"Oh, you poor thing. Come here." I reached down and carefully picked up the kitten. Holding it in midair in front of me, I saw that her whiskers were singed and her paws burnt . . . but she was alive.

"Is your mom going to be glad to see you," I said, as I cuddled the kitten in my arms. Several times I moved her close enough to kiss her dirty pink nose. I could feel her fur dry my tears. The kitten continued to meow, but it was a relieved meow. She knew she was safe.

When I got into the van, I grabbed an extra bandanna and poured some water on it. I laid the damp cloth across my lap and placed the kitten on it. Immediately she started to lick the bandanna, sucking up some of the moisture. It had been three days since she'd had anything to drink or eat. I waited to feed her, not sure how much I should offer her.

As we descended from the Heights, the kitten began to purr. I stroked her forehead, and tiny blotches of white fur began to appear through the black coating. She had started to groom herself but I tried to discourage her. Ingesting that much soot couldn't be good for her. Within a few minutes, the kitten was asleep.

As I got closer to the Red Cross shelter, I began to practice how I was going to tell April about her house. How do you break that kind of news to someone?

April was waiting, as promised. As she ran to my van, I held the kitten up so she could see it, and for a while I forgot the house in Aldercroft Heights. I just wanted to savor the joy of this reunion.

"Agatha!" she screamed. "Agatha!"

April was hysterical when I handed the kitten to her through my open window. She couldn't talk. Instead she laughed and cried, and held the kitten tightly against her chest. Agatha just purred.

As all this went on, I got out of the van and waited for the inevitable question. When April began to calm down, I decided it was time to tell her.

"I can't tell you how happy I am that I found Agatha," I said, then hesitated. "I just wish there might've been some way I could have saved your home, too."

"It's gone?"

I nodded. "I'm so sorry, April. There's nothing left." I couldn't hold back my tears.

April Larkin freed an arm and pulled me toward her.

"You saved what was important," she whispered. "You saved what was important."

Her words still echo in my heart.

Terri Crisp

Pepper's Place

Love stretches your heart and makes you big inside.

Margaret Abigail Walker

As we turned the key to open our little pet shop for the day, we heard the persistent ring of the telephone. I ran for the phone while my husband acknowledged the excited greetings from the cockatiels, canaries and puppies. It wasn't uncommon to receive an early morning phone call, but the voice of this caller seemed different. The voice was raspy, and I detected an air of sadness. The elderly caller did not have a question, but rather a story to tell.

"You see," the gentleman explained, "my wife and I were just sitting down to breakfast alone. We used to have a schnauzer whose name was Pepper." The man went on to share how Pepper had been with them every morning for the past sixteen years as they ate breakfast, drank their coffee and read the morning paper. "He was a member of the family," the man said. Pepper had been with them when their last child left home. He was there when the man's wife became ill and was hospitalized. Pepper had always been there—until this morning.

He went on, "Time passes more quickly than we realize, and time isn't always kind." It happened that Pepper had developed a severe case of arthritis. They waited out the winter, they waited for spring, they waited until yesterday. Pepper was in constant pain, needed to be helped outside, and the man and his wife couldn't watch his suffering any longer. So together, he and his wife, Ruth, and their veterinarian made the decision to "let Pepper go."

His voice cracking, he said, "He was the best dog, and today is our first day alone, and we're having a hard time of it." They didn't want another dog. No other dog could begin to replace Pepper, but they were just curious. "Do you carry schnauzer puppies? Male puppies? Salt-and-pepper male schnauzer puppies?"

I said that we did, in fact, have two male salt-and-pepper schnauzer puppies on hand. "You do?" the aged voice asked incredulously. Not that they would ever or could ever replace Pepper, and besides, "Ruth has an appointment so we won't be coming this morning." We said good-bye and hung up.

The shop filled with people, and soon thoughts of Pepper and his loving family were replaced with the hectic activity of attending to the customers and the attention-seeking residents of the pet shop.

We were still bustling about at mid-morning when two elderly gentlemen came in the door. I knew the one man instantly. His face, weathered and sad, mirrored the voice I heard that morning on the phone.

He introduced himself. "My name is Bill," he said. "Ruth went to an appointment." He explained that he and his neighbor had decided to go for a ride (thirty-five miles) and "just happened over this way." They wondered if they could just take a quick look at a schnauzer puppy while they were here.

I brought out both of the puppies. They wagged their tails and wiggled their roly-poly bodies as they chased each other and tumbled over our feet. They put on their best "take-me-home" faces when Bill's neighbor, picking them up, wondered out loud, "Bill, how could you ever pick just one?" He put them back on the floor, and we continued watching their puppy antics.

Bill seemed reluctant to pick up either of them. He finally yielded to the little one that had contentedly sprawled across his feet, chewing on his shoelaces. He picked him up with the tenderness and wonderment of a young father picking up his first child, and he cradled the puppy against his chest.

"Well," he explained to the puppy, "I can't take you home. Ruth would probably throw us both out." But once in his arms, Bill couldn't put the puppy down. We talked about the weather, his children, our children, and finally, as polite conversation does, it began to wane. There was nothing left to say, no more postponing the inevitable. Bill concentrated on the pups, saying, "Ruth isn't going to like this. Ruth isn't going to like this at all."

We watched as Bill looked from puppy to puppy. At last, shaking his head, he asked with a grin, "If I take this guy home and Ruth kicks us out, would you have a doghouse for us tonight?" With his decision made, I helped Bill to the counter with his puppy, while his brother was returned to his cage to wait for another chance to be adopted.

The brother puppy had never been alone before, and he made us all painfully aware that he did not enjoy his new only-child status. Bill, standing at the counter, watching the remaining puppy expressing its displeasure, remarked, "It's no good to be alone."

Bill paid for his purchase, and then he and the neighbor left with the puppy affectionately secured in Bill's arms. Smiles and back-slapping congratulations accompanied them out the door. With a warm feeling, we returned to our day's chores, as visions of the elderly couple enjoying the new puppy danced through our minds.

Within minutes the door opened again. It was Bill, shaking his head. "We started up the road, and I just couldn't do it. . . ." His voice trailed off. "It's no good to be alone. Ruth's going to be boiling mad at me, and I'm going to need that doghouse tonight for sure. But I'm going home with the brother pup, too. It's just no good to be alone!"

The day ended as it had started, with a ringing phone. It was Bill and Ruth. They were just calling to let us know that Bill wouldn't be needing the doghouse after all. "Well," he said, "Ruth loves the boys and taking them both home was the best decision I've ever made—on my own, anyway."

We heard from Bill and the "boys" just last month. Bill's voice had an uplifted lilt and a smile in it. "The boys are great and are even picking up a taste for toast and eggs. You see," he explained, "Pepper left some pretty big shoes to fill. That's why it takes two."

Dawn Uittenbogaard

Sparkle the Wonder Dog

I met Gene Wilder while we were making the movie *Hanky-Panky* together. I had been a fan of his for many years, but the first time I saw him in person, my heart fluttered—I was hooked. It felt like my life went from black and white to Technicolor. Gene was funny and athletic and handsome, and he smelled good. I was bitten with love and you can tell it in the movie. The brash and feisty comedienne everyone knew from *Saturday Night Live* turned into this shy, demure ingenue with knocking knees. It wasn't good for my movie career, but it changed my life.

Up to that point, I had been a workaholic. I'd taken one job after another for over ten years. But just looking at Gene made me want to stop . . . made me want to cook . . . made me want to start a garden . . . to have a family and settle down.

But Gene was in no hurry to make a commitment. We were together on and off for the next two-and-a-half years. My new "career" became getting him to marry me.

During that time, Gene took me to France. It was a marvelous vacation and I learned to love France as much as Gene did.

But not long after our trip to France, we broke up. Gene said he was suffocating, that my needs were smothering him. I was heartsick, filled with love and with nowhere to put it. I decided to get a dog. I love dogs, but *Saturday Night Live* and New York City and my career weren't conducive to having pets. My cousins in Detroit used to raise and show Yorkshire terriers, so I made a desperate call to them to help me find a dog that was female, already housebroken and small enough that I could travel with her.

They found Sparkle. Glorious Sparkle with her coal-dark eyes and gray-blond hair, and her nose like a tiny black button.

Sparkle was a perfect life-form, so little, only five pounds. I designed her haircut 'cause I didn't like the way Yorkies look ordinarily, so I had her clipped very short on her body and her head cut square like a little bear with Dumbo ears. I put various bows and barrettes in her hair to keep it out of her eyes, and she always seemed pleased with the process.

I became one of those people who show you endless pictures of their dog, and all the pictures look alike.

I took her on television with me when I was afraid to go alone. She was on the David Letterman show where she did a Stupid Pet Trick: she took a bow on command. She did it on camera perfectly right the first time and they did an instant replay of it.

Sparkle always went through things with me. She loved me no matter what I did. I think dogs are the most amazing creatures; they give unconditional love. For me they are the role model for being alive.

Gene and I were split up for about five weeks, and when we got back together it was under new conditions because there was Sparkle—it wasn't just me, it was me and Sparkle.

The next summer, we went back to the south of France and took Sparkle with us. The French people love dogs. They went crazy for ours. She not only opened doors; she opened their faces and their personalities. Sparkle was allowed to go everywhere with us. She ate in the restaurants sitting on her own chair. She got a real chance to go out and see other people, and she was treated like a queen. I called it the dog's holiday.

When we returned, I had a lot of work. But I still had plenty of time to involve Gene in endless conversations about commitment and meaningful relationships and child-rearing and meaningful relationships and commitment. He was still fighting for independence and I was all for smothering suffocation.

It wasn't long before Gene and Sparkle and I were on our way for our holiday in France again. We were taking an early morning flight and because we had the dog, they put us in a private passenger lounge to wait. I put Sparkle down on the floor and she was running around being cute when I saw her sniffing something in a corner. When I knelt down, there were these little turquoise pellets spilling out of a box on the floor. The box clearly said RAT POISON. I gasped—I didn't know if Sparkle had eaten a pellet or not. Gene said, "She wouldn't eat that," but I was frightened. What if she had eaten one?

We called the poison center and gave them the number on the box and the name of the poison. "Get her to a vet immediately," said the voice on the other end. I just picked up Sparkle, said to Gene, "I am going to the vet, I will meet you in New York later," kissed him good-bye and ran out. My luggage was already on the plane, which was scheduled to leave in twenty minutes.

I flagged down a limo that was just dropping somebody off. I was panicked now—the hysterical mother—screaming, "Get us to the nearest vet!"

We found Airport Cities Animal Hospital in Inglewood, and I rushed the dog in. The vet was just getting to work and putting on his coat when I ran in yelling, "My dog ate rat poison!" I was white as a ghost but Sparkle was wagging her tail. He was a wonderful vet; I gave him the information, he called the poison center and they told him what to do. He gave Sparkle an injection that caused her to throw up a turquoise pellet—she *had* eaten one. If I hadn't spotted that box, Sparkle would have gradually gotten ill and then died, and we wouldn't have known why.

I stayed the whole day in the vet's office holding Sparkle. The injection had made her anxious and she trembled all day. She had to go on a program of injections for two weeks, in case any pellet had dissolved and gone into her system. The vet let me take her home. I still had to take her back every day for the injections, so when Gene called me from his stopover in New York, I said to him: "You go on to France. You need the holiday and there is nothing you can do here. I'll take care of Sparkle now and when you get back, everything will be fine."

Gene did go, but he went thinking, *Well, she has definitely grown up.* I wouldn't let him out of my sight before then, and this was me acting in a very responsible way.

When Gene came back from France, he gave me an engagement ring. Our cousin Buddy refers to it as the time when Sparkle tried to commit suicide because Gene wasn't marrying Gilda. He believes that Sparkle's "suicide attempt" was what turned Gene around and made him actually ask me to get married.

So you can see why I owe a great deal to that dog.

Gilda Radner

Pet Love

Animals have always been a way of life with my family. I never thought of myself as an "only child" because our pets were my playmates and confidants. I cannot remember any family high spot, or crisis, or joy, or sorrow that didn't include whatever pets we had at the time. More than once in my life I have dried my tears on soft, silky ears! This was never more true than when my husband, Allen Ludden, died.

Life does not come equipped with an instruction manual, and neither does death. Allen and I had worked together on and off during almost eighteen years of marriage, but in our private life we were always very much a team. As well as lovers, we were each other's critic, editor, fan and friend. While we had had two long years to get used to the idea, when he died I was shattered. My first instinct was to crawl away somewhere to mourn in private, and to some extent I suppose I did. But there were two other gentlemen in my life, my dogs, Timmy, a coal-black miniature poodle, and Sooner, a Labrador-golden retriever mix. They missed Allen, too, but were not about to let me just wither away.

Pets, I discovered long ago, always seem to know what a person is feeling. After Allen's death there was a wonderful outpouring of love and sympathy from our family and friends, all the people we had worked with over the years, plus hundreds of people we had never met but who had come to know how special he was through watching him on television. My mother was incredible in her support, knowing just when to move in, and when to stand back and give me the little space I needed. But still, whenever anybody was around, even those who were the closest, I felt obligated to keep up appearances and try not to show my grief. I suppose that was from not wanting to make them feel even sadder worrying about me. Such games we humans play! Of course I was grieving! My life had been torn apart! And while I was able to put on a great show of strength for my friends and family, I could not pull the same act with Timothy and Sooner. They knew me too well; they could read me loud and clear.

Sensing that Allen's death had left me badly wounded, Timothy and Sooner snuggled in to help. Not that I was so willing to cooperate, at least at first. But can anyone say no to a little black pest who keeps throwing his favorite toy at you, or to a seventy-pound "leaner" who is adamant that dinner is already thirty minutes late?

I had continued to work right up until three days before Allen's death, beginning and ending each day at the hospital. All at once the pattern changed, and the purpose was gone. I had no interest in "lights, camera, makeup," or much of anything else, for that matter. It was, therefore, up to Sooner and Timothy to take over organizing my day. Their needs became my needs. They gave my life definition—a reason to get up in the morning, a firm grasp on today when so much of me wanted to turn back the clock to yesterday. Timothy and Sooner got me through that first week, the first month, the first year—all those terrible "firsts."

Looking at my life I see many segments: childhood, an early marriage, ten years of being a single career girl, then my life with Allen. Move in a little closer and there are segments within segments: Allen well, Allen ill, and then, life without Allen. I have discovered that while I can never forget such a loss, I have, with time, pulled my life together. I am working full tilt, exploring new activities, taking new challenges.

I suppose, in the final analysis, I have invested a lot of time and love in animals over the years. But I have reaped such a great return on each investment. For through the many stages of my life, my feeling for animals has been an unwavering constant . . . a dependable reservoir of comfort and love.

Betty White

Little Lost Dog

Through the living room window I watched our fifteen-year-old son, Jay, trudge down the walk toward school. I was afraid that he might again head out into the snow-blanketed fields to hunt for his missing beagle, Cricket. But he didn't. He turned, waved, and then walked on, shoulders sagging.

Ten days had passed since that Sunday morning when Cricket did not return from his usual romp in the fields. Jay had spent that afternoon searching the countryside for his dog. At times during those first anxious days, one or another of us would rush to the door thinking we'd heard a whimper.

By now my husband, Bill, and I were sure Cricket had been taken by a hunter or struck by a car. But Jay refused to give up. The previous evening, as I stepped outside to fill our bird feeder, I heard my son's plaintive calls drifting over the fields near us. At last he came in, tears in his blue eyes, and said, "I know you think I'm silly, Mom, but I've been asking God about Cricket and I keep getting the feeling that Cricket's out there somewhere."

Although we all attended church regularly, Bill and I

often wondered where Jay got his strong faith. Perhaps the blow of losing a much-loved older brother in an auto accident when Jay was six turned him to the Lord for help.

I wanted to hold Jay close and tell him that he could easily get another dog. But I remembered too well the day four years before when we brought him his wriggling black-white-and-brown puppy.

The two of them soon became inseparable and, although Cricket was supposed to sleep in the garage, it wasn't long before I'd find him peacefully snuggled on the foot of Jay's bed.

However, that night I did tell Jay that I felt there was such a thing as carrying hope too far. Temperatures were very low, and I felt sure no lost animal could have survived.

"Mom," he said, "I know it seems impossible. But Jesus said that a sparrow doesn't fall without God knowing it. That must be true of dogs, too, don't you think?"

What could I do but hug him?

The next day, after sending him off to school, I drove to my real estate office, where I forgot all about missing dogs in the hustle of typing up listings.

At two o'clock, the telephone rang. It was Jay. "They let us out early, Mom—a teachers' meeting. I thought I'd hunt for Cricket."

My heart twisted. "Jay," I said, trying to soften the irritation in my voice, "please don't put yourself through that anymore. The radio here says it's below freezing, and you know there's no chance of—"

"But Mom," he pleaded, "I have this feeling. I've got to try."

"All right," I conceded.

After our phone call, he took off through the field where he and Cricket used to go. He walked about a half-mile east and then heard some dogs barking in the distance. They sounded like penned-up beagles. So he headed in that direction. But then, for a reason he couldn't determine, he found himself walking away from the barking.

Soon Jay came to some railroad tracks. He heard a train coming and stopped to watch it roar by. Wondering if the tracks would be hot after a train went over them, he climbed up the embankment and felt them. They were cold as ice.

Now he didn't know what to do. He pitched a few rocks and finally decided to walk back down the tracks toward where he had heard the dogs barking earlier. As he stepped down the ties, the wind gusted and some hunters' shotguns echoed in the distance.

Then everything became quiet. Something made Jay stop dead still and listen. From a tangled fence row nearby came a faint whimper.

Jay tumbled down the embankment, his heart pounding. At the fence row he pushed some growth apart to find a pitifully weak Cricket, dangling by his left hind foot, caught in the rusty strands of the old fence. His front paws barely touched the ground. The snow around him was eaten away. It had saved him from dying of thirst. Although his left hind paw would later require surgery, Cricket would survive.

My son carried him home and phoned me ecstatically. Stunned, I rushed to the house. There in the kitchen was a very thin Cricket lapping food from his dish with a deliriously happy fifteen-year-old kneeling next to him.

Finishing, Cricket looked up at Jay. In the little dog's adoring eyes I saw the innocent faith that had sustained him through those arduous days, the trust that his master would come.

I looked at my son who, despite all logic, went out with that same innocent faith and, with heart and soul open to his Master, was guided to Cricket's side.

Donna Chaney

"He's about five feet six, has big brown eyes and curly blond hair, and answers to the name of Master."

2

PETS AS TEACHERS

*The power lies in the wisdom
and understanding of one's role
in the Great Mystery, and in honoring
every living thing as a teacher.*

Jamie Sands and David Carson

The Gift of Subira

Do what you can, with what you have, where you are.

Theodore Roosevelt

Forty miles north of Los Angeles, there is a wildlife preserve called Shambala. With a raw beauty reminiscent of Africa, gigantic brown-rock outcroppings lay randomly dispersed throughout the sprawling land of the preserve. Shambala—Sanskrit for "a meeting place of peace and harmony for all beings, animal and human"—is a sanctuary for lions and other big cats. Nestled in the awesome grandeur of California's Soledad Canyon, it is, quite simply, breathtaking.

One day a small group of young people were at Shambala on a field trip from a local rehabilitation center. A lovely woman, the actress Tippi Hedren, who is the founder of Shambala, stood in front of the cheetah enclosure. "Her name is Subira," Tippi said, beaming. "She's a three-year-old cheetah, not even at the height of her game. Magnificent, isn't she?"

As though it were a well-rehearsed script, Subira

turned her head to the audience and gazed into the crowd. The black lines running from her eyes to her mouth were so distinctive that they appeared to have been freshly painted on for the day's exhibition. And the closely set black spots on a tawny-colored backdrop of thick fur were so dazzling that everyone felt compelled to comment. "Oooooh, look at her, she's so beautiful!" they said in unison. I thought so, too.

Tippi, a friend of mine, had invited me to visit her that day; I was sitting in the front row of chairs assembled for the visiting group. All of us continued to stare in awe—except for a teenage boy in the back row. He groaned in what seemed boredom and discontent. When several members of the group turned in his direction, he brushed the front of his T-shirt as though to remove dust particles, and, in a macho gesture calculated to impress us, rolled up the right sleeve of his shirt, further exposing his well-developed muscles.

Tippi continued, ignoring the boy's interruption. "The cheetah is the fastest land animal on earth," she told the small crowd. "Aren't you, honey?" she asked in a playful velvety tone, looking over her shoulder at the exquisite animal lying atop a large, long, low branch of a massive oak tree.

Abruptly, as though disgusted by any affection, the boy in the back row mocked, "Big deal. A big, skinny cat with a bunch of spots that runs fast. So what! Next! Bring out the stupid tigers or whatever so we can get this over with!" Embarrassed, the other members of the group turned and looked at the boy in disapproval.

Tippi also looked at the boy, but she made no response. But the cheetah did. Looking in the teenager's direction, the cheetah instantly began chirping.

Using this cue, Tippi informed the group, "Cheetahs make distinctive noises. A happy sound is a distinct chirp, like the one you are hearing now. Her hungry sound is a throaty vibration, and her way of saying 'watch out' is a noise that sounds like a high, two-pitched hum. But as you can hear by all this chirping, she's pretty happy. In fact, I think she likes you," she said, looking directly at the boy.

"Yeah, yeah, sure! She just loves me," the boy mimicked sarcastically. Again, Tippi ignored the ill-mannered remark. I couldn't help wondering what had happened to make this boy so angry and full of spite.

Tippi now turned the question-and-answer segment over to a young assistant. Then she motioned to me for us to leave. Walking away, we turned back to observe the group and now saw the belligerent young man with the smart mouth from a new vantage point. The boy, with his muscular torso and tight T-shirt, sat tensely in a wheelchair. One empty pant leg, folded under, hung next to his remaining leg and tennis shoe.

Seventeen-year-old Cory had dreamed of playing major league baseball someday. That was his one and only goal. He lived and breathed baseball and dreamed of the day when he would have a following, fans who knew he was "the man." No one doubted Cory's ability, certainly not the lead university scout for baseball talent in the state. The scout had recruited Cory, confirming a promising future. That was before the car accident. Now, it seemed nothing could replace the joy that was dashed when the boy lost his leg.

Cory lost more than a leg in the tragic accident; he also lost his hope. And his spirit. It left him not only physically disabled but emotionally crippled. Unable to dream of a goal other than being a major league baseball player, he was bitter and jaded, and felt just plain useless. Hopeless. Now he sat in a wheelchair, a chip on his shoulder, angry at the world. He was here today on yet another "boring field trip" from the rehab program.

Cory was one of the rehabilitation center's most difficult patients: Unable to summon the courage to dream new plans for the future, he gave up on not only himself but others. "Get off my back," he had told the rehab director. "You can't help me. No one can."

Tippi and I continued to stand close by as the group's guide continued, "Cheetahs never feed on carrion; they eat fresh meat—though in captivity, they do like people food!"

Carrion? The word somehow interested the boy—or perhaps it just sounded perverse. The unpleasant young man called out, "What's that mean?"

"Cadaver, corpse, remains," the young assistant responded.

"The cheetah doesn't eat road kill," the boy smirked loudly. The boy's harsh sound seemed to please the cheetah and she began purring loudly. The audience, enchanted by Subira's happy noise, oohed and aahed.

Enjoying the positive response—and always willing to flaunt—Subira decided to give the audience a show of her skills. As if to say, "Just see how fast these spots can fly," Subira instantly began blazing a trail of speed around the enclosure. "Oh," sighed the crowd, "she's so beautiful."

"She only has three legs!" someone gasped.

"No!" the girl in the front row exclaimed, while the other astonished young people looked on in silence, aghast at what they saw.

No one was more stunned than Cory. Looking bewildered at the sight of this incredible animal running at full speed, he asked the question that was in everyone's mind. "How can she run that fast with three legs?" Amazed at the cheetah's effortless, seemingly natural movements, the boy whispered, "Incredible. Just incredible." He stared at the beautiful animal with the missing leg and he smiled, a spark of hope evident in his eyes.

Tippi answered from our spot behind the group. "As you have now all noticed, Subira is very special. Since no one told her she shouldn't—or couldn't—run as fast as a cheetah with four legs, she doesn't know otherwise. And so, she can." Tippi paused for a moment, and turning to Subira, continued, "We just love her. Subira is a living example, a symbol, of what Shambala is all about: recognizing the value of all living things, even if, for any reason, they are different."

The boy was silent and listened with interest as Tippi continued. "We got Subira from a zoo in Oregon. Her umbilical cord was wrapped around her leg in the womb, so it atrophied, causing her to lose the leg soon after she was born. With only three legs, her fate seemed hopeless. They were considering putting her to sleep at that point."

Surprised, Cory asked, "Why?"

Tippi looked directly into Cory's face, "Because they thought, 'What good is a three-legged cheetah?' They didn't think the public would want to see a deformed cheetah. And since it was felt that she wouldn't be able to run and act like a normal cheetah, she served no purpose."

She went on, "That's when we heard about Subira and offered our sanctuary, where she could live as normal a life as possible.

"It was soon after she came to us that she demonstrated her own worth—a unique gift of love and spirit. Really, we don't know what we'd do without her. In the past few years, the gift of Subira has touched people around the world, and without words she has become our most persuasive spokesman. Though discarded because she was an imperfect animal, she created her own worth. She truly is a most cherished and priceless gift."

Abandoning all wisecracks, Cory asked softly, "Can I touch her?"

Seeing Subira run had switched on the light in Cory's

heart and mind. It completely changed his demeanor. And his willingness to participate. At the end of the tour, the leader of the visiting group asked for a volunteer to push and hold the large rolling gate open so the van could exit the ranch. To everyone's surprise, Cory raised his hand.

As the rest of the group looked on in amazement, the boy wheeled himself over to the large gate and, struggling to maneuver it open, pulled himself up from his chair. Gripping the high wire fence for support, he pushed it open. The expression on his face as he continued to hold the gate until the van passed through was one of great satisfaction. And determination. It was clear that Cory had received the gift of Subira.

Bettie B. Youngs, Ph.D., Ed.D.

The Dog Next Door

When I was about thirteen years old, back home in Indiana, Pennsylvania, I had a dog named Bounce. He was just a street dog of indeterminate parentage who had followed me home from school one day. Kind of Airedale-ish but of an orange color, Bounce became my close companion. He'd frolic alongside me when I'd go into the woods to hunt arrowheads and snore at my feet when I'd build a model airplane. I loved that dog.

Late one summer I had been away to a Boy Scout camp at Two Lick Creek, and when I got home Bounce wasn't there to greet me. When I asked Mother about him, she gently took me inside. "I'm so sorry, Jim, but Bounce is gone."

"Did he run away?"

"No, son, he's dead."

I couldn't believe it. "What happened?" I choked.

"He was killed."

"How?"

Mom looked over to my father. He cleared his throat. "Well, Jim," he said, "Bogy broke his chain, came over and killed Bounce."

I was aghast. Bogy was the next-door neighbors'

English bulldog. Normally he was linked by a chain to a wire that stretched about 100 feet across their backyard.

I was grief-stricken and angry. That night I tossed and turned. The next morning I stepped out to look at the bulldog, hoping to see at least a gash in its speckled hide. But no, there on a heavier chain stood the barrel-chested villain. Every time I saw poor Bounce's empty house, his forlorn blanket, his food dish, I seethed with hatred for the animal that had taken my best friend.

Finally one morning I reached into my closet and pulled out the Remington .22 rifle Dad had given me the past Christmas. I stepped out into our backyard and climbed up into the apple tree. Perched in its upper limbs, I could see the bulldog as he traipsed up and down the length of his wire. With the rifle I followed him in the sights. But every time I got a bead on him, tree foliage got in the way.

Suddenly a gasp sounded from below. "Jim, what are you doing up there?"

Mom didn't wait for an answer. Our screen door slammed and I could tell she was on the phone with my father at his hardware store. In a few minutes our Ford chattered into the driveway. Dad climbed out and came over to the apple tree.

"C'mon down, Jim," he said gently. Reluctantly, I put the safety on and let myself down onto the summer-seared grass.

The next morning, Dad, who knew me better than I knew myself, said, "Jim, after you finish school today, I want you to come to the store."

That afternoon I trudged downtown to Dad's hardware store, figuring he wanted the windows washed or something. He stepped out from behind the counter and led me back to the stockroom. We edged past kegs of nails, coils of garden hose and rolls of screen wire over to a corner. There squatted my hated nemesis, Bogy, tied to a post.

"Now here's the bulldog," Dad said. "This is the easy way to kill him if you still feel that way." He handed me a short-barreled .22-caliber rifle. I glanced at him questioningly. He nodded.

I took the gun, lifted it to my shoulder and sighted down the black barrel. Bogy, brown eyes regarding me, panted happily, pink tongue peeking from tusked jaws. As I began to squeeze the trigger, a thousand thoughts flashed through my mind while Dad stood silently by. But my mind wasn't silent; all of Dad's teaching about our responsibility to defenseless creatures, fair play, right and wrong, welled within me. I thought of Mom loving me after I broke her favorite china serving bowl. There were other voices—our preacher leading us in prayer, asking God to forgive us as we forgave others.

Suddenly the rifle weighed a ton and the sight wavered in my vision. I lowered it and looked up at Dad helplessly. A quiet smile crossed his face and he clasped my shoulder. "I know, son," he said gently. I realized then: He had never expected me to pull that trigger. In his wise, deep way he let me face my decision on my own. I never did learn how Dad managed to arrange Bogy's presence that afternoon, but I know he had trusted me to make the right choice.

A tremendous relief overwhelmed me as I put down the gun. I knelt down with Dad and helped untie Bogy, who wriggled against us happily, his stub tail wiggling furiously.

That night I slept well for the first time in days. The next morning as I leaped down the back steps, I saw Bogy next door and stopped. Dad ruffled my hair. "Seems you've forgiven him, son."

I raced off to school. Forgiveness, I found, could be exhilarating.

Jimmy Stewart
As told to Dick Schneider

OK... COME ON IN.
UGH! YOUR FEET ARE FULL OF SNOW, YOU SHED EVERYWHERE, YOU'RE ALWAYS GETTING INTO TROUBLE!
SOMETIMES I WONDER WHY WE GOT YOU IN THE FIRST–
SLURP!
–DON'T KISS ME WHILE I'M LECTURING YOU!

The Joy of the Run

All the men in my family for three generations have been doctors. That was what we did. I got my first stethoscope when I was six. I heard stories of the lives my grandfather and my father had saved, the babies they'd delivered, the nights they'd sat up with sick children. I was shown where my name would go on the brass plaque on the office door. And so the vision of what I would become was engraved in my imagination.

But as college neared, I began to feel that becoming a doctor was not engraved upon my heart. For one thing, I reacted to situations very differently from my dad. I'd seen him hauled out at three in the morning to attend a child who'd developed pneumonia because his parents hadn't brought him to the office earlier. I would have given them a hard time, but he never would. "Parents want their kids to be all right so bad, they sometimes can't admit the child's really sick," he said forgivingly. And then there were the terrible things like the death of a ten-year-old from lockjaw—that I knew I couldn't handle. What troubled me most was my fear that I wasn't the son my father imagined. I didn't dare tell him about my uncertainty and hoped I could work it out on my own.

With this dilemma heavy on my mind the summer before college, I was given a challenge that I hoped would be a distraction. A patient had given my father an English setter pup as payment for his help. Dad kept a kennel of bird dogs on our farm, which I trained. As usual, Dad turned the dog over to me.

Jerry was a willing pup of about ten months. Like many setters, he was mostly white, with a smattering of red spots. His solid-red ears stood out too far from his head, though, giving him a clown-like look. Just the sight of him gave me a much-needed chuckle. He mastered the basics: sit, stay, down, walk. His only problem was "come." Once out in the tall grass, he liked to roam. I'd call and give a pip on the training whistle. He would turn and look at me, then go on about his business.

When we finished his lessons, I would sit with him under an old pine oak and talk. I'd go over what he was supposed to know, and sometimes I'd talk about me. "Jerry," I'd say, "I just don't like being around sick people. What would you do if you were me?" Jerry would sit on his haunches and look directly at my eyes, turning his head from side to side, trying to read the significance in my voice. He was so serious that I'd laugh out loud and forget how worried I was.

After supper one evening, I took him out to the meadow for exercise. We had walked about 100 yards into the knee-high grass when a barn swallow, skimming for insects in the fading light, buzzed Jerry's head. Jerry stood transfixed. After a moment, he chased the swallow. The bird flew low, zigzagging back and forth, teasing and playing, driving Jerry into an exhilarated frenzy of running. The bird led him down to the pond and back along the meadow fence, as though daring him to follow. Then it vanished high in the sky. Jerry stood looking after it for a while and then ran to me panting, as full of himself as I'd ever seen him.

In the days that followed, I noticed that his interest in hunting faded as his enthusiasm for running grew. He would just take off through the grass, fast as a wild thing. I knew when he'd scented quail because he'd give a little cock of his head as he passed them. He knew what he was supposed to do; he just didn't do it. When he'd finally come back, exhausted and red-eyed, he'd lie on the ground with an expression of such doggy contentment that I had a hard time bawling him out.

I started again from the beginning. For a few minutes he would listen solemnly. Then he'd steal the bandanna from my back pocket and race across the meadow, nose into the wind, legs pumping hard. Running was a kind of glory for him. Despite my intense desire to train him well, I began to feel a strange sense of joy when he ran.

I had never failed with a dog before, but I was surely failing now. When September came, I finally had to tell Dad that this bird dog wouldn't hunt. "Well, that ties it," he said. "We'll have to neuter him and pass him off to someone in town for a pet. A dog that won't do what he's born to do is sure not worth much."

I was afraid being a house dog would kill Jerry's spirit. The next day, I had a long talk with Jerry under the oak tree. "This running thing is gonna get you locked up," I said. "Can't you just get on the birds and then run?" He raised his eyes to my voice, looking out from under his lids in the way he did when he was shamed. Now I felt sad. I lay back and he lay down next to me, his head on my chest. As I scratched his ears, I closed my eyes and thought desperately about both our problems.

Early the next Saturday, Dad took Jerry out to see for himself what the dog could do. At first, Jerry worked the field like a pro. Dad looked at me oddly, as if I'd fooled him about Jerry.

At that very moment the dog took off.

"What in hell is that dog doing?"

"Running," I said. "He likes to run."

And Jerry ran. He ran along the fence row, then jumped it, his lean body an amazing arc. He ran as though running were all ease and grace, as though it made him a part of the field, the light, the air.

"That's not a hunting dog, that's a deer!" my father said. As I stood watching my dog fail the most important test of his life, Dad put his hand on my shoulder. "We've got to face it—he's not going to measure up."

The next day I packed for school, then walked out to the kennel to say good-bye to Jerry. He wasn't there. I wondered if Dad had already taken him to town. The thought that I had failed us both made me miserable. But when I went into the house, to my great relief Dad was in his chair near the fireplace, reading, with Jerry asleep at his feet.

As I entered, my father closed his book and looked directly at me. "Son, I know this dog doesn't do what he should," he said, "but what he does do is something grand. Lifts a man's spirits to see him go." He continued to look at me steadily. For a moment I felt he could see into my very heart. "What makes any living thing worth the time of day," Dad went on, "is that it is what it is—and knows it. Knows it in its bones."

I took a solid breath. "Dad," I said, "I don't think I can do medicine." He lowered his eyes, as though he heard at last what he dreaded to hear. His expression was so sad, I thought my heart would break. But when he looked at me again, it was with a regard I hadn't seen before.

"I know that," he said solemnly. "What really convinced me was when I watched you with this no-account mutt. You should've seen your face when he went off running."

Imagining his intense disappointment, I felt close to tears. I wished I had it in me to do what would make him happy. "Dad," I said, "I'm sorry."

He looked at me sharply. "Son, of course I'm disappointed that you're not going to be a doctor. But I'm not disappointed in *you.*

"Think about what you tried to do with Jerry," he said. "You expected him to be the hunter you trained him to be. But he just isn't. How do you feel about that?"

I looked at Jerry asleep, his paws twitching. He seemed to be running even in his dreams. "I thought I'd failed for a while," I said. "But when I watched him run and saw how he loves it, I guess I thought that was a good enough thing."

"It *is* a good thing," my father said. He looked at me keenly. "Now we'll just wait to see how *you* run."

He slapped me on the shoulder, said good night and left me. At that moment I understood my father as I never had before, and the love I felt for him seemed to fill the room. I sat down next to Jerry and scratched him between his shoulder blades. "I wonder how I'll run too," I whispered to him. "I sure do."

Jerry lifted his head just slightly, licked my hand, stretched his legs, and then went back to the joyful place of his dreams.

W. W. Meade

Summer of the Raccoons

If I'd had my way, the story would have ended that day where it began—on the sixth hole at Stony Brook.

"What was that bawling?" my wife, Shirley, asked, interrupting me in mid-swing. Without another word she marched into a mucky undergrowth and re-emerged carrying something alive.

"Rrrit, rrit, rrit," it screamed.

"It's an orphaned raccoon," she said, gently stroking a mud-matted ball of gray fur.

"Its mother is probably ten yards away, has rabies and is about to attack," I scolded.

"No, it's alone and starving—that's why the little thing is out of its nest. Here, take it," she ordered. "I think there's another baby over there."

In a minute she returned with a squalling bookend—just as mud-encrusted and emaciated as the first. She wrapped the two complaining ingrates in her sweater. I knew that look. We were going to have two more mouths to feed.

"Just remember," I declared, "they're your bundles to look after." But of all the family proclamations I have made over the years, none was wider off the mark.

When, like Shirley and me, you have four children, you don't think much about empty nests. You don't think the noisy, exuberant procession of kids and their friends will ever end. But the bedrooms will someday empty, the hot bath water will miraculously return, and the sounds that make a family will echo only in the scrapbook of your mind.

Shirley and I had gone through the parting ritual with Laraine and Steve and Christopher. Now there was only Daniel, who was chafing to trade his room at home for a pad at Penn State. So I was looking forward to my share of a little peace and quiet—not raccoons.

"What do you feed baby raccoons?" I asked the game protector over the phone the next morning. We had cleaned them up, made them a bed in a box of rags, added a ticking clock in the hope it would calm them, found old baby bottles in the basement, fed them warm milk and got them to sleep, all without floorwalking the first night.

However, they revived and began their machine-gun chant shortly after Shirley had run out the door, heading for classes. In anticipation of a soon-to-be empty nest, she had gone back to college to get a master's degree so she could teach.

Meanwhile, I had my own work to do—various publishing projects that I handle from home. As the only child remaining with us, Daniel was my potential raccoon-relief man. Or so I hoped.

"Whose bright idea was this?" he asked with the tart tongue of a teenager.

"Your mother thought you needed something more to earn your allowance," I cracked. "Will you heat some milk for them?"

"Sorry, I'm late for school," he called over his shoulder. He and I were at that awkward testing stage, somewhere between my flagging authority and his rush for independence.

The major problem with trying to feed the raccoons was one of flow. Milk was flowing out of the bottle too fast and through the kits the same way.

"Thinner milk and less corn syrup," the wildlife man suggested, adding that he would send along a brochure for raising them. "The object," he coached, "is to take care of them until they can go back to the woods and take care of themselves."

"I'll do anything I can to make that happen," I assured him. "They're about eight ounces each"—I had weighed them on my postage scale. "They'll be old enough to be on their own in a couple more weeks, right?"

"Not quite," he said. "Come fall, if all goes well, they'll be ready."

I'll strangle them before then, I said under my breath. I prepared a new formula and tried it on one. The kit coughed and sputtered like a clogged carburetor. The hole in the nipple was too big.

Maybe I could feed them better with a doll's bottle, I concluded, and set out to find one. At a toy store, I found some miniature bottles, one of which was attached to a specially plumbed doll named Betsy Wetsy. "My Betsys are wetsy enough," I told the clerk—declining doll and diapers, but taking the bottle.

Back home, I tried feeding the raccoons again. Miracle of miracles, they sucked contentedly and fell asleep. (Only twelve more weeks to September, I counted down.)

During the next month and a half I functioned faithfully as day-care nanny for Bonnie and Clyde, named for their bandit-like masks. The kits apparently considered me their mother. When I held them at feeding time, they still spoke in the same scratchy voice, but now it was a contented hum. The only time they may have perceived me to be an impostor came when they climbed on my shoulders, parted my hair and pawed in vain for a nipple.

Before long the kits graduated to cereal and bananas. When they became more active, our back-yard birdbath became an instant attraction. Bonnie, the extrovert of the two, ladled the water worshipfully with her paws like a priest conducting a baptism. Clyde followed suit, but cautiously, as if the water might be combustible. Next Bonnie discovered the joy of food and water together, and thereafter every morsel had to be dipped before being eaten.

By July the kits weighed about three pounds. I built a screened-in cage and moved them outdoors. When they had adjusted well to their new quarters, Daniel suggested we free them to explore the woods and forage for food.

"I don't want them to get lost or hurt out there," I said, sounding more like a mother hen than a surrogate father raccoon.

"They should get used to being on their own," Daniel insisted. We left their door ajar so they could wander during the day. At night, we called them home by banging together their food bowls. They came out of the woods at a gallop.

Still, I was afraid we might be rushing their initiation to the wild. One windy afternoon while Daniel and I were playing catch in the back yard, I spotted Bonnie, twenty feet off the ground, precariously tightrope-walking the bouncing branches of a mulberry tree. She had eaten her fill of berries and was trying to get down, or so I thought.

"Be careful, babe," I called, running to the tree. "Quick, Dan, get a ladder!"

"Let her go," he said calmly. "She's on an adventure. Don't spoil her fun." And he was on the money. When I returned later, she was snoozing serenely in the mulberry's cradling arms.

However, the raccoons did get into trouble one night when they let themselves out of their cage with those dexterous forepaws. Shirley and I were awakened at 2 A.M. by a horrendous scream.

"What was that?" I asked, bolting upright.

"The raccoons?" she wondered.

"They're in trouble!" Tossing off the covers, I grabbed a flashlight and ran outside in my skivvies.

As I came around the south side of the house, I heard something rattle the eaves and jump into the maple tree. Next, I got jumped. First by Bonnie, landing on my shoulder, then by her brother, shinnying up my leg. Circling my neck, they jabbered their excitement: *"Rrrrit, rrrit, rrrit!"*

"It's okay, I've got ya, you're safe," I said, cuddling them in my arms. Apparently a wild raccoon, defending its territory, had attacked Clyde. He had a bloody shoulder that didn't appear serious; Bonnie was fine.

July gave way to August, and August to September. Soon the days were getting shorter, and the raccoons were six-pound butterballs. I was fascinated by their creativity and intelligence. One evening after I banged their food bowls together, there was no reply. When I reported anxiously at the breakfast table that they hadn't come in the night before, Daniel laughed at my concern.

"Now we'll see if you're as good a teacher as a mother raccoon."

"I already know the answer," I said. "By the way, what time did you get in last night?"

"About midnight," he answered.

"Your eyes say later."

"I'm not a baby anymore," he shot back.

Outside, I beckoned the raccoons again, and this time they reported: effervescent Bonnie in a flat-out sprint, Clyde in a tagalong amble.

Near the end of September they were missing a week, and I suggested to Shirley that they were probably gone for good.

"You know it's a mistake trying to hold on to anything that no longer needs you," she counseled.

"Who's holding on?" I protested. But when I continued scanning the woods, hoping to catch sight of them, I knew she was right. Reluctantly, I dismantled their pen, stored their bowls and put them out of my mind. Or tried to. But they had got more of a hold on my heart than I ever thought possible. What I had considered a nuisance had, in fact, been a gift; what I had labeled a burden, a blessing. *Why is it,* I asked myself, *that with so many people and things, we only appreciate them fully after they're gone?*

One Saturday near the end of October, Shirley, Daniel and I were in the back yard raking leaves when I spotted a ringed tail beyond the gate that opens to the woods. "Look, Shirley," I whispered. And though I had no idea if it was one of ours, I called, "Bonnie . . . Clyde."

The magnificently marked animal rose on its hind legs and looked us over inquisitively. For a frozen moment, we faced off, statue-like. Then I called again, and the animal moved in our direction. It was Bonnie, and we went to meet her. Kneeling, I held out my hand, which she licked while I rubbed her neck. She purred her most satisfied *rrrit, rrrit, rrrit.*

"Go get a banana for her," I suggested to Daniel.

"No, it's time she made it on her own," he replied firmly. "She's a big girl now. Don't do anything for her that she can do for herself."

I looked at Shirley and winked. Tall, broad-shouldered Daniel wasn't talking raccoons. He was talking parents. *The object is to take care of them until they can take care of themselves,* a haunting voice echoed. It was time to let go.

After rubbing Bonnie's neck one last time, I stepped back. She sensed my release and bounded off joyfully in the direction from which she had come.

"Have a good life," I called after her. Then she dipped behind a tree and was gone.

Fred Bauer

Things We Can Learn from a Dog

1. Never pass up the opportunity to go for a joy ride.
2. Allow the experience of fresh air and the wind in your face to be pure ecstasy.
3. When loved ones come home, always run to greet them.
4. When it's in your best interest, always practice obedience.
5. Let others know when they've invaded your territory.
6. Take naps and always stretch before rising.
7. Run, romp and play daily.
8. Eat with gusto and enthusiasm.
9. Be loyal.
10. Never pretend to be something you're not.
11. If what you want lies buried, dig until you find it.
12. When someone is having a bad day, be silent, sit close by and nuzzle them gently.
13. Delight in the simple joy of a long walk.
14. Thrive on attention and let people touch you.
15. Avoid biting when a simple growl will do.
16. On hot days, drink lots of water and lie under a shady tree.

17. When you are happy, dance around and wag your entire body.
18. No matter how often you are criticized, don't buy into the guilt thing and pout. Run right back and make friends.

Author Unknown

"You have just one more wish.
Are you sure you want another belly-rub?"

Reprinted with permission from Vahan Shivanian.

Birds, Bees and Guppies

The sex education of a child is pretty important. None of us wants to blow it.

I have a horror of ending up like the woman in the old joke who was asked by her child where he came from and, after she explained all the technical processes in a well-chosen vocabulary, he looked at her intently and said, "I just wondered. Mike came from Hartford, Connecticut."

I figured I had the problem whipped the day my son took an interest in fish. What better way to explain the beautiful reproduction cycle of life than through the animal kingdom? We bought two pairs of guppies and a small aquarium. That was our first mistake. We should either have bought four males and a small aquarium, four females and a small aquarium or two pairs and a reservoir. I had heard of population explosions before, but this was ridiculous! The breakfast conversation ran something like this:

"What's new at Peyton Place by the Sea?" inquired my husband.

"Mrs. Guppy is e-n-c-e-i-n-t-e again," I'd spell.

"Put a little salt in the water. That'll cure anything," he mumbled.

"Daddy," said my son, "that means she's pregnant."

"Again!" choked Daddy. "Can't we organize an intramural volleyball game in there or something?"

The first aquarium begat a second aquarium, with no relief in sight. "Are you getting anything out of your experiences with guppies?" I asked delicately one afternoon.

"Oh, yeah, they're neat," my son exclaimed enthusiastically.

"I mean, now that you've watched the male and the female, do you understand the processes that go into the offspring? Have you noticed the role of the mother in all this?"

"Yeah," he said, bright-eyed. "You oughta see her eat her babies."

We added a third aquarium, which was promptly filled with saltwater and three pairs of seahorses.

"Now I want you to pay special attention to the female," I instructed. "The chances are it won't take her long to be with child, and perhaps you can even see the birth."

"The female doesn't give birth, Mom," he explained. "The male seahorse gives birth."

I felt myself smiling, perhaps anticipating a trend. "Ridiculous," I said. "Females always give birth."

The male began to take on weight. I thought I saw his ankles swell. He became a mother on the twenty-third of the month.

"That's pretty interesting," said my son. "I hope I'm not a mother when I grow up, but if I am, I hope my kids are born on land."

I had blown it. I knew I would.

Erma Bombeck

The Star of the Rodeo

As a very young child in Niagara Falls, New York, I was in and out of the hospital with serious asthma attacks. When I was six years old, the doctors told my parents that if they did not take me to a better climate, I would certainly die. And so my family moved to a tiny town high up in the mountains outside Denver. It was beautiful, but very remote. In the late '50s, there were far more animals than people in Conifer, Colorado.

We kids were in heaven. My older brother, Dan, and I would pack food and sleeping bags, take two horses and our dog, and go camping for the weekend in the wilderness around our home. We saw a lot of wildlife on our trips—including bears, bobcats and even a few elusive mountain lions. We learned to be silent and observe the life around us with respect. One time, I remember waking up and looking straight into the enormous nose of an elk. I lay perfectly still until the elk moved on. Blending with our surroundings, riding our horses for days at a time, we considered ourselves real mountain men. My parents knew that as long as the dog and the horses were with us, we would be safe and always find our way home.

I remember that Dan, three years older and stronger, always beat me at everything. It became a burning passion with me to win. I wanted so badly to be the star for a change.

When I was eight, Dad brought home a horse named Chubby. Chubby's owner had suffered a heart attack and was told to stop riding. The owner thought that we would give Chubby a good home, so he gave the sixteen-year-old gelding to my parents for free.

Chubby, a smallish, charcoal-gray horse, had been a tri-state rodeo champion in roping and bulldogging. Strong, intelligent and responsive, he had tremendous spirit, and my whole family loved him. Dan, of course, got first pick of the horses, so I was left with a slower, lazier horse named Stormy. Chubby was probably too much horse for a boy of eight anyway, but I envied my brother and wished fervently that Chubby were my horse.

In those days, my brother and I entered 4-H Club gymkhanas with our horses every year. The year I was nine, I practiced the barrel race over and over in preparation for that year's competition. But Stormy was a plodding horse and even while I practiced, I knew it was a lost cause. It was the deep passion to win that kept me at it—urging Stormy on, learning the moves for getting around the barrels and back to the finish line.

On the day of the gymkhana, my older brother stunned me by offering to let me ride Chubby in the barrel race. I was beside myself with excitement and joy. Maybe this time, I could finally win.

When I mounted Chubby, I sensed immediately that I was in for a completely different barrel race. With Stormy, it was always a struggle to get her moving from a standing position, and then a chore to keep her going. As we waited for the start signal that day, Chubby was prancing in place, alert and obviously eager to be running. When the signal came, Chubby was off like a rocket before I could react, and it was all I could do to hold on. We were around those barrels and back at the finish line in seconds. My adrenaline was still pumping as I slid off the horse and was surrounded by my cheering family. I won that blue ribbon by a mile and then some.

That night I went to bed worn out with the excitement and glory of it all. But as I lay there, I found myself feeling uneasy. What had *I* really done to earn that first place? All I could come up with was that I'd managed not to fall off and humiliate myself or Chubby. It was the horse that had won the blue ribbon, not me. I looked at the ribbon pinned to my lampshade and suddenly felt ashamed.

The next morning, I woke early. I got out of bed, dressed quickly and crept out of the house toward the barn. I pinned the blue ribbon on the wall of Chubby's stall and stood rubbing his neck, feeling him lip my pockets, looking for the sugar cubes he loved so much. Then it hit me: this horse didn't care about ribbons, blue or otherwise. He preferred something he could eat. Chubby had run that way yesterday, not to win, but simply because he loved to run. He truly enjoyed the challenge and the fun of the game.

With a new respect, I got a bucket of rolled oats, his favorite grain, and let him eat it while I got out the currycomb and gave him a thorough brushing. This horse had given me my blue ribbon, but more important, Chubby had shown me what it means to give yourself to what you do with your entire mind, body and soul.

My heart light once more, I vowed that for the rest of his days, I was going to make sure Chubby got his reward in *horse* currency: grain, sugar, brushing, the chance to run—and lots of love.

Larry Paul Kline

Life Lessons from Lovebirds

Recently, my husband and I were walking through a local mall near closing time, when we decided to stop and take a look around the pet store. As we made our way past the cages of poodles and Pomeranians, tabby cats and turtles, our eyes caught sight of something that immediately charmed us: a pair of peach-faced lovebirds. Unlike many other lovebirds we encountered there, this particular pair looked truly "in love." In fact, they snuggled and cuddled next to each other the whole time we watched them. Throughout the next few days, my mind returned to the image of those two delightful birds. I admired their devotion, and felt their very presence inspiring.

Apparently, these birds had the same effect on my husband, because he showed up late from work one night shortly thereafter, clutching an elegant birdcage that housed those two precious creatures, and introduced them as new additions to the family. For days we wrestled with names of well-known couples, coming up with everything from Ricky and Lucy and George and Gracie to Wilma and Fred. But finally we decided on Ozzie and

Harriet—a gentle reminder of a simpler day when love and togetherness between couples were not only a commitment, but a way of life.

And so it is with this in mind that I have watched these lovebirds and made the following observations about life and love:

1. If you spend too much time looking in the mirror, it's easy to lose your balance.
2. Always keep a pleasant look on your face, even if your cage needs cleaning.
3. If your mate wants to share your perch with you, move over.
4. The real treats in life usually come only after you've cracked a few hulls.
5. It takes two to snuggle.
6. Sometimes your mate can see mites you didn't even know you had.
7. Singing draws more affection than squawking.
8. It is only when your feathers get ruffled that your true colors really show.
9. Too many toys can be distracting.
10. When you have love in your heart, everyone around you will find joy in your presence.

Vickie Lynne Agee

3

PETS AS HEALERS

There is no psychiatrist
in the world
like a puppy
licking your face.

Bern Williams

Cheyenne

"Watch out! You nearly broadsided that car!" my father yelled at me. "Can't you do anything right?" Those words hurt worse than blows. I turned my head toward the elderly man in the seat beside me, daring me to challenge him. A lump rose in my throat as I averted my eyes. I wasn't prepared for another battle.

"I saw the car, Dad. Please don't yell at me when I'm driving." My voice was measured and steady, sounding far calmer than I really felt. Dad glared at me, then turned away and settled back.

At home I left Dad in front of the television and went outside to collect my thoughts. Dark, heavy clouds hung in the air with a promise of rain. The rumble of distant thunder seemed to echo my inner turmoil. What could I do about him?

Dad had been a lumberjack in Washington and Oregon. He had enjoyed being outdoors and had reveled in pitting his strength against the forces of nature. He had entered grueling lumberjack competitions, and had placed often. The shelves in his house were filled with trophies that attested to his prowess.

The years marched on relentlessly. The first time he couldn't lift a heavy log, he joked about it; but later that same day I saw him outside alone, straining to lift it. He became irritable whenever anyone teased him about his advancing age, or when he couldn't do something he had done as a younger man.

Four days after his sixty-seventh birthday, he had a heart attack. An ambulance sped him to the hospital while a paramedic administered CPR to keep blood and oxygen flowing. At the hospital, Dad was rushed into an operating room. He was lucky; he survived.

But something inside Dad died. His zest for life was gone. He obstinately refused to follow doctor's orders. Suggestions and offers of help were turned aside with sarcasm and insults. The number of visitors thinned, then finally stopped altogether. Dad was left alone.

My husband, Dick, and I asked Dad to come live with us on our small farm. We hoped the fresh air and rustic atmosphere would help him adjust. Within a week after he moved in, I regretted the invitation. It seemed nothing was satisfactory. He criticized everything I did. I became frustrated and moody. Soon I was taking my pent-up anger out on Dick. We began to bicker and argue. Alarmed, Dick sought out our pastor and explained the situation. The clergyman set up weekly counseling appointments for us. At the close of each session he prayed, asking God to soothe Dad's troubled mind. But the months wore on and God was silent.

A raindrop struck my cheek. I looked up into the gray sky. Somewhere up there was "God." Although I believed a Supreme Being had created the universe, I had difficulty believing that God cared about the tiny human beings on this earth. I was tired of waiting for a God who didn't answer. Something had to be done and it was up to me to do it.

The next day I sat down with the phone book and methodically called each of the mental health clinics listed in the Yellow Pages. I explained my problem to each of the sympathetic voices that answered. In vain. Just when I was giving up hope, one of the voices suddenly exclaimed, "I just read something that might help you! Let me go get the article." I listened as she read. The article described a remarkable study done at a nursing home. All of the patients were under treatment for chronic depression. Yet their attitudes had improved dramatically when they were given responsibility for a dog.

I drove to the animal shelter that afternoon. After I filled out a questionnaire, a uniformed officer led me to the kennels. The odor of disinfectant stung my nostrils as I moved down the row of pens. Each contained five to seven dogs. Long-haired dogs, curly-haired dogs, black dogs, spotted dogs—all jumped up, trying to reach me. I studied each one but rejected one after the other for various reasons—too big, too small, too much hair. As I neared the last pen a dog in the shadows of the far corner struggled to his feet, walked to the front of the run and sat down. It was a pointer, one of the dog world's aristocrats. But this was a caricature of the breed. Years had etched his face and muzzle with shades of gray. His hipbones jutted out in lopsided triangles. But it was his eyes that caught and held my attention. Calm and clear, they beheld me unwaveringly.

I pointed to the dog. "Can you tell me about him?" The officer looked, then shook his head in puzzlement.

"He's a funny one. Appeared out of nowhere and sat in front of the gate. We brought him in, figuring someone would be right down to claim him. That was two weeks ago and we've heard nothing. His time is up tomorrow." He gestured helplessly.

As the words sank in I turned to the man in horror. "You mean you're going to kill him?"

"Ma'am," he said gently, "that's our policy. We don't have room for every unclaimed dog."

I looked at the pointer again. The calm brown eyes awaited my decision. "I'll take him," I said.

I drove home with the dog on the front seat beside me. When I reached the house I honked the horn twice. I was helping my prize out of the car when Dad shuffled onto the front porch.

"Ta-da! Look what I got for you, Dad!" I said excitedly.

Dad looked, then wrinkled his face in disgust. "If I had wanted a dog I would have gotten one. And I would have picked out a better specimen than that bag of bones. Keep it! I don't want it!" Dad waved his arm scornfully and turned back toward the house.

Anger rose inside me. It squeezed together my throat muscles and pounded into my temples.

"You'd better get used to him, Dad. He's staying!" Dad ignored me. "Did you hear me, old man?" I screamed. At those words Dad whirled angrily, his hands clenched at his sides, his eyes narrowed and blazing with hate. We stood glaring at each other like duelists, when suddenly the pointer pulled free from my grasp. He wobbled toward my dad and sat down in front of him. Then slowly, carefully, he raised his paw.

Dad's lower jaw trembled as he stared at the uplifted paw. Confusion replaced the anger in his eyes. The pointer waited patiently. Then Dad was on his knees hugging the animal.

It was the beginning of a warm and intimate friendship. Dad named the pointer Cheyenne. Together he and Cheyenne explored the community. They spent long hours walking down dusty lanes. They spent reflective moments on the banks of streams, angling for tasty trout. They even started to attend Sunday services together, Dad sitting in a pew and Cheyenne lying quietly at his feet.

Dad and Cheyenne were inseparable throughout the next three years. Dad's bitterness faded, and he and Cheyenne made many friends. Then late one night I was startled to feel Cheyenne's cold nose burrowing through our bed covers. He had never before come into our bedroom at night. I woke Dick, put on my robe and ran into my father's room. Dad lay in his bed, his face serene. But his spirit had left quietly sometime during the night.

Two days later my shock and grief deepened when I discovered Cheyenne lying dead beside Dad's bed. I wrapped his still form in the rag rug he had slept on. As Dick and I buried him near a favorite fishing hole, I silently thanked the dog for the help he had given me in restoring Dad's peace of mind.

The morning of Dad's funeral dawned overcast and dreary. *This day looks like the way I feel,* I thought, as I walked down the aisle to the pews reserved for family. I was surprised to see the many friends Dad and Cheyenne had made filling the church. The pastor began his eulogy. It was a tribute to both Dad and the dog who had changed his life. And then the pastor turned to Hebrews 13:2. "'Be not forgetful to entertain strangers: for thereby some have entertained angels unawares.' I've often thanked God for sending that angel," he said.

For me, the past dropped into place, completing a puzzle that I had not seen before: the sympathetic voice that had just read the right article . . . Cheyenne's unexpected appearance at the animal shelter . . . his calm acceptance and complete devotion to my father . . . and the proximity of their deaths. And suddenly I understood. I *knew* that God had answered my prayers after all.

Catherine Moore

The Gift of Courage

This is courage . . . to bear unflinchingly what heaven sends.

Euripides

Mark was about eleven years old, skinny and slouching, when he and his mom first brought Mojo into the clinic where I worked. Baggy clothes dwarfed the boy's small frame, and under a battered baseball hat, challenging blue eyes glared at the world. Clearly we had to earn Mark's trust before we could do anything with his dog. Mojo was around nine then, old for a black Labrador retriever, but not too old to still have fun. Though recently it seemed that Mojo had lost all his spunk.

Mark listened intently as the doctor examined his dog, answered questions and asked more, while nervously brushing back wisps of blond hair that escaped the hat onto his furrowed brow. "Mojo's going to be okay, isn't he?" he blurted as the doctor turned to leave. There were no guarantees, and when the blood work came back, the doctor's suspicions were confirmed. Mojo had liver and kidney disease, progressive and ultimately fatal. With care he could live comfortably awhile, but he'd need special food, regular checkups and medications. The doctor and I knew finances were a struggle, but the moment euthanasia was suggested, Mark's mom broke in. "We're not putting Mojo to sleep." Quickly and quietly they paid their bill and gently led their old dog out to the car without a backward glance.

We didn't hear from them for a few weeks, but then one day, there they were. Mojo had lost weight. He'd been sick, they said, and he seemed listless. As I led Mojo back to the treatment room for some IV fluid therapy, Mark's little body blocked the way.

"I have to go with him—he needs me," the boy said firmly.

I wasn't sure how Mark would handle the sight of needles and blood, but there didn't seem any point in arguing. And indeed, Mark handled it all as if he'd seen it a million times before.

"Oh, you're such a brave old guy, Mojo," Mark murmured as the catheter slipped into Mojo's vein. We seldom had a more cooperative patient. Mojo only moved his head slightly during uncomfortable procedures, as if to remind us that he was still there. He seemed to take strength from the small, white hand that continually moved in reassurance over his grizzled throat.

This became the pattern. We'd get Mojo stabilized somewhat, send him home, he'd get sick again, and they'd be back. Always, Mark was there, throwing out questions and reminders to be careful, but mostly encouraging and comforting his old pal.

I worried that Mark found it too difficult, watching, but any hint that maybe he'd rather wait outside was flatly rejected. Mojo needed him.

I approached Mark's mom one day, while Mark and Mojo were in the other room, "You know Mojo's condition is getting worse. Have you thought any more about how far you want to go with treatment? It looks like Mark is really having a hard time with all this."

Mark's mom hesitated a moment before leaning forward and speaking in a low, intense voice, "We've had Mojo since Mark was a baby. They've grown up together, and Mark loves him beyond all reason. But that's not all."

She took a deep breath and looked away momentarily, "Two years ago Mark was diagnosed with leukemia. He's been fighting it, and they tell us he has a good chance of recovering completely. But he never talks about it. He goes for tests and treatments as if it's happening to someone else, as if it's not real. But about Mojo, he can ask questions. It's important to Mark, so as long as he wants to, we'll keep on fighting for Mojo."

The next few weeks we saw a lot of the quiet little trio. Mark's abrupt questions and observations, once slightly annoying, now had a new poignancy, and we explained at length every procedure as it was happening. We wondered how long Mojo could carry on. A more stoic and good-natured patient was seldom seen, but the Labrador was so terribly thin and weak now. All of us at the clinic really worried about how Mark would handle the inevitable.

Finally the day came when Mojo collapsed before his scheduled appointment. It was a Saturday when they rushed him in, and the waiting room was packed. We carried Mojo into the back room and settled him on some thick blankets, with Mark at his side as usual. I left to get some supplies, and when I reentered the room a few moments later I was shocked to see Mark standing at the window, fists jammed into his armpits, tears streaming down his face. I backed out of the room noiselessly, not wanting to disturb him. He'd been so brave up until now. Later when we returned, he was kneeling, dry-eyed once more, at Mojo's side. His mom sat down beside him and squeezed his shoulders. "How are you guys doing?" she asked softly.

"Mom," he said, ignoring her question, "Mojo's dying, isn't he?"

"Oh, honey . . ." her voice broke, and Mark continued as if she hadn't spoken.

"I mean, the fluids and the pills, they're just not going to help anymore, are they?" He looked to us for confirmation. "Then I think," he swallowed hard, "I think we should put him to sleep."

True to form, Mark stayed with Mojo until the end. He asked questions to satisfy himself that it truly was best for Mojo, and that there would be no pain or fear for his old friend. Over and over again he smoothed the glossy head, until it faded onto his knee for the last time. As Mark felt the last breath leave Mojo's thin ribs and watched the light dim in the kind brown eyes, he seemed to forget about the rest of us. Crying openly, he bent himself over Mojo's still form and slowly removed his cap. With a jolt I recognized the effects of chemotherapy, so harsh against such a young face. We left him to his grief.

Mark never told us anything about his own illness, or his own feelings throughout Mojo's ordeal, but when his mom called months later to ask some questions about a puppy she was considering buying, I asked her how he was doing.

"You know," she said, "it was a terrible time for him, but since Mojo's death, Mark has begun talking about his own condition, asking questions and trying to learn more about it. I think that dealing with Mojo when the dog was so sick gave Mark strength to fight for himself and courage to face his own pain."

I always thought Mark was being brave for Mojo, but when I remember those calm, trusting eyes and gently wagging tail that never failed no matter how bad he felt, I think maybe Mojo was being brave for Mark.

Roxanne Willems Snopek Raht

Saddle Therapy

One morning, as I lay in bed, I watched sparrows peck at the feeder outside my window, then flap their wings and soar away. Stricken with multiple sclerosis, a disease that destroys muscle control, I could barely lift my head. *I wish I could fly away with you,* I thought sadly. At thirty-nine, it seemed my joy-filled life was gone.

I've always loved the outdoors. My husband, Dan, and I had loved to take long walks near our home in Colorado Springs. But in my mid-twenties, my joints began to ache after our hikes. I thought it was just sore muscles.

Motherhood, a dream fulfilled with the adoption of Jenny, eleven, and Becky, thirteen, made me jubilant. But as eager as I was to be a great mom, I would just flop on the couch after work as a recreational therapist, too tired to help the girls with homework. I figured it was just exhausting being a working mom.

Then one morning I tried to reach for the coffeepot and couldn't: my arm was numb. *What's happening?* I thought in alarm. One doctor prescribed a pain reliever for bursitis. Another diagnosed tendonitis.

Then one day, I was out walking with my daughters when my legs buckled.

"Mom, what's wrong with you?" my frightened, now seventeen-year-old Becky asked.

"I must really be tired," I joked, not wanting to upset the girls—but now I was deeply worried. At Dan's urging, I saw a neurologist.

"You have multiple sclerosis," he told me.

All I could think of was a slogan I once heard: "MS—crippler of young adults." *Please, no!* I anguished. Blinking back tears, I asked, "How bad will it get?"

"We can't say for sure," he said gently. "But in time, you may need a wheelchair."

Though Dan tried to console me, that night I lay sleepless. *How will I care for myself and my family?*

That fearful question echoed in my mind over the next weeks and months. As time passed, I could walk only using a painful process of locking a knee and forcing the stiff leg forward with my hip muscle. Then, at other times, my legs grew numb, refusing to respond at all. I steadily lost control of my hands, until I could barely make my fingers work.

"It's okay, Mom, we can help," the girls would say. And they did.

But *I* wanted to be caring for *them*. Instead, I could barely get dressed and wash a few dishes in the morning before collapsing, exhausted, into bed.

The morning that I lay watching the birds, wishing I, too, could fly away, my heart felt heavy. Hope was dying in me.

Then I saw Dan come in, his eyes alight. "Honey," Dan said, "I heard something amazing on the radio." A nearby stable was offering something called therapeutic horseback riding. The technique reportedly helped with many ailments, including MS.

"I think you should give it a try," he said.

Riding as therapy? It sounded impossible. Still, as a child in Iowa, I loved to ride. *And even if it just gets me out of bed, it'd be worth it.*

"I'm going to fall on my face," I joked a few days later, as Dan helped me struggle on canes to the stables. I needed help getting onto the horse, but as I gripped the reins and began circling the riding arena, my body relaxed.

"This is great!" I exulted. When my ride was over, I told Dan I couldn't wait to try again.

Each time I rode, my hips felt looser and my shoulders became more relaxed. I knew something was happening. At home, I didn't feel hopeless anymore. I wasn't tired all the time, I realized happily.

One afternoon, I told the riding-center volunteers I'd like to ride bareback, the way I had as a child. As I galloped across the pasture, the wind tossing my hair, I thought, *For the first time in years, I feel free!*

Then, as Dan helped me off the horse, something seemed different.

"I can feel my legs again," I gasped to Dan. Dan watched, amazed, as I picked up my leg, then easily and smoothly placed it down again.

It had taken me thirty minutes with two canes to reach the stables from my car. But the return walk took less than three minutes—and Dan carried the canes!

"You did it!" he cheered. Tears of joy welled in my eyes.

Soon after, my daughters came home from college for a visit. I walked over and hugged them.

"Mom, look at you!" Becky cried. With an overflowing heart, I told them how the horses had healed me. My doctors cannot explain why the horse therapy works. All I know is that somehow, it does.

Today, I remain nearly symptom-free as long as I ride at least three times a week.

Each morning I bundle up and set off on a long, brisk walk. Breathing in the fresh mountain air around my home, I feel a special rush of joy. I'm so grateful God has given me back my life.

Sherri Perkins as told to Bill Holton
Excerpted from Woman's World Magazine

Kitty Magic

Great golden comma of a cat,
You spring to catch my robe's one dangling thread,
And somehow land entangled in my heart.

Lija Broadhurst

After a meeting one night, I felt very tired. Eager to get home and get to sleep, I was approaching my car when I heard *mew, mew, mew, mew* . . . Looking under my car, I saw a teeny little kitten, shaking and crying, huddled close to the tire.

I have never had a fondness for cats. I'm a dog person, thank you very much. I grew up with dogs all my young life and cats always bugged me. Kind of creeped me out. I especially hated going into houses that had cat boxes. I wondered if the residents just ignored the awful smell. Plus, cats always seemed to be all over everything—not to mention their hair. And I was semiallergic to them. Suffice it to say, I had never in my life gone out of my way for a cat.

But when I knelt down and saw this scared little red tabby mewing like crazy, something inside urged me to reach out to pick her up. She ran away immediately. I thought, *Okay, well, I tried,* but as I went to get into my car, I heard the kitten mewing again. That pitiful mewing really pulled at my heart, and I found myself crossing the street to try to find her. I found her and she ran. I found her again and she ran again. This went on and on. Yet I just couldn't leave her. Finally, I was able to grab her. When I held her in my arms, she seemed so little and skinny and very sweet. And she stopped mewing!

It was totally out of character, but I took her into my car with me. The kitty freaked out, screeching and running at lightning speed all over the car, until she settled herself right in my lap, of course. I didn't know what I was going to do with her, and yet I felt compelled to bring her home. I drove home, worrying the whole way, because I knew my roommate was deathly allergic to cats.

I got home very late, put the kitten in the front yard and left some milk for her. I was half hoping she would run away by the time morning came. But in the morning she was still there, so I brought her to work with me. Luckily, I have a very sympathetic boss. Especially when it comes to animals. Once we had a hurt sparrow in the office for weeks that he had found and nursed back to health. All day at work, I tried to find someone who would take the kitten, but all the cat lovers were full up.

I still didn't know what to do with the kitty, so I took her on some errands with me when I left work. Again she freaked in the car and this time wedged herself under the seat. My last stop that afternoon was at my parents' house.

Recently my father had been diagnosed with prostate cancer. He had undergone hormone treatment and the doctors now felt they had arrested the cancer. At least for the present. I liked to go there as often as I could.

That afternoon, parked in front of my parents' house, I was trying to coax the kitten out from under the seat when she zoomed out of the car and into the neighbors' bushes. There are a lot of bushes in that neighborhood, and I realized after looking for a while that it was a lost cause. I felt a bit sad but consoled myself that this area had many families with kids. *Surely someone would find her and give her a good home,* I told myself.

To be honest, I felt somewhat relieved because I didn't know what I would have done with her. I visited with my parents, and as I was leaving, I told them to call me if the kitty came around their place and I would come pick her up. I kidded my father, saying, "Of course, you could keep her if you wanted," to which he replied, "Not on your life!" I supposed that Dad wasn't that interested in having pets, particularly cats.

That night there was a call on my answering machine from my father. The kitty had actually shown up on their front doorstep! He said he had her in the house and she was okay, but could I come pick her up the next day? My heart sank. *What am I going to do with this cat?* I thought. I didn't have the heart to take her to the pound, and I was sure that my roommate wasn't feeling up for a hospital trip to treat a cat-induced asthma attack. I couldn't see a solution.

I called my father the next day and told him I would come over and pick up the kitty. To my great surprise, he said not to rush. He had gone out and bought a cat box (oh, no!), cat food and a little dish. I was amazed and thanked him for his generosity. He proceeded to tell me what a character the kitten was and how late the previous night she had been zooming back and forth across the floor. I listened, open-mouthed. The topper came when he said that "Kitty" came up and lay on his chest when he was lying down. I asked, "You let her do that?"

"Oh yes. I pet her and I can feel her motor running," he replied lovingly. "So take your time, dear, finding a home for her. I can keep her until you do."

I was floored. My dad, Seymour, Mister "Keep-Those-Dogs-Outside," had a kitty purring on his chest. In his bed, no less!

As the weeks went on, Dad got weaker. His cancer had reappeared. Yet whenever I called Dad, I heard more and more about how cute Kitty was, how she zoomed around, how loud her motor was, how she followed him everywhere. When I was at the house, my father would call for her, have her come up on his lap, pet her, talk to her and say how much he loved her.

"Dad, aren't you allergic to cats?" I asked once, as he was putting his handkerchief away after one of his infamous loud honks. He just shrugged his shoulders and smiled sheepishly.

As he got sicker, and could barely move without terrible pain, one of his few joys was to have Kitty lay on his chest. He would pet her and say, "Listen, her motor is running. That's a good Kitty, good Kitty." We all watched in awe at Dad's unabashed affection for this little feline.

Kitty worked her magic on both Dad and me. Charming a reluctant pet-owner, the little cat became one of my father's single greatest comforts in his final days. And me? Kitty opened my eyes to the wonder and mystery of how life unfolds. She taught me to listen to my heart, even when my head is saying no. I didn't realize on that unusual night that I was simply a messenger. An unknowing courier delivering a most beautiful and needed friend.

Lynn A. Kerman

"The patient in 12-C needs comforting."

The Golden Years

My best friend, Cocoa, and I live in a senior-citizen apartment complex in a lovely small town. Cocoa is a ten-year-old poodle and I am a sixty-nine-year-old lady, so you can see we both qualify as senior citizens.

Years ago, I promised myself that when I retired I would get a chocolate poodle to share my golden years. From the very first, Cocoa has always been exceptionally well-behaved. I never have to tell him anything more than once. He was housebroken in three days and has never done anything naughty. He is extremely neat—when taking his toys from his box to play, he always puts them back when he is finished. I have been accused of being obsessively neat, and sometimes I wonder if he mimics me or if he was born that way, too.

He is a wonderful companion. When I throw a ball for him, he picks it up in his mouth and throws it back to me. We sometimes play a game I played as a child—but never with a dog. He puts his paw on my hand, I cover it with my other hand, he puts his paw on top, and I slide my hand out from underneath the pile and lay it on top, and so on. He does many amusing things that make me laugh, and when that happens, he is so delighted he just keeps it up. I enjoy his company immensely.

But almost two years ago, Cocoa did something that defies comprehension. Was it a miracle or a coincidence? It is certainly a mystery.

One afternoon, Cocoa started acting strangely. I was sitting on the floor playing with him, when he started pawing and sniffing at the right side of my chest. He had never done anything like this ever before, and I told him, "No." With Cocoa, one "no" is usually sufficient, but not that day. He stopped briefly, then suddenly ran toward me from the other side of the room, throwing his entire weight—eighteen pounds—at the right side of my chest. He crashed into me and I yelped in pain. It hurt more than I thought it should have.

Soon after this, I felt a lump. I went to my doctors, and after X rays, tests and lab work were done, they told me I had cancer.

When cancer starts, for an unknown reason, a wall of calcium builds. Then the lump or cancer attaches itself to this wall. When Cocoa jumped on me, the force of the impact broke the lump away from the calcium wall. This made it possible for me to notice the lump. Before that, I couldn't see it or feel it, so there was no way for me to know it was there.

I had a complete mastectomy and the cancer has not spread to any other part of my body. The doctors told me if the cancer had gone undetected even six more months, it would have been too late.

Was Cocoa aware of just what he was doing? I'll never really know. What I do know is that I'm glad I made a promise to spend my golden years with this wonderful chocolate brown poodle—for Cocoa not only shares his life with me; he has made sure that I will be around to share my life with him!

Yvonne A. Martell

Swimming with Dolphins

Two-and-a-half years after I had two massive strokes, the doctors and therapists told me, "This is as good as you're going to get." This happens to most stroke survivors at some point. The patients come to believe this, and so do the people around them. When they told me this, I was only forty-four years old, a hemiplegic, without the use of my left arm and leg. But I told myself I was lucky to be alive, and my husband, children, parents and I began to emotionally adjust to the fact that the rest of my life would be spent with this limited style of functioning. They'd all been great at helping me with therapy, and I was thankful for their wonderful emotional support.

I resisted the doctor's words, but in a way this diagnosis let me off the hook. I knew very well what I was and was not capable of doing. My life was comfortable. Not adventurous, not joyful, but comfortable.

So I was not at all prepared when my parents moved to Florida, and excitedly told me they'd gotten back in touch with our old neighbors from twenty-five years before.

"The Borgusses have founded a dolphin research and education facility in Key Largo," my mother said, "and

Lloyd Borguss has invited you to come and swim with the dolphins!"

Yes, I knew such things made picturesque documentaries, but this was totally out of my comfort zone. In fact, when I realized my parents were serious about wanting me to accept, I was scared silly. There was no way!

"What are you frightened about, Rusty?" Lloyd Borguss asked me over the phone. "This is salt water. You can't sink. We work with quadriplegics. You're only hemiplegic." (First time I'd heard it described as "only.") He explained his belief that stroke survivors have to challenge themselves with new experiences in order to move beyond their apparent boundaries. He finally talked me into visiting, and my parents decided to come along.

I don't have to go in the water if I don't want to, I told myself.

I spent an afternoon at Dolphins Plus and watched those highly-developed mammals interact with the visitors who came to study and swim with them. I saw dolphins and therapists working together with disabled children and I was impressed. But couldn't I stay impressed from the sidelines in my wheelchair?

No! The message came from Lloyd, from my parents and—all of a sudden—from myself as well. I had to get beyond these limits I'd accepted. No more excuses. I said yes to the three sessions offered and vowed to try my best.

The next morning, I used my wheelchair to get myself to a trampoline-like platform just above the water surface. Two staff people lifted me down to the mat. They put fins on *both* my feet—no more rest for the "bad" one. Then they supported me on both sides as the platform moved on its huge lift into the water. When we were partially submerged but still on the platform, they fitted a mask and snorkel to my face, and held me carefully as we all floated together off the platform. Lloyd was right—I didn't sink after all.

My first session was spent mostly getting used to the water and getting acquainted with my therapist, Christy. The mask was uncomfortable, so I wore it only a short time. Floating on my back instead, I lay back and put my ears under the water. I could hear the dolphins beneath me. Christy explained that they were "scanning" my body with their sonar, a fast, clicking noise like showers of buckshot on a hollow block.

Suddenly, as I lay motionless, a dolphin brushed up against me. It knocked me off balance and I completely tensed up. I was terrified of drowning.

"Let's set a goal of spending more time on your stomach," Christy said. "That way you can look through the mask at the dolphins as you swim."

But just being so helpless in the water felt overwhelming. Frankly, I couldn't handle any goals except getting out!

"Try one more thing before your session's over," Christy suggested. "Grasp these floating barbells and hold on to them at arm's length. Then you can swim with fins, without having to use your arms."

I was encouraged to grasp the barbells with both hands. I protested that my left hand was useless, but when I looked, I realized that my fingers, which Christy had carefully placed around the bar, were indeed grasping it. For the first time since my strokes, my paralyzed arm had become part of my body's overall effort. My arm had a purpose again!

The first session lasted a half-hour. I expected to be exhausted, but I wasn't. After lunch and a rest, I was more than ready for another try with my new acquaintances.

My confidence level was definitely higher that afternoon as I slipped into the water for my second session. Christy found me a better-fitting snorkel and mask, and this time I was able to float on my stomach, arms outstretched, both hands balancing my body with my flotation barbells, for longer and longer periods of time.

Being with the dolphins motivated me. Now that I could see them, I liked having them near me. I was amazed at how gentle these big creatures could be. Most striking was the total acceptance I felt emanating from them. They never came on too strong nor did they seem afraid of me. They somehow unerringly matched their energy with my own, as if they could sense my feelings. I found their attention invigorating and especially enjoyed interacting with one named Fonzie. All the dolphins were playful, twisting and spiraling effortlessly through the water. But there were times I swore I saw laughter sparkling in Fonzie's eyes. I found myself laughing, too.

My playmates took me so far out of myself that I felt completely comfortable in the water. Toward the end of the session, I asked my mother, who was watching us, whether my left leg was obeying my "commands" to move. She gestured excitedly for me to look for myself. I turned and found that my leg was moving side to side. It was still a limited motion, but it meant my brain and my leg were communicating again. I was elated.

As the session ended, I swear that Fonzie was grinning—sharing in the responsibility for my success.

When I got back to my motel room, I found myself feeling so "up," so energized, that I couldn't stay still. The old me would have stayed comfortably safe in my room, but now I wanted to get outside, to feel the breeze. To my own surprise, once I was outside I still felt restless. I wanted more than a breeze, I wanted to go down to the bay.

I headed my wheelchair for the water. *My brain and my leg are communicating!* I kept telling myself. If I could swim, it seemed there was little I couldn't try.

Do you really believe that? I asked myself. The answer was an unexpected, unequivocal *yes*!

Before I could come to my senses, I stopped and pulled

myself up out of my wheelchair. The bay was a good 100 yards away, down an uneven gravel road. I grabbed my quad-cane—and began walking.

My parents, walking the same way a little later, found my wheelchair abandoned along the road. Scared to death, they hurried ahead, terrified in what condition they might find me.

Imagine their surprise when they found me walking, my head held high, delighting in the beauty around me. They brought the wheelchair back empty, as I walked back to my room. That was the first time since the strokes that I'd walked so far. I felt like I'd won the Boston Marathon!

The third session with the dolphins was even better than the second. I discovered growing movement in my affected leg and I was able to control the spasms in my limbs, which had been a problem in past sessions. Perhaps the highlight of the session was when Fonzie raced with Christy and me while Christy pulled me around the pool. "See? I knew you could do it!" she exulted.

Nor did I feel any fear as several of the dolphins brushed gracefully against me. Christy explained that that was their way of making sure I felt welcome. I couldn't believe I had ever been frightened of these magnificent creatures. Their acceptance and playful spirit reopened the place in my heart that looks forward with joy to all life can offer. I felt truly renewed.

My three sessions completed, I returned home to my family. I was energized and enthusiastic, and had a greater confidence in myself and my physical capabilities. I had new control over the limbs we'd all given up on.

There was no medical explanation for my improvement, but it was real. What's more, the improvement went far beyond my physical body. The dolphins' total acceptance of me helped me to better accept and love myself, just the way I am. And the act of overcoming my fear and pushing past my limitations had a profound impact on how I approach every aspect of my life.

Since then, I have bought a specially equipped bicycle that I ride regularly. I've also signed up for horseback riding and registered for a special sailing program designed for people with disabilities.

I'm determined not to set any more limits for myself. Whenever I'm tempted to give in to fear, or simply stay in my comfort zone, I picture the grinning Fonzie, pushing me along, beyond the limits of my doctors' prognosis. They said, "This is as good as you'll ever get." I'm glad the dolphins knew better.

Roberta (Rusty) VanSickle

There's a Squirrel in My Coffee!

A person has two legs and one sense of humor, and if you're faced with the choice, it's better to lose a leg.

Charles Lindner

Our house near Jacksonville, Florida, is a veritable zoo. My wife and I wanted our seven-year-old twins to develop the same love for nature and animals that we had when we were children. We have tortoises and turtles, snakes, iguanas, frogs, rabbits and a four-pound attack-Yorkie named Scooter. We even had a wayward baby armadillo for a spell. But when Rocky came to stay, our household—and our lives—changed dramatically.

A career Navy pilot, I was at home recovering from a rare, invisible form of a deadly skin cancer that had required some drastic surgery, and I definitely needed a humor injection in my daily routine. Rocky was just what the doctor ordered. The doctor, however, turned out to be a veterinarian, not an oncologist!

Dr. John Rossi is the local animal doctor. When someone showed up at his vet clinic with a tiny baby flying squirrel that had fallen from his nest, John and his wife, Roxanne, reasoned that if a baby flying squirrel couldn't help a recovering cancer patient, nothing could.

Rocky became an immediate fixture in our home. When Rocky first arrived, he resembled a little ball of dust—like the ones you find in the guest bedroom closet during spring cleaning. He was no bigger than a walnut and he weighed less. His eyes had recently opened and he drank formula and water from a tiny toy baby bottle. He barely moved and his fur was kind of oily, like a "greaser" from the 1950s. His bulging black eyes looked like aviator goggles, and my twins, having just seen an old cartoon rerun of *Rocky and Bullwinkle,* immediately named him Rocky.

He grew quickly and was soon the size of a fresh bar of soap: his adult size. Rocky's fur turned a silky smooth brown as he learned to clean himself regularly, and his eyes grew even more bulgy. His loose skin and his flat rudder-like tail turned him into a rodent Frisbee during his daily flying lessons, which I conducted by gently tossing him from our bathroom onto our bed. Rocky didn't require much training because gliding came so naturally for him.

Flying squirrel movements are extremely fast and are very vertically oriented. In the wild, they rapidly run up and down tree trunks. In the same way, Rocky ran up and down our bodies, moving like a high-scoring furred pinball in a flesh-and-blood pinball machine.

Moving at what seemed the speed of light, he was all over the inside and outside of our clothing as we tried to catch him with our bare hands. The tickling, particularly when he dived into the armpits—one of his favorite haunts—was incredible. This activity has become a daily ritual in our household, wonderfully uplifting our spirits. My doctors are amazed at how quickly my scars have healed. If laughter is the best medicine, then Rocky has delivered it by the truckload.

One morning, I was enjoying my morning coffee like most people do, except that I had a newspaper in front of me and a squirrel on top of me. Rocky was sitting on my head surveying his squirreldom, probably wondering if he had nibbled off the large chunk of my left ear that had been removed during cancer surgery. Suddenly, I sneezed. It was a big sneeze—one that occurred as I was bringing my cup of coffee, now lukewarm, to my lips. Afterwards, as I reopened my eyes while continuing to bring my coffee to my mouth, I saw two of the most enormous, bulging eyes that I had ever come face-to-face with in my life, a furred hyperthyroidic monster if I'd ever seen one.

"Peggy, there's a flying squirrel in my coffee!" I yelled, laughing hysterically as my wife sprinted into the room. In an instant, Rocky had scrambled back onto my head and was preening himself, probably getting a caffeine buzz to boot.

I picked the newspaper back up, then quickly put it back down in a moment of reflection. We've all had those moments, when suddenly everything is brilliantly clear and sharp, and laced with humor and an overwhelming sense of gratitude. I was overcome by the realization that I was an utterly unique being. Unquestionably—absolutely unquestionably—I was the only person in the world, perhaps in the universe, that had the amazing good fortune to have a flying squirrel in his coffee that morning.

By now, Rocky was sound asleep under my sweater. Unaware of my earth-shattering musings, he had curled up directly on a large scar at the base of my neck where my jugular vein, trapezoid muscle and 200 lymph nodes had been surgically removed.

Rocky—and God—were doing their healing magic once again.

Bill Goss

Finders Keepers

When my daughters reached the third and fourth grades, I occasionally allowed them to walk to and from school alone, if the weather permitted. It was a short distance, so I knew they were safe and no trouble would befall them.

One warm spring day, a small friend followed them home after school. This friend was different from any other friend they had brought home. She had short stumpy legs and long floppy ears, with a fawn-colored coat and tiny freckles sprinkled across her muzzle. She was the cutest puppy I had ever seen.

When my husband got home that evening, he recognized the breed—a beagle puppy, not more than twelve weeks old, he guessed. She took to him right away and after dinner climbed into his lap to watch TV. By now the girls were both begging me to keep her.

She had no collar or identifying marks of any sort. I didn't know what to do. I thought about running an ad in the lost-and-found but I really didn't want to. It would break the kids' hearts if someone should show up. Besides, her owners should have watched her more closely, I rationalized.

By the end of the week she was part of our family. She was very intelligent and good with the girls. *This was a good idea,* I thought. It was time the girls took responsibility for another life so they would learn the nurturing skills they'd need if they decided to become mommies when they grew up.

The following week something told me to check the lost-and-found section in the local paper. One particular ad jumped out at me and my heart pounded with fear at what I read. Someone was pleading for the return of a lost beagle puppy in the vicinity of our grade school. They sounded desperate. My hand shook. I couldn't bring myself to pick up the phone.

Instead, I pretended I hadn't seen the ad. I quickly tucked the paper away in the closet and continued with my dusting. I never said a word about it to the kids or my husband.

By now we had named the puppy. She looked like a Molly, so that was what we called her. She followed the girls everywhere they went. When they went outside, she was one step behind them. When they did chores, she was there to lend a hand (or should I say, paw).

Homework proved a challenge with her around. More than once the teacher was given a homework page that the dog had chewed on. Each teacher was understanding and the girls were allowed to make it up. Life was definitely not the same at the Campbell household.

There was only one problem with this otherwise perfect picture: my conscience was bothering me. I knew in my heart I had to call that number and see if our Molly was the puppy they were desperately seeking.

It was the most difficult thing I've ever done. Finally, with sweaty palms, I lifted the receiver and dialed. Secretly I was praying no one would answer, but someone did. The voice on the other end was that of a young woman. After describing the dog to her in detail, she wanted to come right over.

Within minutes she was at my door. I had been sitting at the kitchen table, head cradled in my hands, asking God for a miracle. Molly sat at my feet the whole time, looking up at me with those big puppy-dog eyes—eyes the color of milk chocolate. She seemed to sense something was wrong.

A thousand thoughts crossed my mind before the woman rang the bell. I could pretend I wasn't home or tell her, "I'm sorry, you have the wrong address." But it was too late; the bell rang and Molly was barking. I opened the door, forcing myself to face my fear.

One look at Molly and the woman's face lit up like a Christmas tree. "Here, Lucy," she called. "Come to Mamma, girl." Molly (Lucy) instantly obeyed, wagging her tail in delight at the sound of the woman's voice. Obviously she belonged to the woman.

Tears stung at the back of my eyelids and threatened to spill over at any moment. I felt like my heart was being ripped from my chest. I wanted to grab Molly and run. Instead I smiled faintly and asked her to please come in.

The woman had already bent over and scooped Molly up into her arms. She awkwardly opened her purse and stretched out a twenty-dollar bill toward me.

"For your trouble," she offered.

"Oh, I couldn't." I shook my head in protest. "She's been such a joy to have around, I should be paying you." With that she laughed and hugged Molly tighter to her bosom as if she were a lost child and not a dog.

Molly licked her face and squirmed with delight. I knew it was time for them to go home. Opening the door to let them out, I noticed a little girl sitting in the front seat of the van. When the child saw the puppy, a smile as bright as a firecracker on the Fourth of July exploded across her face.

My glance turned to a small wheelchair strapped to the back of the van. The woman saw me look at the chair and offered an explanation without my asking. Molly (Lucy) was given to the child to promote emotional healing after a car accident had left her crippled for life.

When the puppy disappeared from the yard, the little girl had gone into a deep depression, refusing to come out of the shell she was in. Molly (Lucy) was their only hope their daughter would recover emotionally and mentally.

"She formed a special bond with the puppy and Lucy gave her a reason to live," her mother explained.

Suddenly I felt very guilty and selfish. *God has blessed me with so much,* I thought. My heart went out to this family that had been through such a terrible time. As they pulled out of the drive, the smile on my face was genuine. I knew I had done the right thing—that puppy was exactly where she belonged.

Leona Campbell

Seeing

Love is a language which the blind can see and the deaf can hear.

Donald E. Wildman

Barkley came to me when he was three years old, from a family who just didn't want him anymore. They had badly neglected the big golden retriever and he was in ill health. After attending to his physical problems and spending some time bonding with him, I found he had a very sweet temperament. He was intelligent and eager to please, so we went to basic and advanced obedience classes and to a social therapy workshop to learn everything we needed to know for Barkley to become a certified therapy dog.

Within a few months, we began our weekly visits to the local medical center. I didn't know what to expect, but we both loved it. After I made sure a patient wanted a visit from Barkley, the dog would walk over to the bed and stand waiting for the person in the bed to reach out to him. People hugged him tight or simply petted him, as he stood quietly wagging his tail with what seemed a huge laughing grin on his face. His mellowness made him a favorite with the staff, patients and even the other volunteers.

I dressed Barkley in something different every week. He had costumes appropriate for each holiday—he wore a birthday hat on his birthday, a green bow tie for Saint Patrick's Day and a Zorro costume on Halloween. For Christmas he sported a Santa hat or reindeer horns. Easter was everybody's favorite: Barkley wore bunny ears and a bunny tail I attached to his back end. Patients were always eager to see what Barkley was wearing *this* week.

About a year after we began visiting, I noticed Barkley was having trouble seeing—he sometimes bumped into things. The vet found he had an eye condition caused in part by his lack of care when he was young. Over the next year, this condition worsened, but Barkley was remarkably good at functioning with his failing eyesight. Even I wasn't aware how bad it had become until one evening when Barkley and I were playing with his ball out in the yard. When I threw the ball to the dog, he had a lot of trouble catching it. He had to use his nose to sniff it out on the ground after he repeatedly failed to catch it in his mouth. The next day I brought him to the vet and they told me that surgery was necessary. After three surgeries in an attempt to save at least some of his vision, Barkley became totally blind.

I was very concerned about how he would adjust to such a terrible handicap, but he acclimated to his blindness rapidly. It seemed that all his other senses sharpened to make up for his loss of sight. Soon he was completely recovered and insisted (by standing at the garage door and blocking my exit!) that he wanted to go along with me to the hospital and visit his friends. So we restarted our weekly visits, much to everyone's great joy—especially Barkley's.

He maneuvered around the hospital so well, it was

hard to tell that he was blind. Once after Barkley became blind, someone asked me if Barkley was a seeing-eye dog. I laughed and told them that it was Barkley who needed a seeing-eye person.

He seemed to develop an uncanny ability to perceive things that were beyond the senses. One day, we went into a patient's room and to my surprise, Barkley went over to the patient's visitor, who was sitting in a chair by the bed, and nudged her hand with his nose. Barkley never made the first contact like that, and I wondered why he did it now. As I came up to her chair, it was only by the way the woman interacted with Barkley that I realized the truth. I don't know how, but the completely blind Barkley had sensed that this lady was blind, too.

It was strange, but after Barkley lost his sight, his presence seemed even more precious to the patients he visited.

When Barkley received an award for performing over 400 hours of volunteer service, everyone told me, "It's amazing what a blind dog can do!"

They didn't understand that Barkley wasn't really blind. He could still see. It's just that now, he saw with his heart.

Kathe Neyer

Guardian Angels

"What are *you* doing here?" my wife, Joyce, exclaimed.

I found Joyce on our deck, gazing down ecstatically at a dog. It was a roly-poly, short-legged, blond-and-white Welsh corgi, ears up. He regarded Joyce with a delighted grin.

Uh-oh, I thought.

Our own two dogs, after reaching extreme old age, were buried on a little hill overlooking the pond. Now, on her walks in town, Joyce visited other people's dogs—Spike the basset, Sophia the Samoyed, Pogo the black whatever. She would say, every so often, "Shouldn't we get another dog?" But I had come to relish the freedom of doglessness.

Now this corgi had trotted onto our deck as if he owned it.

"He's tubby," I pointed out. "He obviously has a wonderful home, where they're munificent with kibbles."

We traced the corgi to new neighbors, a half-mile up the road. They were upset to learn their dog had wandered down the road, dodging cars. The corgi's name, we learned, was Nosmo King, inspired by a "No Smoking" sign.

In the months afterwards, when I crossed the road to check our mailbox, I would sometimes look up the hill and see an animal silhouetted against the sky. A wolflike head, pricked-up ears. *A coyote? A fox?* It seemed too short-legged. It would gaze down the hill at me, as if mulling over what to do. Then it would turn and vanish back up the road. Only later did I realize it was a lonesome corgi, mustering the gumption to make another run for it.

On a morning when red maple leaves lay on the lawn, Joyce glanced up from her desk. Through her office's sliding glass door, Nosmo grinned at her.

That day marked a change. Afterwards, no matter how his owners tried to confine him, several mornings a week Nosmo played Russian roulette with the road's rushing chromium bumpers and showed up on our deck. He would stare in the glass door of Joyce's office, grinning. Let in, he would roll belly up, his stubby legs waving in the air, mighty pleased with himself.

One of us would reach for the telephone. But we always found ourselves speaking to our neighbors' answering machine. Since they worked, Nosmo was alone all day.

"If we don't do something, he's going to keep running down the road and he'll be killed," Joyce said.

"What can we do?" I said. "He's not our dog."

Whenever Nosmo appeared at our door, we would drive him home. He hopped into the car eagerly, ready for an adventure. But we would only imprison him in his house's breezeway to wait for his owners to return. He would watch our receding car through the breezeway's glass door, stricken. He had chosen us. We had turned him away. Looking back as we drove off, Joyce looked as stricken as Nosmo.

One day she made an announcement: "From now on, when Nosmo escapes and comes down, he stays with us until somebody is home at his house."

So, every few days, Nosmo would show up. We would take him in until evening, when his owners returned. On his initial visits, he had shot us searching looks before venturing into a different room, unsure about the local regulations. Now he had the air of a nabob who had bought the place . . . and paid cash.

One evening Nosmo's owners called us. They had to go away for two weeks. They asked, "Could you take Nosmo while we are gone?"

A few nights after Nosmo began his visit, I found Joyce looking worriedly at our foster dog as he slept on the rug.

"Do you think Nosmo looks right?" she asked. "He doesn't chase sticks any more."

It was true. He no longer raced back clenching a thrown stick in his teeth, eyes flashing, daring anyone to wrestle for his prize. Now when Joyce tossed a stick, he just watched, wistfully. Then he would sit dully.

"We have to take him to the vet," Joyce announced.

After the examination, the veterinarian told us that Nosmo's condition was serious. He had a herniated colon. He had already had one operation for this condition. Now he needed another operation, and it was no sure thing. But without surgery, he would slowly die.

When Nosmo's owners returned, Joyce gave them the news. A few days later, she called them again to hear what they had decided. When she put the telephone down, she looked shaken.

"They're afraid the operation is useless, and that they may have to have him put to sleep," she told me.

Joyce slumped at the kitchen table, her chin resting on her hands. Her eyes welled with tears. Without the operation, Nosmo had little hope. And even with the surgery, Nosmo would always need extra attention. Since his family worked all day and he was alone . . .

"What more could you do?" I asked. "You've been Nosmo's guardian angel. Joyce, he's not our dog," I said finally.

For a moment Joyce stared out the window at the end-of-summer fields, the grasses already turning gold and tan. And then she recited a line of verse, by Robert Frost. It was one of our favorites: "Home is the place where, when you have to go there, they have to take you in."

After a moment, Joyce added her own line. "He chose us," she said.

Joyce called Nosmo's owners with an offer: "Let us do day care—we'll be his nurses."

After his successful operation, Nosmo became a dog with two homes. En route to work each morning, one of his owners dropped him off at our house. Every evening, on our way into town, we returned Nosmo to his owners.

Mornings Joyce took Nosmo for a long therapeutic walk. I would watch them from my office window, the concerned-looking woman, the little dog, wandering toward the meadow or into the pine woods across the waterfall.

"It's beautiful here—I'd forgotten," Joyce told me one day. "Now that I'm walking Nosmo, I'm appreciating my own backyard."

Two years passed. And then Nosmo's owners changed jobs and moved to a city apartment that allowed no dogs. Our day-care dog officially became our dog, full time.

One month after Nosmo became our dog, Joyce was diagnosed with a life-threatening illness, acute leukemia, and abruptly went into the hospital. Every day I brought Nosmo to her window, so she could look out and see him grinning up at her. "My therapy dog," she called him. When she finally came home, weakened but on the mend, Nosmo was there to greet her. He had no tail, but his entire body wagged with joy.

Joyce was hospitalized again, and then a third time. Each time she returned home, Nosmo greeted her by throwing himself on his back, waving his flipperlike legs in the air and grinning. Joyce could feel her spirits rising. She could almost feel her immune system stepping up. "Nosmo," she would say, "you are helping me to recover."

As I write, I am looking out my office window. On the back lawn, Joyce is throwing a stick, Nosmo is barking, running, leaping for the stick. He must secretly feed on TNT, he has so much pep. And Joyce is laughing. She, too, radiates life and energy.

I stand at my window, watching Joyce play with the dog, and I think about guardian angels.

I know they exist, for I have seen one with my own eyes. As a matter of fact, I've seen two.

Richard Wolkomir

A Real Charmer

Henry was fourteen years old when he received a gift: a four-foot-long boa constrictor. By the time I arrived on the scene, Henry was seventeen years old and George, the boa, was eight feet long. George was thriving, but Henry was declining.

I still smile when I recall the day the three of us met: It was the day I was interviewed by Henry's parents for a nurse's position. Henry had muscular dystrophy and was getting weaker, too needful to be cared for by his folks alone. While the parents studied my résumé, I walked into Henry's room, knelt down and looked this carrot-topped boy in the eye. Taking note of his thin, twisted body strapped in the wheelchair, I said, "Hi, kid. Need some help, do you?"

Intelligence and mischief looked back merrily at me. Henry had concocted a test for me: a kind of baptism by fire. "Yes, I do. How about bringing George over here?"

Unwittingly I replied, "Sure; where is he and what is he?" I looked around the room, expecting to see a cat, a dog, even a stuffed animal. My glance fell on a large, box-like glass structure across the room.

"George is my boa," Henry smirked. "Would you get him for me, please?"

A snake! I was an excellent nurse, in high demand. I knew that I could walk out of there anytime before I actually accepted the job. Considering the situation, I looked at Henry. *Boy, this kid is cute,* I thought. I glanced around his room. Piles of automotive magazines, books, notepads and pencils littered the folding table that served as Henry's desk. Race car posters and photos of football heroes hung on the walls. Here was a real boy, a tiny teenager, shriveled with disease, yet with humor intact and a flair for the bizarre. Always a sucker for a good-looking face and ready for a challenge, I knew I wanted the job.

"So, uh, how do I pick him up?" I asked, looking into the glass-walled cage containing what appeared to be a gigantic, coiled rope big enough to anchor the *Titanic.*

Henry chuckled. "Very carefully. Grasp him gently behind his head with one hand and support his body with your other."

"That's it? That's the extent of your instructions?" I asked. I opened the hinged lid and felt the cold reptile with my trembling fingers. The snake moved ever so slightly at the touch. *I can do this,* I thought. I waited a moment for a surge of courage. But it didn't come. One deep breath, and I took the plunge, grasping the enormous George and lifting him slowly out of his cage. Before I completed the lift, several feet of the beast swiftly wrapped tightly around my arm. "I can do this," I repeated over and over to myself.

Henry watched silently and intently as I crossed the room, bearing the heavy length of pure muscle.

"What do you want me to do with him?" I asked.

Henry said, "Just put his head and upper body on my lap. George enjoys being petted."

That was my introduction to George. As the months

went by, it was apparent that George was a great—if not the sole—motivator in Henry's life.

It was difficult for Henry when we took a rare excursion in public to eat at McDonald's or visit the bookstore. People stared rudely as Henry laboriously ate his meal or tried to flip through the books with three fingers, the only appendages still responsive to his commands.

But each week, we went to the pet store to buy food for George. After Henry was meticulously bathed, groomed and coiffed, I'd carefully place him in his wheelchair and push him out to my car. Next, after much maneuvering, I'd tenderly strap and pillow him into the passenger seat, fold up his chair and fit it into the trunk. This all took about two hours; two grueling hours for me, two painful hours for Henry as we both struggled not to hurt his delicate body—an impossible task. What a testament to Henry's devotion to his gigantic pet.

One time George turned up missing. Henry's uncle had visited over the weekend and left the top of George's cage open. His parents and I looked everywhere in the elegant yet Spartan home, streamlined for easy mobility for Henry's wheelchair. *There is nowhere for George to hide,* we thought. But we couldn't locate the snake anywhere.

A month went by. Henry was surprisingly calm, convinced that George would reappear in due time. I felt bad for Henry, but I couldn't honestly say I missed George in the least.

I arrived early one morning and went in to awaken Henry. There was George, stretched almost full-length beside Henry as they both slept. I was shocked by my own reaction, but I found the sight one of the most charming I have ever seen. George had finally won me over!

Over the following months, Henry continued to deteriorate, his body coiling tighter, his breathing becoming more labored. Yet he maintained the use of those three fingers, doing his school work and spending hours stroking George. Three frail fingers determinedly kept the loving connection of boy and boa—even to the last day.

On that final day, Henry wrote me a note. I found an envelope with my name on it on his desk. I was touched, as I had grown to care deeply for the valiant boy. He started the note by thanking me for helping him so much with George and, acknowledging my reluctant fondness for the snake, said he knew he could count on me to care for George now that he was gone. I panicked for a moment until I noticed his P.S. Under a smiley face, Henry wrote that I didn't really have to worry—the U.P.S. man had agreed to take George.

Oh, Henry, I thought, *you're still teasing me.* But I did make a point of stroking George fondly one last time before I left.

Lynne Layton Zielinski

Socks

When I was about six or seven, I had a little mutt puppy named Socks. Socks and I were inseparable buddies for the half year he was with me. He slept at the foot of my bed. The last thing I felt at night and the first thing I felt again in the morning was his warm, wiggly form. I loved him with a love that has dimmed little as the years have passed.

One day, Socks turned up missing. A neighborhood rumor circulated about someone seen coaxing him into a car, but nothing could ever be proved.

Socks stayed missing, and I cried myself to sleep for many nights. If you've never lost a dog, then you don't know the feeling, but believe me, it only slightly diminishes with time. My parents tried everything to get me to brighten up, with no apparent luck. Maturity and years healed the wound so that it was no longer visible, but it remained inside me.

One day, many years later, my feelings resurfaced. My family and I were visiting my parents at their wooded acreage in northern Michigan when our tagalong family mongrel, Buckshot, turned up missing.

Old Buck was a pretty good hound. He resembled a big, lovable bear cub more than he did a proper dog, and this day he decided to see what was on the other side of the mountain.

His disappearance hit my seven-year-old son, Chris, especially hard, since Chris figured that Buck was his personal property. The other kids were fond of the dog too, but not like Chris.

Chris was the archetypal freckle-faced little guy with missing teeth and chubby cheeks. He had the knack of looking sad and pitiful even when he was happy. When he was broken-hearted, the angels held their breath.

Chris worried that his pal was gone forever, and looking at my son, I could feel the years peel away. I saw myself and Socks all over again. The old pain came back.

The rain started falling softly as I hoisted myself into my Jeep and began driving back roads, stopping to call Buckshot with a disturbing touch of frenzy in my voice. In my mind's eye, I saw Chris out in the rain wearing a slicker that was way too big, searching with falling hopes.

Miles later, with a throat scraped raw from screaming, I still hadn't reduced the family pet to possession. Back at the cabin, I parked the Jeep and took off on foot, avoiding Chris's eyes, not wanting to admit that maybe a city-bred dog could get irretrievably lost in all that wilderness.

I struck out for the depths of a quaint little piece of real estate the locals refer to as Deadman's Swamp, muttering under my breath about dogs and their hold on small boys. If you've ever wandered around alone way back in the woods as nightfall is setting in, then you know what kinds of tricks your mind can play on you. I felt my vision fog up. The old pain was resurfacing.

After five miles of walking, screaming, running and sweating, I sat down on a slab of rock near an open meadow and tried to sort out how I was going to tell the little man that lived at my house that I couldn't find his dog.

Suddenly I heard a rustle from behind me. Whipping around, I saw old Buck bounding up to me with that where-the-heck-have-you-been attitude that runaway dogs muster up when they're finally found. We rolled on the ground together, my frustration dissolving in the wet ferns. After a bit, I put the dog at heel and we half stumbled and half ran back to the cabin.

When we came out of the woods, my son with the long face, my own father and the vagabond pooch grabbed and hugged one another. That was when it hit me.

I felt as if I had been transported back in time to witness a homecoming I'd hoped for but never experienced. My dad was there, looking thirty again. The little boy hugging the spotted hound was me—a quarter century ago. And old Buck? He was another much-loved mutt who'd finally found his way back.

Socks had come home.

Steve Smith

Jenny and Brucie

Jenny Holmes struggled with her weight every day of her young life. When she was twelve, she wasn't heavy, but she thought she was because she wanted to be thin like a model. An aspiring gymnast, Jenny also wanted to be lithe and wiry, like the Olympic athlete, Nadia Comaneci. She didn't lose weight until she was sixteen. Then she lost twenty pounds in the aftermath of a breakup with her first love, a sort of vengeance upon him. Her long battle with food and weight began. This occurred over the course of twelve years, during which time she tried again and again to lose weight, only to gain it back each time.

Little did Jenny know during those years that the change in her self-image would have nothing to do with low-fat shakes, counting calories or even giving up ice cream and chocolate. It would be a gift from a dog.

Brucie appeared in Jen's life on her twenty-ninth birthday, a gift from her husband, John. Jenny was the happily married mother of two by then. She owned a successful small business selling custom-printed T-shirts. Trying to keep a sense of humor about her efforts to lose weight, she designed one for herself that read, "Those who indulge, bulge." No one else ever called her "fat." At five feet, four inches and 150 pounds, her legs were muscular and her hips thick, but her torso was slim. She had become a woman with a woman's shape, but she still hated her backside. Jenny continued to long for the straight, thin, boyish look of a model.

Brucie, a yellow Labrador pup, came complete with big kisses and a bouncy personality. He was never intended to be a diet aid; he was meant to be a running partner. John loved Jenny just as she was, but he knew that Jenny always seemed more at peace with herself and her body when she ran. He couldn't work out with her himself because he had a bad back. So that job was left to Brucie.

In the beginning Brucie and Jenny ran only fifty paces at a time, each set mixed with increments of one hundred paces walking. *I don't look foolish starting this way,* thought Jen, *because Brucie's bones are too young to make him run much harder.* She was right, and Brucie's early limitations gave her time to start slowly without feeling awkward.

After ten months, though, Brucie was old enough to run several miles a day and Jenny was fit enough to keep up! They logged the miles together every day.

Prior to Brucie's appearance in her life, one of Jen's problems with exercising had always been staying motivated. Everything she read advised pairing up with a running partner. Human exercise companions, however, always let her down. One moved away. Another collected running injuries the way some people collect stamps. A third simply quit. She knew that her last exercise companion was cutting out when he made excuses like, "It's my turn to do the dishes"—at six o'clock in the morning! She hated to admit it, but she had let others down in similar ways. Jenny expected the same from Brucie. She knew that he would run with her, but she didn't count on the pup for help with motivation.

Wrong! The first morning that Jen wanted to stay in bed, Brucie licked her face. When she buried her head under her pillow, he dug her toes out from beneath the blanket. Jenny tucked in her toes more tightly, but Brucie jumped onto the bed. After she pushed sixty pounds of Labrador off her, he whined and thumped his tail against the wooden floor like a drummer. He quieted down when she hushed him, only to return to licking her face! That morning and every one thereafter, Jen and Brucie ran.

Jenny didn't think that she had the courage to face the winter running, but Brucie was undaunted. Shaking his head with disbelief while the dog pranced in the snow and barked outside of Jen's window to awaken her, John decided to give his wife a warm, lightweight set of winter running clothes. Spring brought mud and rain, but Brucie still wanted to run, and what could Jenny do? They had endured freezing temperatures and snowdrifts together. Surely they could manage a bit of slush and sogginess. Besides, she had become Brucie's running companion, too. She could no longer even try to say no to the wide brown eyes that gazed at her every morning when Brucie came to her with his leash in his mouth. Sometimes he even delivered her running shoes to her.

They ran together for ten years. When arthritis and age kept him on the step waiting for Jenny to return from a workout with a new puppy, Brucie didn't seem to mind. He would lie with his face between his paws until he saw them loping into sight, then his tail would thump excitedly against the porch. When they got to the driveway he eagerly walked to see them, his whole body quivering with delight as it had when he was a puppy.

Brucie died last year. Jen, John and their kids scattered

his ashes along a wooded path where they had frequently run together. Today Jen continues to run with her new dog as well as her growing children. Just like Brucie, they don't let her sleep in on rainy Saturday mornings.

Jenny still makes T-shirts for people, but no more "Battle of the Bulge" shirts for her. She's working on a shirt to wear in the Boston Marathon next spring. The front shows a hand-painted Labrador retriever. On the back Jenny stenciled, "Brucie, this one is for you."

Cerie L. Couture, D.V.M.

An Extra Ten Minutes

When you rise in the morning, form a resolution to make the day a happy one for a fellow creature.

Sydney Smith

On Monday afternoons at two o'clock, Beau and I would arrive at the Silver Spring Convalescent Center on Milwaukee's northeast side of town for an hour of pet therapy with the seniors who lived there. We'd walk the hallways greeting everyone on our way to the hospitality room, where residents would come to pet Beau and bask in the adoration of this beautiful, happy, ten-year-old, ninety-nine-pound Doberman pinscher. You'd never know this was the same dog that arrived at my doorstep eight years earlier so beaten, scarred and scared that as soon as he made eye contact with you, he'd lie down on his back with his feet up in the air and pee until you petted and soothed him into feeling safe.

On our first visit, as we walked through the canary-yellow Hallway One, I heard an elderly man's excited voice, thick with a German accent, streaming out of room

112. "Ma, Ma, the German dog is here! The German dog is here!"

No sooner did I hear the voice than a wrinkle-faced, six-foot-tall, white-haired pogo stick of a man was greeting us at the door, swooping his big, open hand and strong arm across the doorway, inviting us in. "I'm Charlie. This is my wife, Emma. Come in, come in."

When Beau heard Charlie's friendly, enthusiastic voice, his entire body went into his customary wagging frenzy and lean-against-your-thigh position, waiting for a petting, which was immediately forthcoming from Charlie. As we walked into the room, a frail but lively eightyish, violet-haired Emma sat in bed, smiling, patting her hand on the bed. All she had to do was pat once, and Beau, leashed and always obedient, was up on the bed lying down beside her, licking her face. Her eyes teared up as Charlie told us that he and Emma had immigrated to the United States from Germany during World War II and had to leave their beloved Doberman, Max, behind. Max, according to Charlie, was the spitting image of Beau.

The next door, room 114, was home to Katherine, a woman in her seventies who had stopped talking a few months earlier and had been living in a catatonic state in her wheelchair for the past month. No amount of love, hugs, talking or sitting had been able to stir her. I was told her family had stopped calling or visiting, and she had no friends. When Beau and I walked into her room, a small light was on next to her bed and the shades were pulled. She was sitting in her wheelchair, her back toward us, slouched over, facing the viewless window.

Beau was pulling ahead of me with his leash. Before I could get around to kneel down in front of her, he was at her left side, with his head in her lap. I pulled a chair up in front of her and sat down, saying hello. No response. In the fifteen minutes that Beau and I sat with Katherine, she never said a word and never moved. Surprising as that may be, more surprising was that Beau never moved either. He stood the entire fifteen minutes, his long chin resting on her lap.

If you knew Beau, you'd know that even ten seconds was an eternity to wait for a petting. As long as I'd known him, he would nuzzle whatever person was closest to his nose, whine, soft-growl and wiggle his body against them until they were forced to pet him, or he'd lose interest and find someone else. Not here. He was as frozen as Katherine, head glued to her lap. I became so uncomfortable with the lack of life in this woman that, much as I wished I felt differently, when the clock chimed 2:30 P.M., I rushed to say good-bye, stood up and pulled the reluctant Beau out.

I asked one of the nurses why Katherine was catatonic. "We don't know why. Sometimes it just happens when elderly people have family who show no interest in them. We just try to make her as comfortable as possible."

All the wonderful people and animals who blessed my life flashed in front of my eyes, and then they were gone. I felt what I imagined Katherine must be feeling: lonely, lost and forgotten. I was determined to find a way through to her.

Every Monday thereafter, Beau and I made our rounds to the hospitality room, stopping to make special visits in room 112 to visit Charlie and Emma, and in room 114 to sit with Katherine. Always the same response—Charlie waving us in and Emma patting the bed, waiting for Beau's licks, both so alive. And then on to Katherine, sitting desolately, no sign of life except for her shallow breathing.

Each visit I attempted to engage Katherine in conversation, asking her questions about her life and telling her about mine and Beau's. No response. I grew more and more frustrated with Katherine, not content with just "being" with her. Yet here was Beau, meditative dog-monk, teaching me how to "be" and love quietly, assuming "the position" for the fifteen minutes we sat at each visit.

On our fourth visit, I was ready to bypass Katherine's room, figuring we didn't really make a difference, so why bother, but Beau had other plans. He pulled me into Katherine's room and took his familiar pose on her left side, head on lap. I acquiesced, but since I had a business meeting later in the afternoon with which I was preoccupied, I decided to cut short our usual fifteen minutes with Katherine to five. Instead of talking, I remained quiet, focusing inwardly on my upcoming meeting. Surely she'd never notice or care. As I stood up to walk out and began to pull Beau away, he wouldn't budge.

And then the most miraculous thing happened. Katherine's hand went up to the top of Beau's head and rested there. No other movement, just her hand. Instead of Beau's customary response of nose nuzzling and increased body wagging, he continued to stand like a statue, never moving from his spot.

I sat back down in silent shock, and for the next ten precious minutes, reveled in the stream of life flowing between Katherine's hand and Beau's head. As the clock chimed half-past two, marking the end of our fifteen minutes, Katherine's hand gently slid back into her lap, and Beau turned to walk out the door.

It's been ten years since that visit and eight years since Beau died in my arms from a stroke. Love has many ways of showing its face. Each time I am ready to walk away from a person on whom I've given up, I am reminded of the power of Beau's loving persistence with Katherine and with me. If Beau can give an extra ten minutes, surely I can too.

Mary Marcdante

4

CELEBRATING THE BOND

You become responsible forever
for what you have tamed.

Antoine de Saint-Exupéry

The Language of Horses

My father, a traditional horseman, was a tough authoritarian. He used intimidation and brutality to "break" horses to his will. Unfortunately, he used the same methods on me. At eight years old, after witnessing a particularly vicious example of my father's methods, I vowed that my life would be different. I would use communication, not violence, to enlist the cooperation of the horses I trained. I was sure that horses had a language, and if I could speak that language, I could train horses in a new and entirely different way. So it was at the age of eight that I set a life goal for myself—to be able to communicate fluently with horses.

My father thought this idea was nonsense, so I had to pursue my goal without his help. My mother supported me, but secretly, for she also feared my father's anger. We lived on a horse facility in Salinas, California, at the time, and I spent every waking hour trying to communicate with the untamed domestic horses on the facility.

The summer I was thirteen, I went to Nevada for three weeks for a job. I had been hired to capture wild mustangs. This was the first opportunity I'd had to work with totally wild horses. Determined to make the best use of my time, I rose early each day and rode a long way into the desert, where I used binoculars to study the habits of the mustang herds that lived there.

I was utterly spellbound by these horses. I would sit for hours and hours, watching those beautiful animals as they ran, grazed and played in the wide spaces of the desert.

What astonished me most was how the wild horses communicated with each other. They rarely used sounds; instead, they used a complex language of motion. The position of their bodies, and the speed and direction of their travel were the key elements of their language. And by varying the degree of rigidity or relaxation in the eyes, ears, neck, head and position of the spine, a horse could signal anything it needed to communicate.

As I watched, I thought: *Could I convince a wild horse to let me get close enough to touch him without him running away?*

For easy spotting, I picked a horse with unique markings, and tried to herd him away from the others. For many days I tried every way I could think of to get near him, but he always sensed me and he was off before I was even close. One day, I got lucky and came up behind him in a small canyon. At last, I had his full attention. Then, using only my body to convey the signals I'd seen the horses use with each other, I persuaded the wary stallion to stand still. He watched me silently as I moved closer and closer. He was watchful, but he wasn't afraid. Not breathing, I took the step that brought me within an arm's reach of him. I avoided his eyes as I stretched my hand toward him and laid it softly on his neck. It lasted only a few seconds, but it was enough. I watched him gallop away, my chest exploding with joy. I had communicated with a horse!

When I returned home, I was bursting with excitement and told my mother what had happened in the desert with the mustang. While I could see that she was happy for me, all she said was that I must never speak of it to my father or anyone else, or I would get in trouble. I felt let down, but I knew she was right. My desire to learn to communicate with horses became a deep inner passion that I fiercely hid from the rest of the world.

Unable to share what was most important to me with anyone, I was almost always alone, except for the horses. The only thing that mattered to me was my life's dream.

Every summer, I returned to Nevada for three weeks to work, continuing my research in the desert. Four years later, when I was seventeen, I progressed so far that I not only touched a wild mustang, I saddled, bridled and rode one without once using any pain or intimidation to do so. Proudly, I rode the wild horse back to the ranch. The ranch hands who saw me ride in called me a liar when I told them what I'd done. They ridiculed me and insisted the horse I rode must once have been a domesticated horse who had run away and ended up with the mustangs. Deeply hurt, I realized the futility of my dreams. With no one to believe in me, it was *my* spirit that was broken.

I eventually got over the pain of that devastating humiliation and decided to continue my training methods, but I vowed I would never again tell anyone what I did.

And so I became a horse trainer. I used my experiences with every horse I worked with to learn more and more about the language of horses. It was a slow but satisfying education.

Once, when I was about twenty-five, a family hired me to tackle the problem of their mare, My Blue Heaven. She was a beautiful horse, intelligent and extremely talented. But during her training, a previous owner had inadvertently mishandled her and she had developed a serious problem: She wouldn't stop. She would blast away like a rocket and refuse to be halted—crashing through fences, and slipping and sliding as she made dangerously sharp turns. She was diabolically treacherous. A short time earlier, the mare had almost killed the present owner's daughter. The family was going on vacation and they asked me to sell the horse for them for whatever I could get for her. They had heard I was good with difficult horses and they knew in order to sell her, someone would have to be able to bring her to a stop from a run. No one else was willing to try.

She was the most dangerous horse I had ever seen, but I used everything I had absorbed over the years to help her. Moving slowly and keeping my communication with her to just the basics, I earned her trust. Building on that trust, I continued to communicate with her, and soon she melted. Our progress was swift and remarkable from that point on. It had seemed impossible, but within a few days, she was transformed.

While the owners were still away, I showed her in a competition and she took first place. I brought her prize, a very expensive saddle, to the home of the family who still owned her. I wrote them a note, explaining that she had improved enough to win this saddle and under the circumstances, I felt that they should reconsider selling her. I pinned the note to the saddle and left it in the dining room for them to find upon their return.

They were ecstatic about the change in My Blue Heaven and were thrilled to be able to keep her. My Blue Heaven went on to become a world-class champion. And her owners found in her a new willingness and sweet temper that made her presence in their family even more precious than her show value.

My Blue Heaven was one of my first public triumphs. But this same story repeated itself over and over during the next thirty years. Hopeless cases were referred to me, and using the simple tools of gentleness, respect and communication, I managed to turn them around.

By then, it was hard to keep my work secret. Even though I still met with some skepticism and scorn, I found many more who were open to, and enthusiastic about, what I was doing.

I was particularly well received in England. In fact, in 1989, I was astounded to find myself, the son of an American horse trainer, being presented to Her Royal Majesty, Elizabeth II, queen of England. It had been a long and often painful road from the high deserts of Nevada to the splendor of Windsor Castle.

That was the turning point of my career. The queen then endorsed my methods and provided me with her private car to tour England and demonstrate my techniques all over the country. Today, it is even possible to study my methods of horse training at West Oxfordshire College in England.

I have achieved what I set out to do when I was a boy of eight. But I feel that I am just a scout, marking the trail for all who will follow me. I watch the young people who are studying my work, and I know they will carry it forward to achieve communication with horses I can't even begin to imagine.

In a certain way, I have my father to thank for setting my life on this course. Out of his work with horses, my passion for them began. And from his violence, my dream was born—that all horses be spared the needless pain and suffering of being "broken."

Monty Roberts
As told to Carol Kline

The Rescue

I wish people would realize that animals are totally dependent, helpless, like children; a trust that is put upon us.

James Herriot

In July 1994, the Emergency Animal Rescue Service set up a shelter in Bainbridge, Georgia, in response to the floods generated by Hurricane Alberto. The animal rescue volunteers arrived in this small Southern town, located on the Flint River, before the floodwaters had spread to the neighborhoods bordering the river.

While out looking for animals that had been left behind, a team of volunteers met a man who had two dogs, which he had no intention of taking with him when he finally evacuated. When the volunteers offered to shelter the man's two dogs, he shrugged his shoulders and said, "Hey, it makes no difference to me."

When asked where the dogs were, he moved toward the elevated front porch of his tiny home and bent down. A minute later, he dragged a large black-and-white dog out from under the rundown house. The man gathered the dog in his arms, walked toward one of our trucks, and deposited him in an airline crate. Then he turned and walked away, not bothering to even say good-bye.

Amy, one of the volunteers, asked the man some questions as she completed the animal-intake form. When she asked what the dog's name was, he replied, "He doesn't have one."

Unable to locate the man's other dog, the volunteers returned to the animal disaster relief center with just the nameless dog. When Amy went to the back of the truck and opened the door of the airline crate, the dog sat still, staring at the floor of his cage. No matter how much Amy coaxed, the dog would not budge. Concerned that maybe the dog was frightened by the height, Amy closed the crate door and had another volunteer help her lower it to the ground.

But another attempt at coaxing the dog out of the crate met with the same response. The dog just stared at the bottom of its cage, displaying absolutely no reaction to the volunteer and not once showing any signs of aggression.

It was time to try something else.

Amy clipped a leash to the dog's collar, and then with the help of another volunteer lifted the back end of the crate so that the dog would slide out. When he landed on the ground, he just lay there.

"What's wrong with this dog?" the volunteer asked Amy as they both stared at the dog lying at their feet.

"I'm not sure, but my guess is he's been abused."

Amy was right. The dog had been abused, but it was not physical abuse that had made him this way. It was neglect.

A lot of the rescue program volunteers have had to face animal abuse and neglect for the first time during disasters, and it's never easy to accept the reality that not everyone treats animals the way they should.

The reality hit Amy hard, but she was determined to do something to help the nameless dog. The first thing she did was name him Albert.

For the next two days, Amy carried the sixty-pound dog around the compound, since he still refused to stand up or walk. One of Amy's jobs was to feed the other dogs who were housed in runs that lined our perimeter fence. As Amy moved from one pen to the next, she'd pick up Albert and move him along with her. In spite of all the barking and commotion the other dogs created, Albert did not react. He just sat on the grass, staring at the ground.

In an effort to save her back, we borrowed a golf cart from the neighboring country club. As Amy made her feeding rounds, Albert then sat in the front seat of the cart, staring at the floorboard, still not responding to any of his surroundings.

At night, Albert lay next to Amy's cot. When we ate, Albert sat next to Amy, refusing to accept any of the tidbits of human food she offered him. In the heat of the afternoon, Amy would find a shady spot and stretch out on the ground next to Albert. I remember, one of those afternoons, standing back and watching the two of them as Amy whispered something into Albert's black, floppy ear. I could only imagine what she was saying to the dog that still refused to respond.

Albert had been with us for four days when we had a late-night birthday party for one of the volunteers. As director of the rescue program, I always came up with an excuse to have a party to relieve the tension and momentarily forget the pain and suffering present in disasters. Laughter and chocolate ice cream always do the trick. That is why we never travel into a disaster area without our ice cream scoop.

The volunteers were gathered under the tent loaned to us by Levy Funeral Home, each one wearing his own

Barney birthday hat and acting like a five-year-old. There were outbursts of laughter, storytelling and lots of chocolate being consumed, and sitting in the middle of it all was Albert, still at Amy's side.

"Look!" a volunteer suddenly shouted above the clamor, as he pointed in Albert's direction.

The group immediately quieted down, unable to believe what it was seeing. Albert was still sitting in the same place, but the very tip of his long black-and-white tail appeared to wag. As we all stared in amazement, Albert's entire tail started wagging. The next thing we knew, he stood up and his rear end was switching back and forth. Then he turned his head and his eyes started blinking, and his ears twitched. It was as if someone had suddenly pushed Albert's "on" button. Albert came alive for probably the first time in his life.

After that evening, the once nameless dog never stopped moving. His whole purpose in life was to keep up with Amy. Wherever she went, you could count on Albert being no more than two steps behind her. As she fed the other dogs, Albert trotted along with her, responding to the other dogs as if to say, "I am finally happy."

Amy and Albert were inseparable. Even when Amy walked to the nearby fire station to take a shower, Albert accompanied her. When Amy got into the shower, Albert hopped right in too, refusing to let Amy out of his sight.

I was beginning to notice, though, that Albert still did not have the energy of an eighteen-month-old dog. We decided it would probably be a good idea to have Albert pay a visit to Dr. Hight, the veterinarian in Bainbridge who was a great help to us. The vet confirmed our fear: Albert had heartworm. The good news was that because Albert was a young dog and the problem was not yet advanced, the doctor was willing to try to treat the frequently fatal illness.

This gave me the excuse I'd been looking for to call Albert's owner. When I explained to him that Albert had heartworm and that it would cost at least $300 to treat him, I expected he'd say, "I don't have the money, so you keep the dog."

But I was wrong. He wanted Albert back.

"You understand that if the dog isn't immediately treated for the heartworm, he'll die," I told the man on the other end of the phone, still hoping I could convince him to release the dog to me.

"Yeah. I understand. That's what happens to all my dogs, and when I lose this one, I'll get myself another one," the man replied, without the least bit of remorse in his voice. "Oh, yeah, my house didn't flood, so I'll be out shortly to pick up my dog."

With that, the man hung up.

In the distance, I saw Amy and Albert playing tug-of-war with a towel. "How am I going to tell Amy we have to give Albert back?" I said half-aloud, as tears streamed down my cheeks. "It'll kill them both."

An hour later a dark blue Camaro pulled up to the front gate, and I immediately recognized the man who stepped out of the car. In his hand he carried a heavy chain. As he came through the gate, Amy spotted him too. I had just explained to her that Albert's owner would be there soon to reclaim his dog. It was one of the most difficult things I'd ever had to do.

At that moment, I wished I were not the director of the rescue program. I wished more than anything that I could make one dog mysteriously disappear. Because of my responsibilities, I knew that I couldn't. If we got the reputation of taking people's animals and not giving them back because we didn't like the way they were cared for, it could prevent us from helping animals in the future.

We have, during disasters, reported instances of animal

abuse to local authorities, but as long as an owner is providing food, water and shelter and is not physically abusing the animal, the law protects the person from having his or her animal confiscated. Since emotional neglect is not considered abuse, Albert's owner was within the law.

When I remembered the shell of a dog that had arrived less than a week before, and what Amy had done to bring him to life, I was distraught. How could we just let him die now?

"Where's my dog?" the man asked in a gruff voice when he spotted me near the intake tent.

"One of the volunteers is walking him right now," I replied, looking over his shoulder to where I could see Amy crouched on the ground next to Albert, her arms wrapped around his neck. This time I didn't have to imagine what she was whispering in his ear. I knew she was saying good-bye.

"Well, get him. I have things to do," he replied impatiently. I had to ask one more time. "Are you sure you want your dog back?" I asked. "I expect he's not going to live much longer."

"Yeah. I want him back," the man said as he turned to survey the property. It took him only a second to spot his dog, still cradled in Amy's arms. "There he is," he said as he started toward the far end of the property.

That was when I reached my hand into my pocket.

"Wait!" I shouted, causing the man to stop and turn back toward me. "How about if I buy that dog from you?" I offered, and then held my breath, waiting for his answer, the fifty-dollar bill scrunched in my hand.

I didn't have to wait long. Before I knew it, the man's hand was palm-up in front of him. His reply was exactly what I wanted to hear. "Sure. I'll sell him."

And so Albert went to live with Amy and her family. He was successfully treated for the heartworm, and when I saw Albert about a month after the floods, it was hard to believe he was the same dog. Albert had been dead inside, but now with his shining eyes and happy prance, he was simply overflowing with life and love. He had been rescued in spirit as well as in body.

Terri Crisp

Lucky to Be Alive

Maria, a gentle, soft-spoken woman of seventy, had always managed to view the world with a child's sense of wonderment. She greeted the dawn of each new day with the brightness of the sun itself and found joy in the smallest of things: a dove perched on her birdfeeder, the fresh morning dew, the sweet scent of jasmine in her garden.

A widow, Maria lived alone in a run-down neighborhood in Deerfield Beach, Florida. One day while out tending the small garden in front of her modest home, Maria had been injured in a drive-by shooting. The bullet had pierced through her skin with a ferocious bite and lodged itself in the old woman's right thigh. Crying out in agony, she had dropped to the sidewalk. When the mailman found her unconscious nearly an hour later, her injured leg had been bleeding profusely. She'd made it to the hospital just in time and later, the doctor had told Maria she was lucky to be alive.

Returning home, Maria didn't feel so lucky. Before the shooting, the elderly woman had always been grateful that she was healthy for her age. Now just getting the daily mail required a Herculean effort. In addition, her medical bills were mounting alarmingly, straining her meager income. And although she had watched the neighborhood deteriorate, somehow things had seemed safe in the daylight—but not anymore. For the first time in her life, Maria felt frightened, alone and vulnerable.

"I feel defeated," she had told her friend Vera. "I'm just an old woman with nothing to do and nowhere to go."

When Vera came to pick up Maria for her checkup at the medical center, she hardly recognized her old friend. Maria's soft brown eyes held a haunting sadness and her face was gaunt and haggard. All the curtains were drawn and her hands shook with fear as she hobbled out onto the front porch, a cane stabilizing her injured leg.

They were a little early for Maria's appointment, so to try to cheer up Maria, Vera took a longer, more scenic route. They were stopped at a red light when Maria suddenly shrieked. "Look at that cat! It's trying to run across the street!"

Vera looked up to see a small black-and-white cat bounding out into the middle of traffic. Both women screamed as they saw one car, then another, and finally a third, hit the cat. The cat lay motionless, its small body flung into the grass. Cars slowed, but no one stopped to help.

"We must save that poor creature," said Maria. Vera pulled over, got out of the car and went to the hurt animal. Miraculously, it was still alive, but badly injured.

"Take my jacket and wrap the kitty in it," said Maria. Vera carefully put the cat on the seat between them. It looked up at Maria and gave her a plaintive, barely audible meow.

"Everything will be all right, my little friend," Maria said tearfully.

Finding an animal clinic, they went inside and told the receptionist what had happened.

"I'm sorry," she said, "but we cannot accept stray animals."

It was the same at the next clinic. Finally, at the third clinic, a kind veterinarian, Dr. Susan Shanahan, agreed to help and quickly started working on the cat.

"This little guy is lucky to be alive," she told Maria and Vera. "If you hadn't been there for him, he never would have made it."

The vet took Maria aside. "The cat's injuries are very serious," she said. "He has severe head trauma, crushed paws and a cracked collarbone. He'll need a lot of expensive medical attention. Today's bill alone will cost at least $400."

Maria gasped. But taking her worn cloth wallet out of her handbag, she gave the doctor all the money she had after paying her bills—$50.

"It's all I have right now, but I promise I will pay you the rest over time. Please don't put that kitty to sleep," she pleaded. "I'll take him home. We *need* each other."

Sensing how important this was, Dr. Shanahan kneeled and took Maria's hands in hers. "I could get into trouble with my boss for doing this," she said gently. "You see, I really shouldn't have helped the cat in the first place, but, don't worry . . . I will personally pay for this."

While the cat was at the clinic, Maria went to check on him every day. She spoke softly to him and gently stroked his chin with her little finger. As the days passed, the cat began to purr and the sparkle returned to Maria's eyes.

The day arrived for the cat to come home. As excited as a little girl on Christmas morning, Maria smiled brightly as she walked into the clinic to pick him up.

"What have you decided to name the cat?" asked Dr. Shanahan.

Cradling the cat in her arms, Maria answered happily, "I'm going to call him Lucky, because together we have found a new life."

Christine E. Belleris

Dog of War

Cry havoc and let slip the dogs of war.

from Shakespeare's *Julius Caesar*

In Vietnam, we all made choices with which we now must live. How many bullets do you carry versus how much water? When the rescue chopper says "only three" and there are four of you left, do you leave a guy or "lock and load" on the Huey driver, hijacking the craft? Worst of all, when it's dark and nobody can help you, do you let some fatally injured kid die slowly or just get it over with?

Not all my decisions were ones I regret. And not all my memories are the kind that jerk my breath away at three in the morning and leave me waiting with clenched fists for the first blessed light of dawn. In the darkness of that time, there was one bright spot: a big German shepherd named Beau.

Beau was a scout dog attached to my infantry unit. His job was to sniff out Viet Cong tunnels, ammo caches and booby traps. Like many of us, he was a soldier on the outside and a puppy in his heart.

When we had to wait for our next move, which was

often, Beau was a great source of entertainment. His handler would tie a thin monofilament line across a path, then dare someone to step over it. Beau's job was not to let anyone trigger a booby trap. He'd been taught it was better to attack one GI than have a mine pop into the air and detonate at the level of everybody's head.

I would spend a minute petting Beau and sharing my C-rations with him. Then I'd start walking toward the string. Beau was never won over by my offers of food. As I approached the trip wire, he'd race to get between me and it, then flatten his radar station ears and roll out an awesome set of glowing white, bone-crushing teeth. His eyes looked straight into mine as his huge torso sank into a crouch, preparing to spring. We dealt with pretty scary stuff, but when Beau told you to stop, no one had the guts to take a step.

After nearly getting shredded by the big guy, I'd go back to my food. Immediately we were pals again.

One steamy, miserable day, my unit was moving through an area of light jungle and tall trees. I was about fourth from point; Beau and his handler were behind me. Gunshots, their sharpness blunted by the smothering heat and humidity, exploded overhead. We hit the vine-covered jungle floor. Beau crouched between me and his handler. "In the trees," someone hissed. As I looked, there were more shots, louder this time. Beau flinched but gave no other sign of injury. I emptied three twenty-round clips in the direction of the noise. My frantic and scruffy peers did likewise. In a moment, it was over.

I looked at Beau. He seemed okay. We made him roll over, then stand up. It was then I caught that line of slick, dark blue-red we all knew too well. A bullet had pierced his foreleg. It appeared to be a clean hole, bleeding only slightly. I patted him and he wagged his tail. His sad, intelligent eyes expressed, "It's okay, Joe. I'm not important. I'm just here to protect you."

A chopper took the dog and his handler away. I patted him and wondered if they would send the big guy home. What a naive kid I was. Some weeks later they were back. Beau had learned even more ways to con me out of my dinner.

Mid-summer, 1967. We were a thousand meters from a huge field outside a tiny hamlet called Sui Tres. In that field was an American artillery unit. Around them were 2,500 Viet Cong. Our job was to shoot our way through and secure the Howitzer guys.

We slept on the jungle floor, lying with our heads on our helmets. Just before dawn we heard the unsteady rumble of machine-gun and heavy-weapons fire erupt from the direction of Sui Tres. Time to face the enemy.

I put on my helmet and reached for the rest of my gear. Beau wandered over to see if we had time for breakfast. The dark jungle was filled with the normal din of muttered curses and rustling equipment. Overhead, Russian-made rockets were about to burst in the treetops around us. The approaching rockets sounded like escaping steam, followed by what seemed like a long moment of silence. Then deafening, lung-crushing thunder.

Dust filled the air. I was face down on the ground, not knowing how I got there. People were screaming for medics. My helmet was split open by shrapnel and would no longer fit on my head. Beau's long black tail wagged near me in the confusion. He was crouched by his handler, waiting for orders. But it was no use; the young soldier had given his last command.

I pulled Beau gently away and stroked the fur on his back. Sticky liquid covered my hand and ran down the side of his body. A tiny piece of shrapnel had penetrated his back just below the spine. Again he seemed not to notice, and tried to pull away to be with his handler. "He didn't make it," I said, kneeling and holding him against my chest. "He just didn't make it."

Each GI is issued a large cloth bandage in an olive-drab pouch attached to his web gear. The rule is to use your buddy's bandage for him and save yours for yourself. Beau didn't have a bandage, so I wrapped him with mine.

They took the dog away with the other wounded. I never saw Beau again.

September 18, 1967. After eleven months and twenty-nine days in Vietnam, I was going home. Malaria had reduced me from 165 pounds to 130 pounds. I looked and felt like a corpse in combat boots. My heart was filled with death—the smell, the look, the wrenching finality of it.

I was standing in line to get my eyes checked. We all had clipboards with forms to fill out. The guy in front of me asked if he could use my pen. He'd been a dog handler, he said. Now he was going home to his family's farm in Iowa. "It's a beautiful place," he said. "I never thought I'd live to see it again."

I told him about the scout dog I'd befriended and what had happened to him and his handler. The soldier's next words took my breath away.

"You mean Beau!" he exclaimed, suddenly animated and smiling.

"Yeah, how'd you know?"

"They gave him to me after my dog got killed."

For a moment I was happy. Then two miserable thoughts popped into my brain. First, I'd have to ask him what had happened to Beau. Second, this handler was on his way home, leaving that loyal mutt to stay here till his luck ran out.

"So," I said, looking at the toe of my jungle boot as I crushed out an imaginary cigarette, "what happened to that dog?"

The young soldier lowered his voice the way people do when they have bad news. "He's gone."

I was so sick of death I wanted to throw up. I wanted to just sit down on the floor and cry. I guess this guy noticed my clenched fists and the wetness in my eyes. He lowered his voice and looked around nervously.

"He's not dead, man," he said. "He's *gone.* I got my company commander to fill out a death certificate for him and I sent him back to my parents' house. He's been there for two weeks. Beau is back in Iowa."

What that skinny farm kid and his commanding officer did certainly didn't mean much compared with the global impact made by the war in Vietnam, but for me, it represents what was really in all our hearts. Of all the decisions made in 'Nam, that's the one I can live with best.

Joe Kirkup

The Deer and the Nursing Home

The deer had been struck and killed by a car. A passing motorist on the narrow mountain road saw a slight movement and stopped. Huddled beside the dead deer was a fawn with the umbilical cord still attached. "I don't suppose you have a chance," the motorist told the tiny creature as he tied off the cord, "but at least I'll take you where it's warm."

The nearest place was the powerhouse of New Jersey's Glen Gardner Center for Geriatrics, a state institution. Maintenance men there quickly produced rags to make a bed behind the boiler for the fawn. Then they took a rubber glove, pricked pinholes in a finger, diluted some milk and offered it to the fawn, who drank eagerly.

With the men taking turns feeding the fawn, the little deer's wobbly legs and curiosity soon grew strong enough to bring it out from its bed behind the boiler. On their breaks, the men petted and played with the baby. "If it's a female, we'll call her Jane Doe," they laughed. But it was a male, so they taught him to answer to "Frankie," short for Frank Buck.

Frankie became especially attached to one of the men, an electrician named Jean. On nice days, Frankie stepped outside with his new friend, enjoying the fresh air and scratches behind the ears. Sometimes other deer came out of the woods to graze. When Frankie caught their scent, his head came up.

"You'd better tie him or we'll lose him," someone commented.

Jean shook his head. "He'll know when it's time to go," he said.

Frankie began following Jean on his rounds, and the slight, white-haired man followed by the delicate golden fawn soon became a familiar sight.

One day a resident, noticing Frankie waiting by a door for Jean, invited the deer in. Glen Gardner housed old people who had been in state mental hospitals and needed special care. When Frankie was discovered inside, the staff rushed to put him outside. But when they saw how eagerly one resident after another reached out to touch him, they let him stay. When Frankie appeared, smiles spread and people who seldom spoke asked the deer's name.

Discovering a line in front of the payroll clerk's window one day, Frankie companionably joined it. When his turn came, the clerk peered out at him. "Well, Frankie," she said, "I wouldn't mind giving you a paycheck. You're our best social worker!"

The deer had the run of Glen Gardner until late fall, when the superintendent noticed he was growing antlers. Fearful he might accidentally injure a resident, the supervisor decreed banishment. Frankie continued to frequent the grounds, but as the months passed he explored farther afield. When he was a year old, the evening came when he didn't return to the powerhouse; now he was on his own.

Still, every morning he was there to greet Jean, exploring the pocket for the treat Jean always brought, and in the afternoon he would reappear. Residents who had refused to go outside before would join him on the front lawn to scratch his ears. George, a solitary resident with a speech defect who didn't seem to care if people understood him or not, taught Frankie to respond to his voice, and they often walked together.

When Frankie was two years old—a sleek creature with six-point antlers and a shiny coat—he failed to show up one April morning. Nor did he answer anyone's calls. It was late the next day before Jean and George found him lying on a sheltered patch of ground. His right front leg was shattered, jagged splinters of bone jutted through the skin.

"Oh, you old donkey," Jean whispered. "What happened?" The deer's eyes were clouded with pain, but he knew Jean's voice and tried to lick his hand.

"There's no way to set a break like that without an operation," said the veterinarian who examined Frankie. They would have to haul Frankie out of the woods on an improvised litter and drive him to Round Valley Veterinary Hospital, five miles away.

On the day of Frankie's surgery, the surgeon, Dr. Gregory Zolton, told Jean, "You'll have to stay with me while I operate. I'll need help." Jean's stomach did a flip-flop, but he swallowed hard and nodded. During the two-hour procedure, Dr. Zolton took bone from Frankie's shoulder to make a graft between the broken bones and then screwed a steel plate across it.

"He said a leg that wasn't strong enough to run on wasn't any good to a deer," recalls Jean.

After the surgery, they took Frankie to an unused horse stable on Glen Gardner's grounds, and Jean sat in the straw beside the recovering deer. He stroked Frankie's head and held him whenever the deer tried to struggle to his feet. Finally, as the sun was coming up, Jean took his own stiff bones home, cleaned up and went to work.

By the seventh day, Jean called Dr. Zolton to say it was

impossible to hold Frankie still for his antibiotic injections. The surgeon laughed. "If he's that lively, he doesn't need antibiotics." But he warned that Frankie must be kept inside for eight weeks. If he ran on the leg before it knitted, it would shatter.

"Whenever anyone went to visit him, Frankie showed how eager he was to get out," recalls Jean. "He'd stand there with his nose pressed against a crack in the door. He smelled spring coming."

When word had come that Frankie had survived the operation, the residents' council at Glen Gardner had called a meeting. Mary, the president, told the group, "There's no operation without a big bill. Now, Frankie's our deer, right?" The residents all nodded. "So we've got to pay his bill." They decided to take up a collection and hold a bake sale.

The day Dr. Zolton's bill arrived, Mary called a meeting. The others watched silently as she opened the envelope. "Oh, dear," she murmured bleakly, "we owe $392." They had managed to collect only $135. Not until she shifted her bifocals did she notice the handwriting, which read: "Paid in Full—Gregory Zolton, D.V.M."

When Frankie's confinement was over, Frankie's friends gathered by the stable door. It was mid-June and grass was knee-deep in the meadow. The buck's wound was beautifully healed—but would the leg hold?

Jean opened the barn door. "Come on, Frankie," he said softly. "You can go now." Frankie took a step and looked up at Jean.

"It's all right," Jean urged him. "You're free." Suddenly Frankie understood. He exploded into a run, flying over the field like a greyhound, his hooves barely touching the ground.

"He's so glad to be out," Mary said wistfully, "I don't think we'll ever see him again."

At the edge of the woods, Frankie swerved. He was coming back! Near the stable he wheeled again. Six times he crossed the meadow. Then, flanks heaving, tongue lolling, he pulled up beside them. Frankie had tested his leg to its limits. It was perfect. "Good!" said George distinctly. Everyone cheered.

Soon Frankie was again waiting for Jean by the electric shop every morning. In the fall Jean put a yellow collar around Frankie's neck to warn off hunters. The mountain was a nature preserve, with no hunting allowed, but poachers frequently sneaked in.

One day a pickup truck filled with hunters drove up to the powerhouse. When the tailgate was lowered, Frankie jumped down. The hunters had read about him and, spotting the yellow collar, figured it must be Frankie.

Every hunting season, George and the other people at Glen Gardner debate whether to lock Frankie in the stable for his own safety—and their peace of mind. But each fall, the vote always goes against it. Frankie symbolizes the philosophy of Glen Gardner, which is to provide care but not to undermine independence.

"A deer and a person, they each have their dignity," Jean says. "You mustn't take their choices away."

So Frank Buck, the wonderful deer of Glen Gardner, remains free. He runs risks, of course, but life is risk, and Frankie knows he has friends he can count on.

Jo Coudert

Turkeys

Something about my mother attracts ornithologists. It all started years ago when a couple of them discovered she had a rare species of woodpecker coming to her bird feeder. They came in the house and sat around the window, exclaiming and taking pictures with big fancy cameras. But long after the red cockaded woodpeckers had gone to roost, the ornithologists were still there. There always seemed to be three or four of them wandering around our place and staying for supper.

In those days, during the 1950s, the big concern of ornithologists in our area was the wild turkey. They were rare, and the pure-strain wild turkeys had begun to interbreed with farmers' domestic stock. The species was being degraded. It was extinction by dilution, and to the ornithologists it was just as tragic as the more dramatic demise of the passenger pigeon or the Carolina parakeet.

One ornithologist had devised a formula to compute the ratio of domestic to pure-strain wild turkey in an individual bird by comparing the angle of flight at takeoff and the rate of acceleration. And in those sad days, the turkeys were flying low and slow.

It was during that time, the spring when I was six years old, that I caught the measles. I had a high fever, and my mother was worried about me. She kept the house quiet and dark and crept around silently, trying different methods of cooling me down.

Even the ornithologists stayed away—but not out of fear of the measles or respect for a household with sickness. The fact was, they had discovered a wild turkey nest. According to the formula, the hen was pure-strain wild—not a taint of the sluggish domestic bird in her blood—and the ornithologists were camping in the woods, protecting her nest from predators and taking pictures.

One night our phone rang. It was one of the ornithologists. "Does your little girl still have measles?" he asked.

"Yes," said my mother. "She's very sick. Her temperature is 102."

"I'll be right over," said the ornithologist.

In five minutes a whole carload of them arrived. They marched solemnly into the house, carrying a cardboard box. "A hundred and two, did you say? Where is she?" they asked my mother.

They crept into my room and set the box down on the bed. I was barely conscious, and when I opened my eyes, their worried faces hovering over me seemed to float out of the darkness like giant, glowing eggs. They snatched the covers off me and felt me all over. They consulted in whispers.

"Feels just right, I'd say."

"A hundred two—can't miss if we tuck them up close and she lies still."

I closed my eyes then, and after a while the ornithologists drifted away, their pale faces bobbing up and down on the black wave of fever.

The next morning I was better. For the first time in days I could think. The memory of the ornithologists with their whispered voices was like a dream from another life. But when I pulled down the covers, there staring up at me with googly eyes and wide mouths were sixteen fuzzy baby turkeys, and the cracked chips and caps of sixteen brown speckled eggs.

I was a sensible child. I gently stretched myself out. The eggshells crackled, and the turkey babies fluttered and cheeped and snuggled against me. I laid my aching head back on the pillow and closed my eyes. "The ornithologists," I whispered. "The ornithologists have been here."

It seems the turkey hen had been so disturbed by the elaborate protective measures that had been undertaken on her behalf that she had abandoned her nest on the night the eggs were due to hatch. It was a cold night. The ornithologists, not having an incubator on hand, used their heads and came up with the next best thing.

The baby turkeys and I gained our strength together. When I was finally able to get out of bed and feebly creep around the house, the turkeys peeped and cheeped around my ankles, scrambling to keep up with me and tripping over their own big spraddle-toed feet. When I went outside for the first time, the turkeys tumbled after me down the steps and scratched around in the yard while I sat in the sun.

Finally, in late summer, the day came when they were ready to fly for the first time as adult birds. The ornithologists gathered. I ran down the hill, and the turkeys ran too. Then, one by one, they took off. They flew high and fast. The ornithologists made Vs with their thumbs and forefingers, measuring angles. They consulted their stopwatches and paced off distances. They scribbled in their tiny notebooks. Finally they looked at each other. They sighed. They smiled. They jumped up and down and hugged each other. "One hundred percent pure wild turkey!" they said.

Nearly forty years have passed since then. Now there's a vaccine for measles. And the woods where I live are full of pure wild turkeys. I like to think they are all descendants of those sixteen birds I saved from the vigilance of the ornithologists.

Bailey White

Tiny and the Oak Tree

. . . a family cat is not replaceable like a worn-out coat or a set of tires. Each new kitten becomes his own cat, and none is repeated. I am four-cats old, measuring out my life in friends that have succeeded, but not replaced one another.

Irving Townsend

He was scary-looking. Standing about six-foot, six-inches tall, he had shoulders the width of my dining room table. His hair hung to his shoulders, a full beard obscured half of his face; his massive arms and chest were covered with tattoos. He was wearing greasy blue jeans and a jean jacket with the sleeves cut out. Chains clanked on his motorcycle boots and on the key ring hanging from his wide leather belt. He held out a hand the size of a pie plate, in which lay a tiny, misshapen kitten.

"What's wrong with Tiny, Doc?" he asked in a gruff voice.

My exam revealed a birth defect. Tiny's spine had never grown together, and he was paralyzed in his back legs. No amount of surgery, medicine or prayer was going to fix him. I felt helpless.

The only thing I could tell this big, hairy giant was that his little friend was going to die. I was ashamed of my prejudice but I felt a little nervous anticipating the biker's reaction. Being the bearer of bad news is never pleasant, but with a rough-looking character like the man in front of me, I didn't know what to expect.

I tried to be as tactful as possible, explaining Tiny's problem and what we could expect, which was a slow, lingering death. I braced myself for his response.

But the big fella only looked at me with eyes that I could barely see through the hair on his face and said sadly, "I guess we gotta do him, huh, Doc?"

I agreed that, yes, the best way to help Tiny was to give him the injection that would end his poor, pain-filled life. So with his owner holding Tiny, we ended the little kitten's pain.

When it was over, I was surprised to see this macho guy the size of an oak tree just standing there holding Tiny, with tears running down his beard. He never apologized for crying, but he managed a choked "Thanks, Doc," as he carried his little friend's body home to bury him.

Although ending a patient's life is never pleasant, my staff and I all agreed that we were glad we could stop the sick kitten's pain. Weeks passed, and the incident faded.

Then one day the oak-sized biker appeared in the clinic again. It looked ominously like we were about to repeat the earlier scenario. The huge man was wearing the same clothes and carrying another kitten in his pie-plate hand. But I was enormously relieved upon examining "Tiny Two" to find he was absolutely, perfectly, wonderfully normal and healthy.

I started Tiny Two's vaccinations, tested him for worms and discussed his care, diet and future needs with his deceptively tough-looking owner. By now, it was obvious that Mr. Oak Tree had a heart that matched his size.

I wonder now how many other Hell's Angel types are really closet marshmallows. In fact, whenever I see a pack of scary-looking bikers roaring past me on the road, I crane my neck to see if I can catch a glimpse of some tiny little kitten poking its head up out of a sleek chrome sidecar—or maybe even peeking out from inside the front of a black leather jacket.

Dennis K. McIntosh, D.V.M.

The Captain

Humankind has not woven the web of life. We are but one thread within it. Whatever we do to the web, we do to ourselves. All things are bound together. All things connect.

Chief Seattle

In the middle of Iowa, on acreage just on the outskirts of a little town, sits an old farmhouse. Inside the house there are lots of couches and soft comfortable chairs, hand-built perches and scratching posts, kitty doors that lead to outside pens with grass and trees and lots of sunny spots to stretch out in. Every day volunteers come to groom and pet and feed freshly cooked food to the many cats who have this farmhouse all to themselves. There is also a small staff who keep the cats' house sparkling clean.

There are dogs there, too. Out back behind the house, near the garden and the orchard, are large dog kennels with insulated and heated doghouses in them. Volunteers come to walk and feed and "love up" the rescued dogs who are brought there when their time is up at the city pound.

As you can tell, the Noah's Ark Animal Foundation runs an unusual kind of no-kill sanctuary. Yet it is a state-licensed animal shelter, officially run as a non-profit charitable organization for over a decade.

For many years I dreamed of running a shelter for lost, stray and abandoned animals. But I wanted the shelter to be comfortable and home-like. Plus, I wanted to feed the animals healthy high-quality food and treat any ailments with natural remedies. Noah's Ark has been that dream-come-true for me. It has been wonderful to watch as the often malnourished animals who come to the shelter start blossoming with health. Their shining coats and bright eyes make all the hard work worthwhile.

Their personalities blossom, too. Some of the cats assume the role of official greeter, strolling out to inspect anyone who comes to visit.

Freddy, a large and beautiful gray Persian, was one of these greeters at Noah's Ark. In fact, I called Freddy "the Captain." He was not a cuddly cat, being far too macho for that, but he was a friendly sort and no one came to the shelter who was not subject to the Captain's inspection, and perhaps a rub or two against the leg. Freddy had been at the shelter six or seven years and had become a personal favorite of mine.

One Saturday morning, I received a frantic call from one of the volunteers who had gone to feed the cats that morning. Something terrible had happened—I had to come over right away.

Nothing could have prepared me for what I found when I arrived at the shelter. During the night, someone had broken into the locked shelter and gone on a killing spree, using blunt instruments to murder and maim over twenty-five cats.

The shock was devastating, and I was almost numb as I called the police and other volunteers to come and help me care for the injured, gather up the dead and attempt to put the shelter back into some semblance of order. As the word quickly spread, a local church sent a crew of ten men to help out, including two of the ministers. It was the compassionate and conscientious labor of all these volunteers that got me through the worst moments of that morning.

After about an hour, I had a panicked thought. *What about the dogs?* Running out to the kennels to check, I was immensely relieved to find them all unharmed. Two of the dogs in our care, Duke and Dolly, are Rhodesian ridgeback-mastiff mixes, enormous and powerful-looking dogs with the hearts of puppies—when it comes to people they know and love. For once I was glad they looked so formidable, even though it's probably why they haven't found homes yet, for I was sure that was why no stranger had been foolish enough to take them on.

When I returned to the house, volunteers were placing the cats that had died in a cart for burial. I felt the tears come to my eyes as I recognized so many of my little friends. Then I saw the gray body, partially covered by a towel.

"Not Freddy," I moaned. "Please don't let it be Freddy." But the Captain was nowhere to be found, and I had to face the fact that Freddy was gone.

I felt physically sick when I thought that it was probably his friendly, trusting nature that had killed him—walking right up to people who had evil intentions toward this sweet and innocent animal.

The outpouring of concern and sympathy from supporters in our community was amazing. And after the local paper reported the incident, the national news services picked up the story, and soon calls and letters flooded in from all over the country. People even drove from neighboring states to adopt the survivors of the attack.

It was a painful time for me. I felt the grief of losing so many beings I had come to love, and I was bewildered by the senselessness of the whole thing. Three young men from the local high school were convicted of the crime.

The incident caused a tremendous uproar in our little town. The violence that ravaged the shelter was the subject of intense debate. A small but vocal minority felt the victims were "just cats," so what was the big deal? But the majority of people, outraged animal lovers, demanded justice.

I felt dazed, trapped in a bad dream that wasn't going away. Nothing could bring back the cats that had died. As we went about the sad business of looking for the terrified cats who had escaped to hide, and of caring for the traumatized and injured cats who remained, I mourned my friends, especially Freddy.

A few days later, as I was stepping out of the house, I saw a large gray Persian coming slowly toward me. I scared us both by yelling "Freddy!" at the top of my lungs. It couldn't be—but it was. He was wobbly and shaken, no longer the suave and debonair greeter of old, but he was alive! I scooped him up into my arms and held him to my chest, my tears falling on his head as I hugged and stroked him. Freddy had come back.

In the chaos of that terrible morning, I had confused Freddy with another gray Persian, lying dead, half-hidden by a towel, on the burial cart. Freddy had been one of the lucky ones to make it outside and escape the others' appalling fate.

Miraculously, it took only a few weeks for Freddy to come around. Eventually, he even resumed his duties as official greeter.

In my grief after the incident, I had felt like giving up—I just hadn't had the heart to continue. It was the gray cat's courage and willingness to trust again that helped mend my own shattered spirit. Ultimately, my love for

Freddy and others like him made me decide to continue Noah's Ark's life-saving rescue work in spite of what had happened.

Today, if you visit our shelter, you will be greeted by a large and confident gray cat walking proudly forward to meet you. His green eyes miss nothing as he inspects you from head to toe. If you pass muster, then you may feel his large bulk pressing affectionately against your shins. For the Captain, I am happy to report, it's business as usual.

David Sykes

The Woman Who Took Chickens Under Her Wing

Years may wrinkle the skin, but to give up enthusiasm wrinkles the soul.

Samuel Ullman

Minnie Blumfield never lost her enthusiasm. She believed that with age came courage, vision and a true appreciation of life—all life. That's why, at the age of eighty-six, Minnie became the sole caretaker of a flock of chickens abandoned alongside one of Southern California's busiest freeways after a poultry truck mishap. For reasons known only to the bureaucracy of the day, the chickens were never rescued. Instead, they simply took up residence in the roadside brush, becoming known to locals as the Hollywood Freeway Chickens.

Like many seniors, Minnie lived alone and survived on a meager pension. But to her, life was precious and not to be callously surrendered or ignored—not even the lives of slaughter-bound livestock. Minnie simply saw creatures in need and without hesitation, stepped into action.

For nine years, while others sped past unaware and unconcerned, Minnie made two pilgrimages a day to provide food and water for the abandoned chickens, using what little money she had available. As the years passed, she worried about the day when she would no longer be able to care for her adopted flock. Who would look after these poor helpless creatures if she could no longer make her journey?

At ninety-five, just when the cruelties of time began to ravage Minnie's body, a heroine appeared. Jodie Mann, a young actress and a founding member of the organization Actors and Others for Animals, was Minnie's neighbor. Jodie had observed Minnie on her sojourns and noticed that the older woman also fed many of the homeless cats in the neighborhood. Jodie approached Minnie to see if her neighbor could identify the owner of a stray dog that Jodie had recently rescued. A quick and lasting friendship resulted. Learning of Minnie's concern for the fate of her flock, Jodie vowed to "fight City Hall" and find the chickens a new home.

Jodie located a ranch where the chickens would be able to live out their natural lives, and organized a rescue party to capture the birds. This was a daunting task that tested Jodie's patience and determination and Minnie's will to live. As the chickens settled into their new home, Minnie was forced to relocate to a convalescent hospital after a series of debilitating strokes.

Jodie maintained a close and loving relationship with Minnie, visiting her often. She found a good home for Minnie's cat, Blacky, and made sure that the stray cats that had come to depend on the older woman's kindness were still provided with care.

Later, as president of Actors and Others for Animals, I was honored to present Minnie Blumfield—then ninety-six years old—with our organization's inaugural

Humanitarian Award. Inspired by and aptly named for Minnie, the award is a delicate bronze statue of a graceful, straw-hatted woman with robust chickens standing sentry at her feet, and a dozing cat nestled safely in her arms. To all of us in attendance that day, the bizarre plight of the cast-off chickens, superimposed with Minnie's undaunted spirit, was awe-inspiring. Many were moved to tears by the soft heart of this frail but determined woman, who with tears streaming down her own paralyzed face, managed to whisper, "Thank you."

Minnie is gone now, but her concern for her fellow creatures lives on in the award that bears her name and likeness. Her courage and selfless example continue to be a source of inspiration and strength for me, for Jodie and for everyone within our organization, as we continue our work of caring for all living creatures who share our planet, our homes and our hearts.

Earl Holliman
President, Actors and Others for Animals

Miracles Do Happen

Where there is great love there are always miracles.

Willa Cather

As a shiny new veterinarian in my mid-twenties, I was sure of everything. The world was black and white with very little gray. In my mind, veterinary medicine was precise and structured, with little room for anything but the rules of science. An experience I had just a few years out of school loosened several stones in that wall of inflexibility.

Two of the most pleasant clients in my small, mountain town practice were an older retired couple. Two kinder, more gentle people could not be found. Their devotion to each other and their pets was luminous. Whenever and wherever they were seen in our little town, their dogs were constant companions. It was assumed that these lovable and loyal dogs were the children they never had. And there was a clear but unobtrusive awareness of this couple's very profound religious faith.

One cold winter morning, they arrived at our clinic with their oldest dog, Fritz. Their big old canine friend could not bear the pain of placing any weight on his hind legs. The great old dog avoided movement as much as possible. When he did feel compelled to move, he pulled himself along with his front legs like a seal, his shrunken, atrophied hind legs dragging outstretched behind him. No amount of encouragement or assistance enabled Fritz to stand or walk on his afflicted rear legs. His owners, with the best of intentions, had been attempting a variety of home treatments for most of the winter, but now his condition had deteriorated to this point. The look in his eyes was of remarkable intelligence and gentleness, but also of great pain.

My partner and I hospitalized the lovable old dog for a few hours so that we could thoroughly examine him, obtain X rays and complete other tests. Sadly, we concluded that a lifetime of living with hip dysplasia had taken its full toll on Fritz. His advanced age, atrophied muscles and painful, disfigured joints left no hope that any type of medical or surgical treatment could allow the old couple's dog to enjoy a happy, painless life. We concluded that his only salvation from excruciating pain was to be humanely euthanized.

Later that day, as cold winter darkness fell on our little mountain town, the old couple returned to the clinic to hear our verdict about their beloved pet. As I stood before them in the exam room, I felt a chill pass over me as if I were out in that winter evening. Clearly they knew what I was going to say because they were already softly crying before I began talking. With great hesitation, I explained their old friend Fritz's dire condition. Finally, I struggled to tell them that the kindest act would be to "put him to sleep" so he would suffer no more.

Through their tears, they nodded in agreement. Then the husband asked, "Can we wait to decide about putting him to sleep until the morning?" I agreed that would be fine. He said, "We want to go home and pray tonight. The Lord will help us decide." They told their old friend good night and left him to rest at the clinic overnight. As they left, I sympathetically thought to myself that no amount of praying could help their old dog.

The next morning I came in early to treat our hospitalized cases. The elderly couple's big old crippled dog was just as he had been the evening before—a look of pain on his face, unable to stand, but still showing that kind, intelligent expression. Within an hour the old couple came into the clinic. "We have prayed all night. Can we see Fritz? We will know what the Lord wants when we see him."

I led them through the clinic to the ward where Fritz lay. As I opened the door and peered into the ward, I was numbed by the sight of Fritz eagerly standing in his cage, wagging his tail and bearing an obvious expression of enthusiastic joy at the sound of his owners. He bore not one indication of any pain or dysfunction.

The reunion of Fritz and the old couple was a blur of canine and human cries of joy, kisses and tears. Fritz bounded youthfully out to the car as the couple rejoiced. In their wake, they left a bewildered young veterinarian who was beginning to see that life is not black and white, but includes rather a great deal of gray. I realized that day that miracles do happen.

Paul H. King, D.V.M.

DON'T WORRY, MICHAEL. I'M SURE FARLEY WILL BE JUST FINE.

CAN I SAY SOME PRAYERS FOR HIM?
THAT WOULD BE A NICE IDEA.

CAN I GO DIRECTLY TO GOD?–OR DO I ASK FOR SOME-ONE IN THE PET DEPARTMENT?
Lynn

Darlene

The first duty of love is to listen.

Paul Tillich

For three years, my dog, Pokey, and I worked side-by-side as volunteers in the Prescription Pet Program at The Children's Hospital in Denver. I often referred to Pokey as a "terror" instead of a terrier because in those younger days, she was a perpetual motion machine. The only time she was different was during our hospital visits, and then she seemed to find some inner force that made her behave. Every time that Pokey and I visited patients, we saw little miracles, but one day something special happened that changed my perspective on how deeply Pokey could give.

On this day the volunteer office asked us to see a patient on the fourth floor—the oncology ward. So, along the way on our rounds, we made a special point to stop in at Darlene's room.

Darlene was sixteen years old, with shoulder-length blonde hair and a ready smile. I asked, "Would you like to visit with Pokey?" and she accepted. I immediately knew that something unusual was going on. You see, my ball-of-fire terrier-mix climbed onto the bed and quickly went to the girl's side to tuck in under her arm. Pokey laid her head on the girl's shoulder, with her little dog face pointed up toward Darlene's.

As Darlene looked down into those liquid brown eyes, she whispered to Pokey. This was definitely a change from the usual patient contact, where doggie tricks were the order of the day. Still, these two were obviously doing some serious work here, so I sat back and watched the television. After about thirty minutes, Darlene spoke up. "Thanks so much for visiting. I know you have other patients to see, so I'd better let you go. You'll never know how much this meant to me." And she flashed us a brilliant smile.

Three weeks later, I got a phone call from Ann, our supervisor in the volunteer office, with whom I had shared this story. She said, "I just wanted to let you know that Pokey's friend, Darlene, is in heaven."

Darlene, that brave and beautiful sixteen-year-old child, had received terrible news the day that we visited her. Her cancer had relapsed for a third time. In her treatment protocol, there were no more options. She was destined to die—very soon.

Darlene had to have been afraid. Still, she couldn't trust her family, friends, doctors or caregivers with her fears. There wasn't a human alive who she could talk to—but she could share herself with this little dog! She knew that Pokey wouldn't tell anyone her secrets . . . wouldn't ridicule her dreams that would never come true.

We'll never truly know what Darlene said that day or just how much good Pokey accomplished with her thirty minutes of loving silence. But Darlene instinctively knew what all dog lovers have known through the ages: No friend can be as trusting, loyal and loving as a dog.

Sara (Robinson) Mark, D.V.M.

The Little Dog That Nobody Wanted

If a dog's prayers were answered, bones would rain from the sky.

Old Proverb

When Dad found Tippy—or rather, Tippy found Dad—it was a hot day in my southern Missouri hometown, in the summer of 1979.

For most of his life, Dad had never cared too much for pets, but the sight of that skinny, mange-infested pup seemed to open a door in his heart. Then that little lost pup slipped ever so meekly through the door.

That morning, Dad had been visiting with customers in the electronics shop where he had landed a part-time job after retirement. Suddenly a terrified, yelping stray puppy bolted through the door.

"I've lived many a year," Dad said that evening as he stepped into the house, "but I've never seen anything so pitiful as this." In his arms he cradled a cardboard box, and inside the box was a tiny wayfarer from an unimaginable hell.

Dad couldn't hold back the tears any longer. "I just

couldn't put her back out on the streets. Look at her . . . we've got to do something to help her. She was just crying and crying and so scared," Dad said as Mom took the box from his arms. "Look at those open sores. Who could be so cruel as to let her get in this condition?"

Mom peered down into the box and was repulsed by what she saw. "Oh, she's too far gone," she told my dad, shaking her head in disbelief. "Let's just have the vet put her out of her misery."

No bigger than a teakettle, the wretched little terrier was being consumed by disease and starvation. Lifeless marble eyes bulged sadly atop a thin pointed nose; bony long legs curled around each other like limp spaghetti on a plate.

"I'm awfully sorry," the vet told Dad the next day. "There's really nothing I can do to help her now. She's too far gone."

But Dad insisted.

"Well, okay—if you want to try, here are some pills and some medicated cream to rub on her mange sores. But don't get your hopes up. I doubt if she makes it through the weekend."

Dad wrapped the sick, homeless pup back into the old bath towel and carried her to the car. That afternoon, he carried her gently out under the maple trees in the backyard and began the medication treatments.

"Every day your father totes that poor, miserable little creature out under the trees and massages the ointment into her skin," Mom said. "Those oozing sores cover her entire body. He can't even tell what color she's supposed to be—all her hair has been eaten away by the mange and infection."

"I won't keep her if she gets better," he promised Mom. "I'll find a good home for her if the medicine works." Mom was not too happy about helping a dirty, uncomely runt with no fur and spaghetti legs.

"I don't think we'll have to worry," Mom sighed. "But don't feel bad when the medicine doesn't work. At least you tried."

Nevertheless, every day, out in the shade of the big maple trees, Dad faithfully doctored the pup with no hair and bony legs, the little lost dog that nobody wanted.

For the first few days after the stray pup entered Dad's life, there was slim hope for her survival. Disease and starvation had taken the little dog down a cruel path. It seemed only a miracle could help.

For seemingly endless days, Mom watched through the kitchen window as Dad continued to cart the little dog in the box out under the maple trees, where he doctored the wounds of neglect.

No one remembers exactly how long it took to see a glint of hope in my dad's countenance—and in the marble eyes of that pup. But slowly, with timidity and reserve, the pup began to trust my dad, and the first waggle of her skinny tail brought intense joy to my father.

Mom never wanted any part of that rescue effort, for she was not interested in bringing a dog into the house and their lives. But when she saw her husband's face the first time that pup showed an ounce of playfulness, she knew that Dad was struck with more than compassion.

Dad came from a rugged hill family who farmed the rocky ridges of the Ozark Mountains. He knew little joy as a child and worked hard at manual jobs as an adult. Reaching down to rescue that weak, mangy pup seemed to mend his wounded spirit, especially when he succeeded at beating the odds by nursing Tippy back to health.

"Just look at her!" Mom smiled. "You've really done it! She's growing her hair back and she's starting to play a little bit. No one thought she'd even live another day, but you stood by her and believed that she could make it."

As the pup continued healing, she began showing her

true colors—except they weren't the prettiest of colors in the prettiest of patterns. A white patch here and there, a crowd of hazy black spots around the snout and chest, mottled white blotches against a black torso. And because of the white tip on her tail, she was given a common name for a common dog: Tippy.

"Now, honey, I've tried to find her a good home but nobody needs a little dog right now," Dad lamented. "I've asked around everywhere. I promise, I've tried real hard." Mom knew he was trying about as hard as a man choosing between a lawn mower and a good hammock on a hot summer afternoon.

"Well, I don't know who would want her," Mom said. "Even with her hair grown in and all those sores gone, she's still kind of ugly and gangly."

A few weeks later, after unsuccessfully trying to trade her off on someone, Dad said, "Now, I know she's not a cute little dog, but I guess she'll have to do. Nobody else wants her."

There. He'd said it. And Mom knew the little lost dog that nobody wanted had curled up to stay.

She would have to sleep out in the laundry room, not in the house, Mom scolded. Dad and Tippy complied with the rules, and their singular friendship sprouted and blossomed in comforting ways—for they came to need each other during Dad's worst of times.

"That pup saw your dad through all his pain and cancer for the next three years," Mom recalled. "Sometimes I think God sent that little dog to be with your dad in the end."

After Dad died, Mom went out to the laundry room one day and gazed down at the quiet little creature curled up obediently in her cardboard box bed.

"Hmmm . . . okay, Tippy," she said softly. "Maybe it won't hurt having you come inside the house just once in awhile. It's awfully lonesome in there." At that moment, Mom felt connected to the homely little dog, as if Dad's hands were still reaching down to help them both in time of need.

In the following months, Tippy and Mom became soul mates of sorts. The cardboard-box bed was brought in from the laundry room to Mom's bedroom, where it stayed for the next fourteen years.

"As long as I had that little dog," Mom said, "it was like a part of your dad was still here. She brought life back into the house."

Eventually, the rigors of time and age took their toll on Mom's little friend; blindness and painful joints set in. With overwhelming sadness and regret, Mom asked my brother to help take Tippy for her final trip to the vet.

"I reached down to cradle her head in my hands," Mom said, "and she leaned her face against mine as if to say thanks for all we had done for her."

Tippy lived seventeen years after that fateful journey of terror through traffic, rundown warehouses, pain and suffering to find my dad. And looking back over the years, it seems to me now that the true miracle was not in the healing forces of Dad's loving hands and kindness toward the little lost dog that nobody wanted—but in the difference they made in each other's lives.

Jan K. Stewart Bass

5

AMAZING ANIMALS

I have learned to use the word impossible *with the greatest of caution.*

Wernher von Braun

LASSIE!
GET HELP!!

Buffalo Games

All animals except man know that the ultimate of life is to enjoy it.

Samuel Butler

[EDITORS' NOTE: *During the Iditarod, the dogsled race across Alaska, a rookie driver came upon a musher who had stopped his team and was gazing down a hill with rapt attention. The rookie driver stopped to see what the other man found so absorbing.*]

We were looking down on a frozen lake—one of the Farewell Lakes. But it wasn't the lake that held his interest. Below and to the right, a group of four buffalo were standing on the shore. Two of them were in the grass at the edge and the other two were out on the ice.

"Somebody told me that there was a herd of buffalo here, but I hadn't expected to see them along the trail," he said.

"Yes," I told the other musher. "Buffalo. I know. They told us . . ."

"No—*watch.*"

I turned back, thinking frankly that he was around the bend. So it was buffalo—so what?

Then I saw what he meant.

The surface of the lake was bare of snow and the two buffalo out on the ice were having a rough time of it trying to stand. One of the buffalo on the shore backed away from the lake, up the sloping side of the ridge, pawed the ground a couple of times and ran full bore for the lake.

Just as he hit the edge of the ice, his tail went straight up in the air. He spread his front feet apart, stiffened his legs and slid away from shore, spinning around in a circle as he flew across the ice.

When he slowed to a stop he bellowed, a kind of "Gwaaa" sound, then began making his tortuous way back to the shoreline.

While he was doing this, the fourth buffalo came shooting out on the ice, slid farther (also tail up) than the last, made a louder noise, and started back slipping and falling.

I couldn't believe it and blinked rapidly several times, thinking I was hallucinating.

"No—it's real," he laughed. "I was passing when I heard the bellow and came up to check it out. I've been here an hour, maybe a little more. They've been doing this the whole time. Great, isn't it?"

We lay there for another half-hour watching them play. The object seemed to be who could slide the farthest, and each of them tried several times, tails up, happy bellows echoing on the far shore of the lake as they slid across the ice.

Buffalo Games . . . who would have thought it could happen?

Gary Paulsen

Doctola

The . . . dog, in life the firmest friend, the first to welcome, foremost to defend.

Lord Byron

I graduated from veterinary school in June of 1984. In July, I hopped a plane for the deepest, darkest heart of Africa and assumed my post as the Thyolo district veterinary officer in August. My life as a new Peace Corps volunteer was moving at warp speed.

My duties were to provide veterinary care and administer the disease control programs for the Thyolo and Mulanji districts in the central African country of Malawi. With nothing more than a cabinet of mostly outdated drugs and a 100-cc motorbike, I was to supervise twenty-three veterinary technicians scattered around my districts and maintain the health of the cattle, sheep, goats, swine, poultry and pet animals in the entire area.

After a month in my new position, I returned to my office one evening after sundown. There, I was greeted by an older gentleman. He sat in the chair that I kept outside my office door. In his lap, he held a box full of puppies. I returned his greeting and then showed him into my office. We conversed in the local language of Chichewa.

The gentleman was Dr. Mzimba, one of the well-known medicine men in the district. In Africa, the medicine man is a spiritual leader and wise man, as well as a healer, for his people. I estimated his age around sixty, but my estimate could easily have been off twenty years in either direction.

In order for him to reach me, he had walked two hours to the nearest bus stop and then taken a six-hour bus ride to my office. He had left his home at 5:00 A.M. and had been waiting for me at my office since his arrival at 4:00 P.M. It was now 7:00 P.M. He went on to explain that there was very little he could do for the sick puppies he had brought me, since his medicine only worked on people. He cared very much for these puppies and had "seen" that some were destined to do great things. He asked that I do all in my power to save them.

The six puppies were very ill. I explained that intensive care would be needed for many days if any of the puppies were to be saved. He agreed to leave them with me. He stated that when he felt it was time, he would return to collect them. With that, he left.

The puppies required round-the-clock care. The pups went with me wherever I went. Homemade electrolyte solution and antibiotics were all that I had available. Yet despite all my efforts, one puppy after another slowly faded away. On the sixth night, the last two remaining puppies and I bedded down for the evening. I fully expected that these two would go the same way as their litter-mates. They were not showing any improvement, and I was sure that they didn't have another day's worth of fight left in them.

I was overjoyed to wake to two happy and perky puppies whining for attention. They looked like puppy skeletons, but they were alive and alert puppy skeletons. Their appetites were ravenous. Frequent small meals soon became frequent large meals, and it didn't take long for them to fill out.

They stayed with me an additional ten days, and I was wondering if Dr. Mzimba would ever return for them. On the tenth day of their recovery period, Dr. Mzimba showed up. He was overjoyed with the two pups that had survived and were now thriving. One pup was black with four white paws and a large white star on his chest. The other pup was brown with a large white patch on the right side of his face. Both pups had prominent ridgebacks.

I watched as the pups licked and kissed the old man's face while he gently cuddled and hugged them. He pulled out a few coins and some old crumpled bills and asked what the fee came to. I charged him my standard consultation fee—a total of $3.50. He gladly paid, but before he left he gave me the honor of naming the pups. I thought long and hard and finally chose the name Bozo for the black pup and Skippy for the brown one. I told him that I once had dogs with those names, and they had been my best friends.

"Come and visit me often, Doctola," he said. "These pups now know you as mother and father. They will not forget and some day will return the great kindness you have shown them." Then Dr. Mzimba and I shook hands and parted company.

Over the course of the next eighteen months, I saw Dr. Mzimba, Bozo and Skippy at least once a month. Every two to four weeks, I took a three-day trip traveling from one village to the next around the Thyolo district, performing various veterinary duties as needed. At the end of each trip, I stopped at Dr. Mzimba's village. He kindly offered me his home and gracious hospitality every time I swung through the neighborhood.

I watched Bozo and Skippy grow into fine dogs. They each reached around eighty pounds. They were twice the size of the local village dogs and were fiercely loyal to Dr. Mzimba. I vaccinated them and dewormed them regularly, and treated their various wounds and ailments. For me, it was like seeing family. Whenever they saw me, they instantly turned into playful puppies.

The dogs were treasured by the people of their village. On every visit, I heard a new story of how the dogs had run off someone trying to steal cattle, or how they had defended the village against roaming hyenas or jackals.

One time, the dogs killed a leopard. They were badly injured in the fight. Both dogs had multiple puncture wounds, lacerations and a great deal of blood loss. I worked through the night to stitch up their endless wounds. Yet in the morning, I was amazed to see each dog stand and eat a little breakfast.

As I packed up my motorbike, I left Dr. Mzimba with after-care instructions and some follow-up antibiotics. He thanked me profusely and hugged me with tears in his eyes.

"That is the second time that you have saved their lives, Doctola. From this time on, they will be your protectors. I have seen it!"

Five months later I was again in the area on one of my regular three-day tours. I was approaching Dr. Mzimba's village and having a rough time. Heavy rain had turned the dirt roads to rivers of mud. I had fallen four times in the last forty minutes and was having a terrible time climbing the hill to Dr. Mzimba's village. It was drizzling and I was wet, muddy, cold and in a bitter mood as I tried to maneuver my motorbike along the slippery one-lane path.

I stopped short. Ahead, in the beam of my headlight, a hyena stood blocking the path. It was slowly making its way toward me, unafraid of the light or sound of my motor. I honked the horn, to no effect. The hyena's advance continued, slow and steady. *How strange,* I thought. In the past, they had always run off in fright. Then I saw the blood and saliva dripping from its mouth and the blank stare in its eyes. Rabies!

As the hyena came toward me, I slowly backed up and tried to keep my distance. The mud was much too thick and slippery to make a run for it, and the path too narrow to turn around.

The only real option was to run anyway and hope the hyena would choose to attack the motorbike instead of me. Despite my efforts to keep a reasonable distance, I was unable to backpedal fast enough. The hyena was gaining on me. It gave a ghoulish laugh as it snapped its powerful jaws in the air. I was about to make a run for it when, on either side of me, Bozo and Skippy appeared. They jumped onto the path between me and the hyena. Their muscles were rock-steady and the hair on their backs stood straight up. They held their ground, teeth bared.

The ensuing battle was fierce and bloody. Not once did the dogs cry out as they fought with a speed and endurance I never thought possible. The life-and-death battle unfolded in the beam of my motorbike headlight. When it was over, the hyena lay dead and the dogs were nowhere to he found. I called and called but there was no sign of them.

I hurried to Dr. Mzimba's home. As I slipped and stumbled along the path, I was thinking about my treatment plan: stitches, antibiotics, a rabies booster, fluids, shock treatment. I owed those wonderful dogs so much. I had to find them and I had to thank them and they had to live and I wasn't going to settle for anything less.

When I arrived at Dr. Mzimba's house, I found him waiting patiently in a chair on the porch outside his hut. I ran to him, explaining all that had happened in a combination of Chichewa and English. I was breathless and hyperventilating and I wasn't sure if he understood me. It seemed that he did.

"Come with me and I'll show you the dogs," he said, and he motioned for me to follow.

I grabbed my medical cases and followed him to the back of his hut. He stopped and pointed to two graves. "Bozo and Skippy sleep there. Three days ago, a pack of hyenas came down from the hills and attacked our cattle. Bozo and Skippy fought like ten dogs and they chased the hyenas away and saved our cattle. But it was too much for them, Doctola," he said with tears streaming down his cheeks. "They both died shortly after the fight. There was no time to send for you."

I shook my head. "No! It can't be. They just saved my life fifteen minutes ago. I know it was them. I saw them and I know it was them." I fell to my knees and looked up at the black sky. The pelting drizzle now mixed with my own tears. "There aren't two other dogs in this country that look even close to Skippy and Bozo. It had to be them!" I said, half pleading, half arguing, wishing and hoping it was not so, and all the time sobbing uncontrollably.

"I believe you, Doctola," said the wise African as he knelt down next to me. "I told you that someday the dogs would return your kindness. They will always protect you!"

Herbert J. (Reb) Rebhan, D.V.M.

A Mother's Love

I am a New York City fireman. Being a firefighter has its grim side. When someone's business or home is destroyed, it can break your heart. You see a lot of terror and sometimes even death. But the day I found Scarlett was different. That was a day about life. And love.

It was a Friday. We'd responded to an early morning alarm in Brooklyn at a burning garage. As I was getting my gear on, I heard the sound of cats crying. I couldn't stop—I would have to look for the cats after the fire was put out.

This was a large fire, so there were other hook and ladder companies there as well. We had been told that everyone in the building had made it out safely. I sure hoped so—the entire garage was filled with flames, and it would have been futile for anyone to attempt a rescue anyway. It took a long time and many firefighters to finally bring the enormous blaze under control.

At that point I was free to investigate the cat noises, which I still heard. There continued to be a tremendous amount of smoke and intense heat coming from the building. I couldn't see much, but I followed the meowing to a spot on the sidewalk about five feet away from the front of the garage. There, crying and huddled together, were three terrified little kittens. Then I found two more, one in the street and one across the street. They must have been in the building, as their fur was badly singed. I yelled for a box and out of the crowd around me, one appeared. Putting the five kittens in the box, I carried them to the porch of a neighboring house.

I started looking for a mother cat. It was obvious that the mother had gone into the burning garage and carried each of her babies, one by one, out to the sidewalk. Five separate trips into that raging heat and deadly smoke—it was hard to imagine. Then she had attempted to get them across the street, away from the building. Again, one at a time. But she hadn't been able to finish the job. What had happened to her?

A cop told me he had seen a cat go into a vacant lot near where I'd found the last two kittens. She was there, lying down and crying. She was horribly burnt: her eyes were blistered shut, her paws were blackened, and her fur was singed all over her body. In some places you could see her reddened skin showing through the burned fur. She was too weak to move anymore. I went over to her slowly, talking gently as I approached. I figured that she was a wild cat and I didn't want to alarm her. When I picked her up, she cried out in pain, but she didn't struggle. The poor animal reeked of burnt fur and flesh. She gave me a look of utter exhaustion and then relaxed in my arms as much as her pain would allow. Sensing her trust in me, I felt my throat tighten and the tears start in my eyes. I was determined to save this brave little cat and her family. Their lives were, literally, in my hands.

I put the cat in the box with the mewing kittens. Even in her pathetic condition, the blinded mother circled in the box and touched each kitten with her nose, one by one, to make sure they were all there and all safe. She was content, in spite of her pain, now that she was sure the kittens were all accounted for.

These cats obviously needed immediate medical care. I thought of a very special animal shelter out on Long Island, the North Shore Animal League, where I had taken a severely burned dog I had rescued eleven years earlier. If anyone could help them, they could.

I called to alert the Animal League that I was on my way with a badly burned cat and her kittens. Still in my smoke-stained fire gear, I drove my truck there as fast as I could. When I pulled into the driveway, I saw two teams of vets and technicians standing in the parking lot waiting for me. They whisked the cats into a treatment room—the mother on a table with one vet team and all the kittens on another table with the second team.

Utterly exhausted from fighting the fire, I stood in the treatment room, keeping out of the way. I didn't have much hope that these cats would survive. But somehow, I just couldn't leave them. After a long wait, the vets told me they would observe the kittens and their mother overnight, but they weren't very optimistic about the mother's chances of survival.

I returned the next day and waited and waited. I was about to completely give up hope when the vets finally came over to me. They told me the good news—the kittens would survive.

"And the mother?" I asked. I was afraid to hear the reply.

It was still too early to know.

I came back every day, but each day it was the same thing: they just didn't know. About a week after the fire, I arrived at the shelter in a bleak mood, thinking, *Surely if the mother cat was going to make it, she'd have come around by now. How much longer could she hover between life and death?* But when I walked in the door, the vets greeted me with big smiles and gave me the thumbs up sign! Not only was she going to be all right—in time she'd even be able to see again.

Now that she was going to live, she needed a name. One of the technicians came up with the name Scarlett, because of her reddened skin.

Knowing what Scarlett had endured for her kittens, it melted my heart to see her reunited with them. And what did mama cat do first? Another head count! She touched each of her kittens again, nose to nose, to be sure they were all still safe and sound. She had risked her life, not once, but five times—and it had paid off. All of her babies had survived.

As a firefighter, I see heroism every day. But what Scarlett showed me that day was the height of heroism—the kind of bravery that comes only from a mother's love.

David Giannelli

"If I was Noah, I'd have taken a whole BUNCH of cats instead of just two."

Reprinted by permission of Bil Keane.

Daughter of Sunshine

The baby gorilla was born in the zoo. Her mother, Lulu, could not produce enough milk to adequately feed her, so the zoo keepers stepped in. They worked in shifts to hold the two-month-old ape in their arms around the clock, imitating the way real gorilla mothers take care of their young. The baby thrived and grew to be an exceptionally loving and gentle creature. The keepers named her Binti Jua, which means "daughter of sunshine" in Swahili.

Since Binti Jua was born in captivity, she was content with the life of a zoo gorilla, climbing the trees in her enclosure and playing happily with the other gorillas.

There was an old male gorilla living at the zoo, a large silverback, who had never shown any interest in fathering any offspring. Something about Binti Jua appealed to the elder ape and when Binti was six, she became pregnant.

The zoo keepers were concerned that because the young gorilla hadn't had any maternal role models, she might not be fully prepared to mother her own young. So they gave her lessons. They used a stuffed animal as a baby substitute and taught her to put the "baby" to her breast and to hold the "baby" constantly, the way gorillas do in the wild.

She was a good student and when her daughter, Koola, was born, Binti Jua was the perfect mom. This combination of natural motherliness and her comfort with humans would later make her an internationally celebrated heroine.

One day, when Koola was about a year-and-a-half old, Binti Jua was in her outdoor enclosure, holding and grooming her baby as usual. The zoo visitors were all enjoying the sight of the gorillas, when suddenly a little three-year-old boy who had been playing along the barrier of the enclosure toppled over the edge and fell over twenty feet to the concrete floor below.

There was a sickening thud, and the little boy's hysterical mother began screaming for help.

Immediately, Binti Jua, still holding Koola, made her way over to the unconscious child. The watching crowd gasped in horror. Unconsciously, people tend to associate gorillas with the movie monster King Kong. What would the huge ape do to the little boy?

First the mother gorilla lifted the boy's arm, as if checking for signs of life. Then, gently, she picked him up and held him tenderly to her chest. Rocking him softly as she walked, she carried him over to the door the zoo keepers always used to enter and exit the enclosure. When another larger female gorilla approached her, Binti Jua made a guttural sound, warning the other gorilla to stay away. By this time, the door was open and the keepers were there with the paramedics, who had been called to rescue the injured boy. The gorilla carefully placed the boy on the floor in front of the door, and the paramedics whisked the child away. When the door closed again, Binti Jua calmly walked back to her tree and began grooming her own baby once more.

The people watching were stunned. The event would have been dramatic enough without the role of the heroine being filled by a gorilla. And Binti Jua was the best type of heroine, not caring for either fame or reward.

The boy recovered without any lasting harm resulting from his adventure. And the world was moved by Binti Jua's good deed; letters and gifts came pouring in for her from all over the world. She even received a medal from the American Legion and an honorary membership in a California PTA.

Acting from her heart, Binti Jua did what any mother would do: She protected and helped a child. But this gorilla didn't care that the child was of another species. She showed the qualities we humans hold most dear—love and compassion for all.

Carol Kline

The Eyes of Tex

Eric Seal thought the scrawny puppy at his feet was perhaps five weeks old. Sometime during the night, the little mixed-breed female had been dumped at the Seals' front gate.

"Before you ask," he told Jeffrey, his wife, "the answer is an absolute *no*! We are not going to keep it. We don't need another dog. When and if we do, we'll get a purebred."

As though she hadn't heard him, his wife sweetly asked, "What kind do you think it is?"

Eric shook his head. "It's hard to tell. From her color markings and the way she holds her ears in a half-lop, I'd say she's part German shepherd."

"We can't just turn her away," Jeffrey pleaded. "I'll feed her and get her cleaned up. Then we'll find a home for her."

Standing between them, the puppy seemed to sense that her fate was being decided. Her tail wagged tentatively as she looked from one to the other. Eric noticed that although her ribs showed through a dull coat, her eyes were bright and animated.

Finally, he shrugged his shoulders. "Okay, if you want

to fool with her, go ahead. But let's get one thing straight: We don't need a Heinz-57 mongrel."

The puppy nestled comfortably in Jeffrey's arms as they walked toward the house. "One other thing," Eric continued. "Let's wait a few days to put her in the pen with Tex. We don't want Tex exposed to anything. He has all the troubles he can handle."

Tex, the six-year-old cattle dog the Seals had raised from a puppy, was unusually amiable for a blue-heeler, a breed established by ranchers in Australia. So, although he already shared his doghouse with a yellow cat, soon Tex happily moved over and made room for the new puppy the Seals called Heinz.

Not long before Heinz showed up, the Seals had noticed that Tex appeared to be losing his eyesight. Their veterinarian said he thought the dog had cataracts that might be surgically removed.

But when they brought Tex to a specialist in Dallas, he determined that the dog's poor eyesight was only partially due to cataracts. He made an appointment for Tex at the local college's veterinary laboratory.

Doctors there determined that Tex was already blind. They explained that no medical or surgical procedure could have halted or delayed Tex's progressive loss of vision.

As they talked on their way home, the Seals realized that over the last few months, they had watched Tex cope with his blindness. Now they understood why Tex sometimes missed a gate opening or bumped his nose on the chain-link fence. And why he usually stayed on the gravel walkways traveling to and from the house. If he wandered off, he quartered back and forth until he was on the gravel again.

While the couple had been preoccupied with Tex's troubles, Heinz had grown plump and frisky, and her dark brown-and-black coat glowed with health.

It was soon obvious that the little German shepherd crossbreed would be a large dog—too large to continue sharing a doghouse with Tex and the yellow cat. One weekend, the Seals built another doghouse next to the one the dogs had shared.

It was then they recognized that what they had assumed was puppy playfulness—Heinz's pushing and tugging at Tex while romping with him—actually had a purpose. Without any training or coaching, Heinz had become Tex's "seeing eye" dog.

Each evening when the dogs settled in for the night, Heinz gently took Tex's nose in her mouth and led him into his house. In the morning, she got him up and guided him out of the house again.

When the two dogs approached a gate, Heinz used her shoulder to guide Tex through. When they ran along the fence surrounding their pen, Heinz placed herself between Tex and the wire.

"On sunny days, Tex sleeps stretched out on the driveway asphalt," says Jeffrey. "If a car approaches, Heinz will nudge him awake and guide him out of danger.

"Any number of times we've seen Heinz push Tex aside to get him out of the horses' way. What we didn't understand at first was how the two could run side by side, dashing full speed across the pasture. Then one day, the dogs accompanied me while I exercised my horse, and I heard Heinz 'talking'—she was making a series of soft grunts to keep Tex on course beside her."

The Seals were awed. Without any training, the young dog had devised whatever means were necessary to help, guide and protect her blind companion. It was clear that Heinz shared more than her eyes with Tex; she shared her heart.

Honzie L. Rodgers

The Christmas Mouse

By having reverence for life, we enter into a spiritual relation with the world.

Albert Schweitzer

Once upon a time, we lived in part of a massive, hundred-plus-year-old stone building with an interesting past. Located at a fork in the road at the top of a ridge in rural Lockport, New York, it had once been a blacksmith shop; before that, we heard, it had served as a stagecoach stop. Though it resembled a fortress, it was a grand old place and we loved it. It had character and charm—and leaks, drafts and holes. Pipes froze. So did we. Our cats regularly left us tiny, gory gifts, remnants of the house mice that entered as they pleased after we were asleep.

It was the Christmas of 1981. We had emerged from some difficult times, and I, after the summer's cancer surgery, had a new awareness of the worth of each day, as well as a deeper appreciation of love and family. It was an especially excellent Christmas because all six of our children were with us. Although we didn't know it then, my husband, David, and I would move to Florida the following summer, and never once since that Christmas have we all managed to be gathered in the same place at the same time.

At one end of the big area that served as living room, dining room and kitchen, I was putting dinner together. Things were noisy, what with the Christmas music on the stereo, the clatter in the kitchen corner, and nine young adults horsing around (a few had brought friends). The cats, in typical cat fashion, had absented themselves upstairs, away from the hullabaloo.

Just then, out of the corner of my eye, I caught a small, unexpected movement and turned to focus on an astonishing sight. There in the midst of all this uproar, smack in the middle of a kitty bowl on the floor, sat a tiny, exquisite deer mouse eating dry cat food. Incredulous, I stared, but didn't say a word. For one thing, I wanted to make sure he wasn't a figment of my imagination; for another, I'll admit, I wanted to keep him to myself for a few minutes. He was very charming.

Up on his haunches he sat, chubby rear firmly planted, little front paws holding a piece of cat food. The pieces were round, with holes in the middle; our mouse firmly clutched his morsel with a hand on each side, looking for all the world like a little fat guy munching a doughnut. When he finished one, he'd help himself to another, turning it about and adjusting it in his small fingers till it was perfectly situated, then he'd start nibbling again.

I squatted down and looked at him, catching his shiny dark eye. We gazed at each other, then he looked away and nonchalantly went on eating. It was time to call in the witnesses.

"Hey!" I softly called to the assembled multitude. "Come and look at this." When eventually I got their attention, I thought it would be all over—he'd run and hide from the mob advancing on him. Not so! He sat right there while eleven bent-over people stood in a circle, gawking (not silently, either) at him. He glanced confidently at the crowd, gave his doughnut a quarter-turn, and kept munching.

We were amazed. He wasn't in the least afraid of us. What made the little guy so brave? Some of us brought cameras into the circle, and while the flashes popped, the mouse proceeded serenely onward with his Christmas feast. From time to time, he paused to regard us with that sparkly, confiding glance, as the pile of food in the bowl grew smaller.

For some time we watched in delight while he, apparently bottomless, stuffed himself with goodies. However, enchanted as I was to entertain him, I was uneasily aware that it was also dinnertime for the resident Predators Two. When the cats appeared on the scene, as they were bound to any minute, our Christmas mouse could be seriously hurt or killed in the ensuing pandemonium, even if we were able to prevent the cats from transforming the diner into dinner (a perfectly appropriate denouement from their point of view).

I leaned closer. "Listen," I murmured, "we have been honored. But now you have to go back outside with the other mice. Good company though you are, your life is in jeopardy here. If you will permit, I will escort you."

With that, I reached into the dish and picked him up. He neither attempted to bite nor gave way to panic, but sat in my hand, calm and comfortable, awaiting developments, front paws resting on my thumb. I had not expected this; I thought there would be fear, protest, a struggle. Instead, he looked at me, a veritable paradigm of the intelligent, friendly fairy-tale mouse, exactly like something out of a Disney movie.

"What are you, really?" I silently inquired. "Are you really a mouse?" The cool, rational part of me jeered at the question, yet there was something undeniably uncanny about this Christmas visitor.

I carried him outdoors, followed by the family. It had grown dark—one of those blue-and-white Northern winter nights with snow on the ground, the air crisp and sharp.

Squatting down near the cover of bushes in back of the house, I released him. He sat on my palm and looked about, taking his time. Then he jumped to my shoulder and for a long moment we sat there, I in the snow and he on my shoulder, woman and mouse together looking out into the night. Finally, with a mighty leap for one so small, he flew through the air, landed in the shadow of the bushes out of sight and was gone. We humans stayed outside for a while, wishing him well and feeling a little lonely.

His visit left us with astonishment that has never diminished, the more so because, as country people, we knew perfectly well that wild mice are terrified of humans. Furthermore, deer mice are particularly timid; unlike common house mice, they avoid inhabited homes. Engaging and winsome they may be (in the wild, they are known to sing), but not with our kind.

These rare, luminous occasions when wild things in their right minds cross the line that separates us leave us full of wonder. We resonate with remembrance of something ancient and beautiful. As all together we surrounded him, his little wild presence silently conveyed joy, peace, trust and wonder. He was a delightful mystery and a tiny miracle.

Diane M. Smith

Juneau's Official Greeter

All those who travel to Juneau, Alaska, by water are welcomed at the dock by a dog named Patsy Ann. She doesn't bark. She doesn't wag her tail. She doesn't even respond when you call her.

That's because Patsy Ann is a bronze statue that sits imposingly and silently in the middle of Patsy Ann Square, which borders Juneau's Gastineau Channel.

The real Patsy Ann was a Staffordshire bull terrier who arrived in Juneau as a newborn pup in late 1929 with her human family. Her family didn't keep her once they realized she was deaf and could not bark.

The dog was taken in by a second family, but for unknown reasons was later abandoned by them as well. Patsy then became an orphan who freely roamed the streets of Juneau.

Patsy Ann limited her daily wanderings to the downtown area, where local merchants and residents grinned at the sight of her happily loping from business to business.

Though Patsy Ann was an orphan, the Longshoremen's Hall became her nightly home. For her, it was the most logical place for warmth and sleep because she spent so much of her time on the docks. The deaf dog possessed a most remarkable ability. Whenever a ship neared Gastineau Channel, Patsy Ann was somehow able to "hear" its whistle, even if the ship was as much as a half-mile away. At once, the terrier would scamper down to the wharf to await the ship's arrival.

Juneau's residents had no idea how Patsy Ann was able to sense the imminent approach of a ship, anymore than they could figure out how the dog knew at exactly which dock she should wait. But they learned to trust her unerring judgment.

One afternoon, townspeople gathered at the appointed dock to await an incoming ship. Patsy Ann joined the expectant crowd and then suddenly ran to a different dock. Everyone was perplexed by her behavior until they realized they had been given misinformation. The ship entered the channel and berthed at the very dock where the terrier was waiting!

Patsy Ann may have loved the local people who fed her and fondly patted her. She may have felt cared for by the longshoremen. But Patsy Ann's primary happiness came from sitting on the docks as she waited to welcome the ships.

It was appropriate, then, in 1934, for Juneau's mayor to proclaim Patsy Ann "the official greeter of Juneau, Alaska."

That same year, the city passed an ordinance stating that all dogs must be licensed. After an animal-control worker impounded Patsy Ann and threatened to euthanize the stray, several of the locals chipped in to pay for her license and to buy a bright red collar for her. She was again free to continue her lookout duty.

For thirteen years, nearly all the days of her life, the wagging tail and the happy-go-lucky presence of the little dog brought a pleasant constancy to the lives of

Juneau residents. She could not hear them say "good girl," but she saw their smiles and felt their affection.

Then, in 1942, Patsy Ann died of natural causes.

Members of the saddened community placed Patsy Ann's body in a small wooden casket and lowered it into Gastineau Channel. Now she would forever be tied to the hearts of Juneau's people and to the tranquil waters she loved to watch.

Nearly fifty years after Patsy Ann's death, a campaign was waged to memorialize the terrier. A small patch of land at the Gastineau wharfside was converted into what is now Patsy Ann Square, and a larger-than-life bronze statue was commissioned—complete with a bronze collar that rests at its base.

Today at the foot of the square, gaily-colored flowers bloom, and people sit on benches and gaze out at the horizon, just as the bronze Patsy Ann does.

Patsy Ann, adopted and loved by all the residents of Juneau, is still the official greeter for her city. The statue of the little dog who could not hear sits forever next to a wooden sign, her bronzed presence echoing the words printed there: Welcome to Juneau, Alaska.

Roberta Sandler

Simon

There are no ordinary cats.

Colette

Only fifty-three animals in the world have ever received the Dickin Medal, an award presented to animals connected with the British armed forces or civil defense who have displayed "conspicuous gallantry or devotion to duty." The medals, named for the founder of the People's Dispensary for Sick Animals (PDSA), Maria Dickin, were given to the animals for their heroism during World War II or in conflicts directly following the war. The recipients were eighteen dogs, three horses, thirty-one pigeons and one cat. That one cat was Simon, of His Majesty's Ship *Amethyst.*

In the early morning of April 20, 1949, the British warship *Amethyst* was anchored in China's Yangtze River. The crew included a small black-and-white cat named Simon.

All seafaring ships need cats. Mice and rats love to live on ships, creeping in on hawser cables, jumping aboard from docks, coming in along with freight shipments. Mice and rats damage ships, raiding the food storage areas and chewing fabrics to make nests for their young. They also carry viruses, which can be passed on to crew and passengers by mosquitoes or fleas that bite infected rodents and in turn bite a person. Having Simon on board was better than 100 rat traps.

That April morning, the captain was waiting for daylight to continue his voyage up the dangerous river. The Chinese Nationalists, in control of the river, had forbidden all night traffic. Civil war was ready to explode at any moment, and the captain of H.M.S. *Amethyst* had been ordered to sail upriver to Nanking to protect the British embassy there.

Shortly after dawn, before the *Amethyst* could escape, the Yangtze river became a war zone. Explosions shook the air. Shells screeched over the ship, and one rocket and then another crashed into the ship. When the shelling stopped a short time later, many British sailors lay dead on the *Amethyst*'s deck. A large number of crew members were wounded, including Simon. The disabled *Amethyst* was trapped right where she was, and it looked as if the British ship would be stranded for political reasons for quite some time. When the captain checked their stores of food, water and fuel, he found supplies enough for about two months. *Surely they would be able to escape before then,* he thought.

Life on the Yangtze settled into a dull, hot, humid procession of boring days of sweat and ship repair. Simon recovered from his injuries sufficiently to continue his duties as chief rat-catcher.

One day during this time, the ship's doctor saw Simon limping past the sick bay on his way to the hold to look for rats.

"Why don't you come in here and visit these chaps?" the doctor asked, and held the door open. Simon walked inside, where row on row of cots each held an injured lad.

"I'm going to try something," the doctor told his attendant. He picked Simon up and carried him over to a bed in the corner, where Seaman Mark Allen lay with his eyes closed. The boy, who was only sixteen, had lost both legs below the knee in the shelling. For four days, since regaining consciousness, he had refused to talk or eat or even open his eyes.

The doctor set Simon on the boy's bed. Simon sat looking at him, but the boy's eyes remained closed. The doctor moved Simon onto the boy's chest and placed the limp hand on the cat's back.

"Somebody's here to see you, Mark," said the doctor.

Mark opened his eyes just a little. When he saw Simon's steady gaze, he opened them further. The corners of his mouth quirked ever so slightly.

"I have a cat at home," he said. "But I'll never see him again." He pushed Simon away and turned his face into his pillow.

The next day the doctor took Simon to see Mark again and left him sitting on Mark's bed. Simon crawled up on Mark's stomach and began kneading, as he often did before settling down. Mark opened his eyes. His thin hand reached out and stroked Simon's rough fur. The boy began to sob.

The doctor hurried over. "Cook's got some good vegetable soup in the galley. How would you like me to get you a bowl of it? Simon will stay here with you."

Mark nodded ever so slightly. He stroked Simon, who settled down by him and began purring.

From that day on, Mark began eating and gaining strength. Simon visited every day. By the time a month had passed, Mark was able to get around the ship in a wheelchair.

Day after day passed; the days turned into weeks. The thermometer rose to 110 degrees Fahrenheit every day below decks. Between the heat and the severely limited rations, life on the ship became almost intolerable.

The crew looked thin and pinched about their mouths as their energy deserted them in the sweltering heat. Only one sailor kept up his daily activities with spirit and good will: Able Seaman Simon. He patrolled the ship, visited the sick, killed mice and rats, and made life bearable for his fellow shipmates. He never complained about the heat or his health.

On July 19, the temperature reached 110 degrees on the decks and 118 degrees in the engine room. Even Simon walked the decks very slowly. They wouldn't be able to last much longer. Their stores were almost depleted and there was barely enough water to drink, a terrible hardship in the unrelenting heat. The ship was fixed now, but they were held hostage by the warring Chinese and could not sail without again risking serious damage to the ship and her crew.

By the start of August, they couldn't stay where they were any longer. They decided to make a run for it under cover of darkness. It was a serious gamble, but they had no other option.

A combination of weather conditions, some cleverly executed deceptions and sheer good luck enabled the ship to escape. On August 3, the *Amethyst,* free at last, sailed down the China coast to Hong Kong. Hundreds of British citizens waited on the docks to cheer the ship as she steamed into the harbor.

Soon after, one of the ship's officers wrote to the PDSA in England to nominate Simon for the Dickin Medal. While they were docked in Hong Kong, a reply came—the awards committee unanimously conferred the Dickin Medal on Simon. The presentation ceremony would occur after the *Amethyst* returned to England. In the meantime, they sent a tricolor collar for Simon to wear and made an announcement to the world press: "Be it known that from April 22 to August 4, Simon of the H.M.S. *Amethyst* did rid the ship of pestilence and vermin with unrelenting faithfulness. Throughout the incident Simon's behavior was of the highest order and his presence was a decisive factor in maintaining the high level of morale in the ship's company."

Simon became an instant hero. The little black-and-white cat's photograph appeared in hundreds of newspapers and magazines. For weeks, Simon received more than 200 pieces of mail a day. Simon seemed unimpressed with the attention. He posed reluctantly for pictures and continued killing rats.

While en route to England, Simon picked up a virus. Weakened from the wounds he had suffered during the shelling, the cat died. The ceremony to honor Simon, scheduled for when they reached England, turned out to be his funeral.

The PDSA Pet Cemetery has an arched wrought iron gate with the words "They Also Serve" stretched over the entrance. On the day of Simon's funeral, a small casket covered by a Union Jack stood surrounded by baskets and sprays of flowers in the special cemetery.

As the ceremony was about to begin, a handsome young man in a navy uniform with H.M.S. AMETHYST on his cap walked slowly through the gate and joined the small crowd of people grouped around the open grave. He used crutches, but he stood tall and the shoes on his feet shone in the sun. It was Mark Allen, the sailor who perhaps more than anyone owed his life to Simon.

And as they buried the little hero of the *Amethyst,* it seemed fitting that it was Mark's strong, young voice that rang out in the morning air: "The Lord is my shepherd, I shall not want . . ."

Rosamond M. Young

6

ON COMPANIONSHIP

*Animals are such agreeable friends—
they ask no questions,
they pass no criticisms.*

George Eliot

The Ugly Pupling

Things are beautiful if you love them.

Jean Anouilh

In the spring of 1980, I was living in Woodstock, New York, when my Tibetan terrier dog, Shadow, had a litter of six puppies.

The one pup I couldn't sell was considered homely. Tibetan terriers are known for their lustrous double coats. The underlayer of their coat is thick and cottony, while the outer layer resembles human hair—silky and shiny. This combination makes for a very fluffy look. People also prize their well-proportioned faces. This pup had neither trait. She had a rather long nose and a terribly unattractive coat. She had no underlayer, and this made her topcoat look thin, flat and wiry. It gave her the appearance of a tramp just coming in from the rain. People who came to see her would say, "She seems like a pleasant dog," they'd say, "but she looks kind of scraggly and ugly." No one wanted our little friend, not even for free!

What amazed me was that no one recognized this dog's rare quality. She was by nature always very happy, and although most puppies are happy, she had an unexplainable inner joy about her, a sixth sense, a certain spiritual presence, as if she could read your mind and move you to a more contented place.

In June, I still had the pup with the perpetual "bad hair day." I was going back to school in less than a week and I felt hesitant to leave without finding her a proper home.

One night an idea came to me. There was a Tibetan monastery about a mile from my home, and I'd been there a few times to participate in their meditations. I'd even introduced myself to some of the Tibetan monks living there. Maybe someone there would be willing to adopt her. It was worth a try.

The following morning, I took my little friend to the monastery. When I arrived, a lot of cars were in the parking lot. I thought, *Gee, this place has always been so quiet. I wonder what's going on?* I got out of the car with the pup in hand and went up the stairs to the familiar front doors. I entered the foyer and found people lined up wall to wall, apparently waiting for something to occur beyond the hand-carved interior doors. Then I saw a familiar face—one of the monks I'd met on a previous visit. When he saw me holding the dog, he gave me a wide grin and said, "Ah, follow me now!"

He pulled on my sleeve and dragged me to the front of the line. Using what appeared to be a special code, he knocked on the door. The double doors swung open and we were greeted by another monk. The first monk whispered something in the second monk's ear, then the second monk also said, "Ah." With that, the pup and I were pulled to the front of yet another line of people, all bearing gifts of fruit, candy, plants, odd bowls and handmade crafts.

I turned to face the front of the room and there before me was a very bright and cheery-eyed fellow, dressed to the hilt in red and golden-yellow velvets. He glanced at my puppy, then directly at me. Then he put his hands out, fingers open, and said, "Yes, yes. Oh, yes." This magnificent-looking person placed a red string around my puppy's neck, sang a foreign chant, and proceeded to place a second string around my neck. He continued his chant while slowly lifting my puppy from my arms. He carefully embraced her within his velvet robe. He then nodded and bowed, saying something in a foreign language. He tapped me on the head and turned around as he walked toward his chair, still holding my puppy in his arms.

The monk who brought me into the room now quickly ushered me out. In the foyer, met by other monks, I was swept through the halls, pup-less and out the front door of the monastery. I was asked to stand at the top of the steps and wait until further notice.

At this point, a wave of maternal concern moved through me. *Where is my dog and what will happen to her?* I thought. Turning to a Buddhist onlooker for understanding, I related the events of the last fifteen minutes.

He smiled and explained that I had met the "Karmapa," a monk who is quite high in the Tibetan Buddhist tradition—second only to the Dalai Lama. He told me that I was very fortunate because today the famous and beloved Karmapa was here from Tibet to bless this monastery along with its surrounding land. People from all over the world had come to pay him their respects, but rarely did anyone enter into his private receiving room. To enter there and be blessed by His Holiness, and then for him to accept my generous gift, was an auspicious event, one that rarely happens in a lifetime! He shook his head, "You must have earned a lot of merit in past lives; you are very fortunate, my dear." Closing his eyes, he pondered for a moment, then added, "Then again, perhaps it is your dog's good fortune!"

At that moment the door flew open again, and this wondrous Buddhist monk exited from the building and down the red-carpeted exterior steps, holding his head up high while greeting the people. Women and children gathered around, holding baskets of flowers to throw at his feet.

I was so caught up in the magic of it that I didn't notice her at first. But then to my surprise, I saw my pup—the pup that was considered ugly—now looking like a beautiful star! The Karmapa held her up high with what seemed to be the greatest of pride, and the crowd roared with delight. I would swear that the puppy appeared to be smiling, too.

From that point on, everything seemed to happen in slow motion. They continued down the stairs. Slowly they entered the waiting black limousine. Through the closely-hovering crowd, I caught my last view of the dog and the monk, glimpsing them through the tinted-glass windows. Something in the way they sat together told me she was going to be all right. It wasn't just that she was with the Karmapa; it was the way she sat on the lap of the Karmapa. They seemed to have gained a great deal of respect and trust for one another in a short period of time. The limousine drove them away, leaving behind a path of colorful rose petals.

After that, the monks at the monastery kindly kept me posted on her adventures and whereabouts. Over the years, I heard that the Karmapa traveled all over the world with his Tibetan terrier. The Karmapa grew to genuinely adore his canine companion and they were rarely apart during her entire lifetime. The sight of her funny face always brought him and others a feeling of joy, and therefore, he gave her a name that translates from the Tibetan language as Beautiful Happy One. She became his friend and devoted companion, and they were rarely apart during her entire lifetime.

Once considered an ugly puppy, few appreciated what she possessed, yet from the moment she was born, she emanated happiness. It was as if she knew she'd eventually meet her wonderful friend, the Karmapa, who would recognize her true beauty and love her great soul.

Angel Di Benedetto

Babblers Anonymous

During my college days, I began cultivating myself to fit the image I held of an aspiring author. I fancied myself a connoisseur of language and shuddered at others' misuse of it. Most of all, I scoffed at people who spewed drivel at babies or, even more loathsome, at pets. Although neither babies nor pets were part of my life, I felt quite certain that when they were, I would be a role model for mothers and animal lovers everywhere.

Then one day my friend Marcia called and asked if I would take in a stray cat. "He's cold and scared," she said. "He's been living on my neighbor's garage roof. Someone dumped him from a car."

Cats are sensible animals, I thought. I had always admired their regal bearing and independence. Besides, Charles Dickens, H. G. Wells and Mark Twain had all owned cats. I imagined a cat curled at my feet as I typed, perhaps inspiring my creativity to new heights. I invited Marcia to bring over the stray.

As Marcia approached my apartment, I heard rather than saw the cat. He protested loudly until she set the carrier on my living room rug. The moment she opened the door of the carrier, a skinny black cat streaked out, raced into the bedroom, jumped into the bathroom and bathtub, leapt out, then charged back into the living room and onto my lap.

"I've got to run," Marcia said, grabbing the carrier and stepping outside in one smooth move. "Yell if you need anything."

By this time, the cat was kneading his paws on my stomach in frantic rhythm, much like a boxer jabbing a punching bag. "You're not shy," I said wryly. Although the cat was bony, his coat shone blue-black in the lamplight. His mustard-yellow eyes blinked at me momentarily before he resumed his activity.

"I guess I need to call you something." I choked on my words. *Listen to me,* I thought. *I'm talking to this animal as if he understands.*

"Ralph," I continued, despite myself. "Ralph is a nice, no-nonsense name." No cutesy Boo-Boos or Fluffys for me.

That night I set down the rules of cathood. Ralph would not be allowed on my bed. He would sleep on the rug in the living room. He would learn to respond appropriately to simple, one-word commands. For my part, I would speak to him like the intelligent animal he was.

After a two-night cycle of putting Ralph on the floor and awakening to find him beside me in bed, I gave in on that rule. I told myself that this was for my good rather than his, because his purring relaxed me, and his warm, fuzzy body felt wonderful against my back.

As the week wore on, we seemed to understand each other perfectly. I made sure not to speak to Ralph other than as master to animal. Then one morning, I accidentally stepped on his tail. Such a pitiful wail! I scooped him up and held him close.

"Oh, Mommy's so sorry!"

I looked around. Who said that? Oh, no! It was happening. I was beginning to talk like one of *them.*

Over the next few days, I desperately tried to curb my maternal feelings. I decided to squelch the Mommy business first, but nothing else seemed appropriate. Master was a bit much. Kathy? No, too familiar—I would lose my authority. "Mommy" best summed up my role. So grudgingly, I became Ralph's mommy . . . but I promised myself I would make no further concessions.

Then one night Ralph was sick on the carpet. After cleaning up, I hugged and stroked him.

"Poor baby," I cooed. "Him was sick."

Him was sick! I envisioned my English professor tightening a noose around his neck. As Ralph napped, I reviewed my worsening condition. I could no longer deny the facts. I was rapidly becoming a pet owner-babbler.

During the next few weeks, I resolved to control every word that came from my lips, but the unthinkable happened. Such aberrations as "You is a widdle baby boy" flowed freely, as though the evil spirit of grammar atrocities possessed me every time I looked at Ralph. Worse yet, he seemed to expect such talk.

One night I decided to go cold turkey. I placed Ralph on my lap so he faced me. "Now," I began, consciously resisting the babble, "you're a sensible, intelligent animal. You want an owner who treats you as such, don't you?"

Ralph's eyes never moved. I read understanding there, encouraging me to go on. "Henceforth, I will treat you with the dignity and respect such a noble cat deserves."

Ralph's mouth was opening. So intent was his stare that for one insane moment, I thought he would speak. He yawned in my face.

"You silly, pweshus baby," I said, laughing and cuddling him to me.

Now the rules are gone. I never had the authority anyway. Only love and the babbling remain. Does anyone know of a Babblers Anonymous?

Kathleen M. Muldoon

"Was it a 'ittle putty tat?
'es it was. It was a putty!
Tum tum tum!
Tum on, pwetty putty,
tum det on Mommy's wap."

A Damaged Dog

A jarring cry roused me from my sleep early one Friday morning. Running to my window, I saw what I expected—the canine victim of yet one more hit-and-run driver. The gaunt, wolf-like creature lay huddled against a doorway. I knew there was no owner. The dog was clearly one of the many homeless, hungry mutts prowling the streets of Kiev, where I was temporarily working as a journalist.

Perhaps he isn't too badly injured, I hoped vainly. But when he tried to walk, he kept falling on his hurt shoulders, leaving a blood-soaked path on the pavement behind him. *He could be dangerous,* I worried. Wrong again. He kept nudging passersby with his head in an obvious plea for help.

In no time, I was one of a small group of people surrounding the shocked animal, debating what could be done. "I'll take him," I said, startled by my own words. "Temporarily."

Someone brought out a bed sheet, and I smiled as the dog immediately tried to roll himself onto it. My neighbor, Yelena, volunteered her services and we soon drove around in her car, from one primitive clinic to another. The recommended treatment was a merciful death. The bone in one of the dog's legs was shattered and no one had the facilities, skills or medication to treat him. Ukraine in 1992 was a cash-strapped country.

The dog looked at me plaintively, his eyes glazed from the effects of morphine. I became determined, with an advantageous wad of American dollars in my pocket, to save this creature's life. "Surely something can be done," I said.

"If anyone can do anything, it's Oleg Feodoseyevych, a professor at the Agriculture Academy. He's the best veterinary surgeon this country has," I was told. Yelena and I were soon carrying our canine patient through a stable of pigs and cows into a large teaching surgery full of giggling students in funny white paper caps. The famed Oleg Feodoseyevych gingerly felt around the dog's body, smiled, and said the magic words: "He'll be all right."

The operation lasted four hours, and I watched as the professor patiently inserted a metal rod into one of the dog's legs. The dog, awake throughout, yelped whenever the local anesthetic started to wear off. "He needs more anesthetic," someone would volunteer. Usually it was me.

Just minutes after the operation, we were back in the car, the dog with two new white casts, and me with a sheet of instructions on post-operative care and medicine to buy. Where was I supposed to get gauze or painkillers in a city whose pharmacies carried little more than vitamins and herbal teas?

"Don't worry," said Yelena. "The pharmacies are empty but home medicine cabinets are full." Sure enough, Yelena came over that evening with a bag full of vials, tubes, syringes and tablets.

For three days and nights my sick patient groaned, lying motionless on a blanket. He moved nothing but his tail, which thumped loudly against the parquet floor each time I entered the room. I fed him chicken soup through an eyedropper. Six times a day I changed the bandages over a partial opening in the casts, causing him obvious pain as the gauze ripped his bloody shaven skin.

Foolishly hoping he perhaps had an owner, I placed ads in the local papers. I received many calls, but none from a long-lost master. Several people offered to adopt him, and I began compiling a list of possible owners for the day he would be recovered.

Before long the dog was ready for solid food, and I called my cleaning woman, Nadia, in a panic over what to feed him—Western-style commercial dog food was not yet available in Ukraine. Chubby Nadia, dog-lover extraordinaire, soon stood at my stove, brewing a concoction of mashed potatoes, carrots and chopped beef. She instructed me, who had never owned a dog, on the basics of dog care.

Eventually my patient started walking and I ventured outside with him after carrying him down the final twenty steps of my building. Teetering along on his two plastered legs, tail wagging, he was met with a wave of sympathy. Grannies on their balconies shook their heads, making little *tsk-tsk* sounds, children jumped around us asking if it would hurt to pet his head, and every dog owner in sight stopped to offer his favorite canine home remedy for broken bones.

"Eggshells," said one woman, who ran half a block to tell me this.

Finally the day came when Oleg Feodoseyevych arrived to remove the casts. We heaved the dog into the bathtub, and I held him as the doctor cut away the plaster.

"You know, a dog has to have a name," he said.

"Oh, no," I answered, waving the list of potential owners at him. "I'm not planning on keeping him. You can see, my lifestyle, the traveling I have to do . . ."

The good doctor looked up, and smiled.

Olivier, as I came to name him, never did leave. He fully recovered and showered me with his love, repaying me tenfold for my spontaneous decision that traumatic Friday morning. Many a day he pulled me away from my solitude, anger, laziness and greed. He gave me exquisite sunrises over the river Dnieper at the break of dawn, introduced me to endless people in the park, and enchanted me for hours as I watched his ridiculous antics with his four-legged friends. He covered me with wet sappy kisses and warmed me with big howling welcomes.

Did I save him, I wondered, *or did he save me?*

Two years later, Olivier left as abruptly as he arrived. One day, while playing with his favorite dog pal in the park, he fell over, convulsed, and died. A subsequent autopsy showed a ruptured liver enlarged to twice its size. He had no chance, the doctor said, a woman who was another specialist from the Agriculture Academy. Olivier had plenty of other internal problems, she said, as a result of years of impoverished living on the streets of Kiev.

Seeing my distress, she tried to comfort me in the typical gruff Slavic manner. "You know, you shouldn't just pick up any old dog off the street. They're too damaged to live long. It's just not worth the emotional cost."

And what of the emotional gain? I wondered, considering her words.

As I stepped out of the clinic, I resolved never to heed her advice.

Roma Ihnatowycz

A French Cat

Recently my husband Gene and I traveled throughout Europe. We rented a car as we always do and drove along the back roads, staying in quaint, out-of-the-way inns. The only thing that distracted me from the wonder of the trip was the terrible longing I felt for our cat Perry. I always miss him when we travel, but this time, because we were gone for more than three weeks, my need to touch his soft fur and to hold him close became more and more intense. With every cat we saw, the feeling deepened.

We were high in the mountains of France one morning, packing the car before resuming our trip, when an elderly couple walked up to the car parked next to ours. The woman was holding a large Siamese cat and speaking to him in French.

I stood watching them, unable to turn away. My yearning for Perry must have been written all over my face. The woman glanced at me, turned to speak to her husband and then spoke to her cat. Suddenly she walked right over to me and, without one word, held out her cat.

I immediately opened my arms to him. Cautious about the stranger holding him, he extended his claws, but only for a few seconds. Then he retracted them, settled into my embrace and began to purr. I buried my face in his soft fur while rocking him gently. Then, still wordless, I returned him to the woman.

I smiled at them in thanks, and tears filled my eyes. The woman had sensed my need to hold her cat, the cat had sensed that he could trust me, and both, in one of the greatest gifts of kindness I have every received, had acted upon their feelings.

It's comforting to know the language of cat lovers—and cats—is the same the world over.

Jean Brody

"I'm afraid we'll have to keep him overnight. Are you going to need a loaner?"

Tailless Tom

Tailless Tom has been gone a long time now, but I still see him in my mind's eye as clear as if he had died only yesterday. I see him strutting along proud as punch, his rear end with only the tiniest stump of tail on it twitching in the breeze. I like to think of Tailless Tom as my cat, which he was, but he wasn't . . . the way the Statue of Liberty belongs to me, but it doesn't. The truth is that Tailless Tom belonged to a whole regiment, and I think every man in that regiment belonged to him.

Tailless Tom's proud way of walking might make you think he was a Manx cat, but he wasn't. He was just an ordinary brown alley cat who had lost his tail—he never told me how—in his early years before we met. That was back in the early 1930s, when I first opened my animal hospital in Mount Vernon, New York.

Tom lived near the hospital with a nice but terribly squeamish lady. She couldn't stand the things Tom brought home from his daily outings in the fields that used to be plentiful around Mount Vernon.

Because he was such a friendly, gregarious cat who seemed to truly like people, Tom dropped in on me one day and I showed him around my hospital, which stood clean and empty while I waited for customers to discover me.

Shortly afterward, I met the lady with whom he lived. She dropped in for some advice about Tom. Was there any way she could stop him from bringing home the mice, moles and birds he caught?

"He puts them right at my feet, Dr. Camuti, and sometimes they're still alive!"

I told her she should feel complimented. And she should be proud that her cat was such a good hunter. She sniffed at that, and dabbed at her eyes with a lacy handkerchief. "Well, I can't stand it. I'm a very nervous woman and I find it upsetting."

The woman knew that I thought Tailless Tom was a terrific cat. That was why she called me a week later. She sounded close to hysteria.

"Do you want Tom? He's yours right now. I can't take it anymore."

"What happened?"

Her voice rose, and the words came tumbling out in a wild rush. "Do you know where he is this very minute? Sitting outside the screened porch door with a snake in his mouth, and it's still alive! You have to come and get him right away, Dr. Camuti, or I'll find some other way to get rid of him. I can't have this happening anymore!"

I said I'd be right over. Sure enough, Tom was sitting exactly where she said he was. The snake turned out to be a racer, absolutely harmless and a baby, not much larger than a big worm. Tom dropped it at my feet. I patted his head, and the snake shot off into the grass.

I brought Tom back with me to the hospital. He immediately sensed it was his new home. I told Tom that the hospital would have to be a temporary home for him because as my practice grew, the hospital was bound to fill up with all sorts of animals, and a cat in residence just wouldn't work out. I told him that I would certainly do my best to find him a good, permanent home. Tom said nothing. He just rubbed against my pants leg and purred.

With his personality, I thought I'd have no trouble finding a home for Tailless Tom. People seemed interested when I told them about the cat's warm, friendly disposition, but when I got to the part about his talents as a hunter, I lost many of them. And the one or two that asked to meet Tom didn't seem to find this tailless wonder as attractive as I did.

One day, I thought of a perfect solution. I was the commanding officer at the White Plains Armory on South Broadway. There were lots of people around over there, and Tom liked people. It would be a great home for him. There were plenty of open fields around the place, so Tom would have good hunting.

Tom took to army life like a duck to water, and the men fell for him. One of the sergeants made him his own dog tag and put it on a chain around his neck. Wearing the proof of how special he was, Tom strutted more proudly than ever.

Tom's favorite time was when the 102nd Medical Regiment moved out to Camp Smith, near Peekskill, New York, for two weeks each summer. As a member of the regiment, Tom naturally went along.

As commanding officer of the service command at Camp Smith, one of my duties was to supply the food to the thirteen companies in the regiment. All the supply sergeants tried to give special treats to Tom as a way of pleasing me, but Tom let them know he couldn't be bought. He would just turn up his nose and march on.

Though he wasn't officially assigned to the post, Tom made mess hall inspection his job. It was a big undertaking, since there were eleven mess halls for the enlisted men and two for the officers, all strung out in a 400-foot line. Tom dropped by many of the halls two or three times a day to look things over. Obviously he had his favorite kitchens, and the men who ran them felt honored by Tom's visits. Those he ignored tried desperately to lure him over, as though Tailless Tom was in charge of bestowing some terrific award, like the Duncan Hines Seal of Approval.

Tom actually made the whole camp his command, but he would always check in at my company several times a day just to give me a rub and a purr and let me know that I still stood high in his affection. But he refused to sleep in my officer's tent. Tom was a born diplomat. He always bedded down with the enlisted men.

When we returned from Camp Smith, Tom went back to hunting the open fields around the armory. No matter how far he wandered, he always kept the armory in his sights, and the minute he saw men gathering for a meeting, he came racing back.

Life went on for Tom at the armory for several years. And then one day, coming back from one of his field patrols, he was run over by a car right in front of the armory. It was a loss every man felt.

There was no question about Tom's funeral. It was automatically decided that he should have a full military send-off.

I don't think there was one man attached to the armory who skipped Tom's funeral. He was placed in a small casket and buried in the front yard of the armory while a military salute was fired in his honor and taps was sounded. I looked down the line of men standing at attention as Tailless Tom went to his glory, and I could see the sun picking up wet spots on many faces. I admit the tears were running freely down my face.

Today there is a small marker on Tailless Tom's grave in the front yard of the armory. When I'm out driving, I often stop to pause a minute and look at Tom's grave and remember him. I can still hear the sound of his dog tag rubbing against the chain around his neck as he strutted around with his stump of tail high in the air, and all four feet marching in proud cadence. He was a great cat and a good soldier.

Louis J. Camuti, D.V.M.

The White House Dog

My name is Mildred Kerr Bush and I came to live with the Bush family on February 13, 1987. Their previous dog, C. Fred Bush, had died on January 20, and George, who was then Vice President of the United States of America, knew that his wife, Bar, missed C. Fred and needed a dog. But he also knew that Bar did not need a puppy.

"Training puppies on your own rugs is a challenge. Training pups on government rugs is impossible."

So George turned to his great friend Will Farish. Bar had fallen in love with my mother and sister in South Texas when she and George had joined Will and Sarah there on a trip after Christmas. Sarah had mentioned that my mother had had a big litter. So George called Will, who said he was sure that he had a dog, and called back later to ask if a girl would be all right. The Bushes had never had a female dog before, but George said, "That would be great." Will said he had the perfect dog . . . but she was liver-colored and white, not black and white like her beautiful mother and sister. George said, "Fine."

Will brought me from Versailles, Kentucky, to Cincinnati, where we met the Bushes at the foot of the steps of *Air Force II*. It was love at first sight. Both Bushes kissed me and I sat on Bar's lap all the way home. I'm going to be honest (this is a confession that is difficult for me to make and you will understand why as you read on). Bar did whisper to me that night, "You are so sweet, but you are so ugly. You have a pig's nose, you are bowlegged, and your eyes are yellow." I knew immediately that I was going to have to try harder. She also told me that she really loved me, and I believed her.

That was sort of a rocky start, but I have since heard her tell others that she will never have a male dog again, and that I am the best dog they ever lived with. I believe that too.

Being a vice-president's dog does have its perks. You often get to meet celebrities. Several months after I arrived at the V.P. House we got a letter from Benji, the famous dog movie actor, asking if he could come by for a courtesy call. He was on a tour promoting his latest movie. You can imagine my excitement . . . I would get to meet a real live macho movie star. We invited two of the "grands," Jenna and Barbara, to bring over their Horace Mann kindergarten class to see the famous fella. He drove up in a big limousine, surrounded by aides, leaped out on command (as Bar pointed out), and then I discovered the awful truth. Benji turned out to be an aging (twelve-year-old) female. To add insult to injury, she also turned out to be the nicest, best-behaved, friendliest dog I have ever met. The next day the papers had a big article and picture of Benji visiting the U.S. Marine barracks with the Marine mascot. I was barely mentioned. Not that I cared.

I've learned publicity is a double-edged sword. My babies and I were once on the cover of *Life* magazine. I could only conclude that I was their selection for 1989 Mother of the Year. The babies and I looked smashing. I was glad to have a family picture before they all took off for new homes. If only the puppies' father, Tug, had been with us.

Just when I was riding high, out of the blue and with absolutely no provocation, the July 1989 issue of *The Washingtonian* magazine came out with their "Best & Worst" list. Guess whose picture was on the cover? Mine! Guess which I was . . . best or worst? Worst. The President advised me to "shake it off," ignore it, and not let it get my goat.

It reminded him of the time that Dick Schaap (a sportswriter for *New York* magazine) wrote an article entitled "The Ten Most Overrated Men in N.Y.C." He told me that as the U.S. Ambassador to the United Nations, his name headed the list. George invited the other nine men, the nervous author and several ambassadors to a reception honoring "The Overrated." It was a great party.

The newspapers and the Bushes had lots of fun with *The Washingtonian* article. George immediately came to my defense. Bar was a little quieter. After what she had whispered to me that first night, I guess she felt this was one battle she should stay out of. The editors of *The Washingtonian* even apologized and sent me some marvelous dog biscuits. George accepted their apology. He wrote the editor of the guilty magazine: "Dear Jack: Not to worry! Millie, you see, likes publicity. She is hoping to parlay this into a Lassie-like Hollywood career. Seriously, no hurt feelings; but you are sure nice to write. Arf, arf for the dog biscuits—Sincerely, George Bush." Easy for the President to accept the apology. I did not.

It was bad enough to have my face on the cover, beside which they had written, "Our Pick as the Ugliest Dog: Millie, the White House Mutt," but the picture they had inside was taken the very afternoon of my delivery. Show me one woman who could pass that test, lying on her side absolutely "booney wild" (family expression for undressed) on the day she delivered six babies! I also objected to the word "mutt." I am a blueblood through and through.

After *The Washingtonian* attack we got lots of letters. Many came to my defense. There were letters to the editor, and many letters sent directly to the White House. I guess the most pleasing message of all came directly from the office of Senator Bob Dole, who personally brought the following press release to the White House:

FOR IMMEDIATE RELEASE:

LEADER: *WASHINGTONIAN* ATTACK ON FIRST DOG MILLIE:
AN "ARF" FRONT TO DOGS EVERYWHERE

WASHINGTON—CALLING IT AN "ARF" FRONT TO DOGS EVERYWHERE, LEADER, FIRST K-9 ASSISTANT TO SENATE REPUBLICAN LEADER BOB DOLE (R-KS) SAID TODAY THAT *THE WASHINGTONIAN* MAGAZINE WAS BARKING UP THE WRONG FIRE HYDRANT WHEN IT PICKED FIRST DOG MILLIE AS WASHINGTON'S UGLIEST DOG IN ITS CURRENT "BEST & WORST" LIST.

"I TALKED WITH MILLIE ABOUT THIS TODAY," LEADER SAID, "AND ADVISED HER TO START USING *THE WASHINGTONIAN* TO PAPER-TRAIN HER PUPPIES."

LEADER ANNOUNCED HE'S FORMING A NEW ORGANIZATION CALLED P.A.W.S.—WHICH STANDS FOR POOCHES AGAINST WASHINGTON SMEARS.

"WHATEVER HAPPENED TO ALL THIS 'MAN'S BEST FRIEND' STUFF I'VE BEEN HEARING ALL THESE YEARS? IF THE EDITORS OF *THE WASHINGTONIAN* KEEP UP THESE DOGMATIC ATTACKS, THEY HAD BETTER WATCH THEIR STEP—LITERALLY WATCH THEIR STEP," LEADER SAID.

"AS FIRST DOG, MILLIE HAS SET A GREAT EXAMPLE FOR MILLIONS OF AMERICAN DOGS. SHE IS RAISING A FAMILY, DOESN'T STRAY FROM THE YARD, AND DOES HER BEST TO KEEP HER MASTER IN LINE. IT'S JUST NOT RIGHT FOR HER TO BE HOUNDED LIKE THIS.

"LET'S MAKE NO BONES ABOUT IT. DOGS EVERYWHERE ARE WHINING ABOUT THIS. LET IT BE KNOWN, WE WON'T SIT FOR IT."

Millie Bush
As dictated to Barbara Bush

Barney

Mary Guy figured that becoming a national celebrity was probably about as much as a squirrel could hope to achieve in one lifetime. But Barney is not your average squirrel.

Mary has a bottled water business in Garden City, Kansas. She is also a known animal lover. One day in August of 1994, one of her customers showed her an orphaned baby fox squirrel that he had found. When he asked if she could care for it, she felt she had to at least give it a try.

It so happened that a week earlier, Mary's cat, Corky, had had four kittens. Mary's husband, Charlie, suggested they try adding the squirrel to the litter of kittens—and it worked! Barney (named by a grandson after a particular purple dinosaur) was not only adopted by Corky, he was accepted as a sibling by all four kittens. He became especially close with one feline sister, Celeste.

Some of the Guys' guests thought this cat/squirrel family was so adorable that they contacted the local newspaper about it. The paper ran a story with a photo of the mother cat nursing her four kittens and Barney under the headline: "One of these kittens seems sort of squirrelly."

The unusual story was picked up by the Associated Press and sent to newspapers all over the country. As a result, Mary received calls and letters from all over the country, and even Canada, by people who were impressed with the story and picture. Barney was a celebrity!

Unfortunately, there was a downside to Barney's fame.

The article was seen by employees of the Kansas Department of Wildlife and Parks. A state official contacted the Guys and told them that it is illegal to keep a squirrel as a pet in the state of Kansas. They would have to return Barney to the wild.

Mary was thunderstruck. Not only had she become attached to her unusual pet, she feared for his life if he was turned loose. He had no fear of cats—he'd been raised by one! But squirrels are rodents and cats are natural enemies of rodents. If Barney was turned loose, he'd be lunch for the first stray cat he met. She explained this to the authorities, but to no avail. The law's the law.

"Well, ma'am," suggested one officer, "if you buy a hunting license, you can legally keep him until the end of squirrel season. It runs until December 31."

It was a temporary solution, but Mary hurried out to pay the thirteen dollars for a hunting license.

Mary grieved as the end of the year approached. She had come to truly love the mischievous little guy and was certain that turning him loose was tantamount to a death sentence.

Also, by this time, all of the kittens had been adopted except Celeste; and she and Barney were now best friends. They played together, slept together and chased each other all over the house. If Mary separated them, Celeste wailed miserably. And Barney showed not the slightest interest in life in the great outdoors.

Mary again approached the newspapers. Perhaps the

same notoriety that had landed Barney in this mess could lead to a solution.

The story of Barney's plight went out over the Associated Press wires. By early December, Mary was deluged with calls and letters from all over the country offering their prayers and moral support. Some callers who lived in states with differing laws even offered to take in both Barney and Celeste.

The Wildlife and Parks Department also received calls and mail from around the country. Not wanting to look heartless, they suggested that Barney might be released at the Garden City Zoo's park. The Kansas Attorney General called Mary and suggested that she give Barney to a "rehabilitator" who would teach him to survive in the wild before releasing him.

Still, Mary feared for the safety of her beloved pet—and knew he didn't want to leave his happy life any more than she wanted to lose him.

As New Year's Eve approached, the Guys saw one slim chance. The new year would bring a new administration into the Kansas statehouse. Mary arranged for friends who were invited to the new governor's inaugural celebration to take information about Barney with them.

One of the first acts of the Kansas governor's office in 1995 was to issue the Guys a special permit to keep their squirrel.

And so Barney became the first squirrel in history to not only become a national celebrity, but to receive a pardon from the governor.

No, not your average squirrel at all.

Gregg Bassett
President, The Squirrel Lover's Club

Mousekeeping

Until a certain sunny morning in early September, I had never sought the company of mice. On that day, my husband, Richard, called me out to the barn of our Rhode Island farm, where I found him holding a tin can and peering into it with an unusual expression of foolish pleasure. He handed me the tin can as though it contained something he had just picked up at Tiffany's.

Crouched at the bottom was a young mouse, not much bigger than a bumblebee. She stared up with eyes like polished seeds. She was a beautiful little creature and clearly still too small to cope with a wide and dangerous world.

Richard had found her on the doorstep. When he picked her up, he thought the little mouse was done for. By chance he had a gumdrop in his pocket, and he placed the candy on his palm beside the limp mouse. The smell acted as a stimulant. She flung herself upon the gumdrop, ate voraciously and was almost instantly restored to health.

Richard made a wire cage for Mousie, as we now called her, and we made a place for her on a table in the kitchen. I watched her while I peeled vegetables. I found myself fascinated by her—I had no idea there were so many things to notice about a mouse.

Her baby coat was a dull, gun-metal gray, but it soon changed to reddish brown with dark gray anklets and white feet. I had thought the tails of mice were hairless and limp. Not so. Mousie's tail was furred, and rather than trailing it behind like a piece of string, she held it up quite stiffly. Sometimes the tail rose over Mousie's back like a quivering question mark.

She cleaned herself like a cat. Sitting on her small behind (she could have sat on a postage stamp without spilling over), she licked her flanks, then moistened her paws to go over her ears, neck and face. She would grasp a hind leg with suddenly simian hands while she licked the extended toes. For the finale she would pick up her tail and, as though eating corn on the cob, wash its length with her tongue.

Mousie became tame within a few days. She nibbled my fingers and batted them with her paws like a playful puppy. She liked to be petted. If I held her in my hand and rubbed gently with a forefinger, she would raise her chin, the way a cat will, to be stroked along the jawbone. Then she would lie flat on her back in the palm of my hand, eyes closed, paws limp and nose pointed upward in apparent bliss.

Our little friend slept in a plastic Thermos cup, lined with rags that she shredded into fluff as soft as a down quilt. After a while I replaced the cup with half a coconut shell that I inverted, cutting a door into the lower edge. It was a most attractive mouse house, quite tropical in feeling. Mousie stuffed it from floor to ceiling with fluff.

The cage was equipped with twigs for a perch and an exercise wheel on which Mousie traveled many a league to nowhere. Her athletic ability was astounding. Once I put Mousie in an empty garbage pail while I cleaned the cage. She made a straight-upward leap of fifteen inches, nearly clearing the rim.

Mousie kept food in a small aluminum can we had screwed to the wall of the cage. Richard and I called it the First Mouse National Bank. If I sprinkled bird seed in the cage, Mousie worked diligently to transport it, stuffing the seeds in her little cheeks for deposit in the bank.

Though Mousie kept busy, I feared that her life might be lonely. I asked a biologist I knew for help. He's the one who determined Mousie's sex (to a lay person, the rear end of a mouse is quite enigmatic), and he provided a male laboratory mouse as a companion.

The new mouse had a stout body, hairless tail and a mousy smell—unlike our Mousie, who was seemingly odorless. I named him Stinky and with some misgivings put him in Mousie's cage.

Stinky lumbered about, squinting at nothing in particular, until he stumbled across some of Mousie's seeds. He made an enthusiastic buck-toothed attack on these goodies. Flashing down from her perch, Mousie bit Stinky's tail. He continued to gobble. Disgusted, Mousie went to bed.

From this unpromising start, a warm attachment bloomed. The two mice slept curled up together. Mousie spent a great deal of time licking Stinky, holding him down and kneading him with her paws. He returned her caresses, but with less ardor. He reserved his passion for food.

One day as an experiment, I put Mousie's food bank on the floor of the cage. Stinky sniffed at the opening. Mousie watched, whiskers quivering, and I had the distinct impression of consternation on her face. With a quickness of decision that amazed me, Mousie seized a wad of bedding, stuffed it into the bank, effectively corking up her treasure. It was a brilliant move. Baffled, Stinky lumbered away.

In spite of their ungenerous behavior toward each other, I felt that Stinky made Mousie happy. Their reunions after being separated were always joyous, with Mousie scrambling all over Stinky and just about licking him to pieces. Even stolid old Stinky showed some excitement.

I wasn't aware when Stinky became ill. But one day after about a year, I saw Mousie sitting trembling on her branch when she should have been asleep. I looked in the cage and found Stinky stone-cold dead.

Alone the rest of her days, Mousie lived a total of more than three years. That, I believe, is a good deal beyond the span usually allotted to mice. She showed no sign of growing old or feeble. Then one day, I found her dead.

As I took her almost weightless body in my hand and carried it out to the meadow, I felt a genuine sadness. She had given me much. She had stirred my imagination and opened a window on a Lilliputian world. Beyond that, there had been moments when I felt contact between her tiny being and my own. Sometimes when I touched her lovingly and she nibbled my fingers in return, it felt as though an affectionate message was passing between us.

I put Mousie's body down in the grass and walked back to the house. I was sad, not for Mousie, but for me. The size of a friend has nothing to do with the void he or she leaves behind. I knew I would miss my littlest pet.

Faith McNulty

The Cat and the Grizzly

Cats seem to go on the principle that it never does any harm to ask for what you want.

Joseph Wood Kruth

"Another box of kittens dumped over the fence, Dave," one of our volunteers greeted me one summer morning. I groaned inside. As the founder of Wildlife Images Rehabilitation Center, I had more than enough to do to keep up with the wild animals in our care. But somehow, local people who didn't have the heart to take their unwanted kittens to the pound often dumped them over our fence. They knew we'd try to live-trap them, spay or neuter them, and place them through our network of approximately 100 volunteers.

That day's brood contained four kittens. We managed to trap three of them, but somehow one little rascal got away. In twenty-four acres of park, there wasn't much we could do once the kitten disappeared—and many other animals required our attention. It wasn't long before I forgot completely about the lost kitten as I went about my daily routine.

A week or so later, I was spending time with one of my favorite "guests"—a giant grizzly bear named Griz.

This grizzly bear had come to us as an orphaned cub six years ago, after being struck by a train in Montana. He'd been rescued by a Blackfoot Indian, had lain unconscious for six days in a Montana hospital's intensive care unit, and ended up with neurological damage and a blind right eye. As he recovered, it was clear he was too habituated to humans and too mentally impaired to go back to the wild, so he came to live with us as a permanent resident.

Grizzly bears are not generally social creatures. Except for when they mate or raise cubs, they're loners. But this grizzly liked people. I enjoyed spending time with Griz, giving him personal attention on a regular basis. Even this required care, since a 560-pound creature could do a lot of damage to a human unintentionally.

That July afternoon, I approached his cage for our daily visit. He'd just been served his normal meal—a mix of vegetables, fruit, dog kibble, fish and chicken. Griz was lying down with the bucket between his forepaws, eating, when I noticed a little spot of orange coming out of the blackberry brambles inside the grizzly's pen.

It was the missing kitten. Now probably six weeks old, it couldn't have weighed more than ten ounces at most. Normally, I would have been concerned that the poor little thing was going to starve to death. But this kitten had taken a serious wrong turn and might not even last that long.

What should I do? I was afraid that if I ran into the pen to try to rescue it, the kitten would panic and run straight for Griz. So I just stood back and watched, praying that it wouldn't get too close to the huge grizzly.

But it did. The tiny kitten approached the enormous bear and let out a purr and a mew. I winced. With any normal bear, that cat would be dessert.

Griz looked over at him. I cringed as I watched him raise his forepaw toward the cat and braced myself for the fatal blow.

But Griz stuck his paw into his food pail, where he grabbed a piece of chicken out of the bucket and threw it toward the starving kitten.

The little cat pounced on it and carried it quickly into the bushes to eat.

I breathed a sigh of relief. That cat was one lucky animal! He'd approached the one bear of the sixteen we housed that would tolerate him—and the one in a million who'd share lunch.

A couple of weeks later, I saw the cat feeding with Griz again. This time, he rubbed and purred against the bear, and Griz reached down and picked him up by the scruff of his neck. After that, the friendship blossomed. We named the kitten Cat.

These days, Cat eats with Griz all the time. He rubs up against the bear, bats him on the nose, ambushes him, even sleeps with him. And although Griz is a gentle bear, a bear's gentleness is not all that gentle. Once Griz accidentally stepped on Cat. He looked horrified when he realized what he'd done. And sometimes when Griz tries to pick up Cat by the scruff of the cat's neck, he winds up grabbing Cat's whole head. But Cat doesn't seem to mind.

Their love for each other is so pure and simple; it goes beyond size and species. Both animals have managed to successfully survive their rough beginnings. But even more than that, they each seem so happy to have found a friend.

Dave Siddon
Founder, Wildlife Images Rehabilitation Center
As told to Jane Martin

Fine Animal Gorilla

Those of us who study apes have always known that gorillas are highly intelligent and communicate with each other through gestures. I had always dreamed of learning to communicate with gorillas. When I heard about a project in which other scientists tried to teach a chimpanzee American Sign Language (ASL), I was intrigued and excited. I thought ASL might be the perfect way to talk to gorillas because it used hand gestures to communicate whole words and ideas. As a graduate student at Stanford University, I decided to try that same experiment with a gorilla. All I had to do was find the right gorilla.

In 1971, on the fourth of July, a gorilla was born at the San Francisco Zoo. She was named Hanabi-Ko, a Japanese word meaning "fireworks child," but everyone called her Koko. She was three months old when I first saw her, a tiny gorilla clinging to her mother's back.

Soon after that, an illness spread through the entire gorilla colony. Koko almost died, but she was nursed back to health by doctors and staff at the zoo. Her mother was unable to care for her, and even though Koko was healthy again, she wasn't old enough to live among older gorillas. It seemed the perfect solution that I begin my work with her.

I started visiting Koko at the zoo every day. At first, the baby gorilla clearly didn't like me. She ignored me or bit me when I tried to pick her up. Then slowly, because I never failed to come see her every day, Koko began to trust me.

The first words I attempted to teach Koko in sign language were "drink," "food" and "more." I asked the zoo assistants who helped in the nursery to form the sign for "food" with their hands whenever they gave Koko anything to eat. I signed "drink" each time I gave Koko her bottle and formed her small hand into the sign for "drink," too.

One morning, about a month after I began working with Koko, I was slicing fruit for her snack and Koko was watching me.

"Food," she signed.

I was too surprised to respond.

"Food," she clearly signed again.

I wanted to jump for joy. Koko could sense I was happy with her. Excited, she grabbed a bucket, plunked it over her head and ran wildly around the playroom.

By age two, Koko's signs were more than just simple, one-word requests. She was learning signs quickly and stringing them together.

"There mouth, mouth—you there," Koko signed when she wanted me to blow fog on the nursery window to draw in with our fingers. And "Pour that hurry drink hurry," when she was thirsty.

The next year, Koko moved into a specially remodeled trailer on the Stanford University campus, where I could be with her more of the time and she could concentrate on her language lessons with fewer distractions.

We had a big birthday party for Koko when she turned three. She carefully ate almost all of her birthday cake with a spoon. But when it came time for the last bite, the little gorilla couldn't resist. She scooped the cake up with her hand and stuffed it into her mouth.

"More eat," she signed.

By the age of five, Koko knew more than 200 words in ASL. I recorded every sign that she used and even videotaped her actions so I could study her use of sign language later. The more signs Koko learned, the more she showed me her personality. She argued with me, displayed a very definite sense of humor and expressed strong opinions. She even used sign language to tell lies.

Once I caught her poking the window screen of her trailer with a chopstick.

"What are you doing?" I signed to her.

Koko quickly put the stick in her mouth like a cigarette. "Mouth smoke," she answered. Another time I caught her chewing a crayon when she was supposed to be drawing a picture.

"You're not eating that, are you?" I asked her.

"Lip," Koko signed, and she quickly took the crayon out of her mouth and moved it across her lips, as if putting on lipstick. I was so amazed, I almost forgot to reprimand her.

Like any naughty child, when Koko behaved badly, she was sent to a corner in her trailer. She was quite aware that she had misbehaved: "Stubborn devil," she would sign to herself. If it was only for a small thing, she would excuse herself after a little while in the corner. But if she felt she had been very bad, she soon turned around to get my attention. Then she would sign, "Sorry. Need hug."

I decided to find a companion for Koko and so Michael, a three-year-old male gorilla, came to live with us. I wanted to teach him sign language and I also hoped that one day, Koko and Michael would mate. Would they teach their baby ASL? It was a question I was eager to have answered.

Michael was a good student. He often concentrated even longer on his lessons than Koko did. At first, Koko was very jealous of her new playmate. She called Michael names and blamed him for things he hadn't done. They squabbled like a couple of typical human toddlers.

"Stupid toilet," she signed, when asked about Michael.

"Stink bad squash gorilla," Michael answered back.

Koko loved to see Michael get scolded, especially when it was for doing something that Koko had encouraged him to do. She would listen to me telling Michael to be a good gorilla, and a deep breathy sound would come out of her—it was the sound of a gorilla laughing.

But they loved to play together and spent a lot of time wrestling, tickling and signing to each other.

If you asked Koko what her favorite animal was, she would invariably sign "gorilla." But she also loved cats. Her two favorite books were *Puss in Boots* and *The Three Little Kittens*. Still, nothing prepared me for the way Koko reacted when a small, gray, tailless kitten came to live with us.

When asked what presents she wanted for her birthday or Christmas, Koko always asked for a cat. When she was twelve, we brought her three kittens to choose from and she picked the one kitten who didn't have a tail. The very first time she picked up the little kitten, she tried to tuck him in the crease of her thigh, and then on the back of her neck, two of the places mother gorillas carry their babies. She called him her "baby" and picked the name "All Ball." Without a tail, the kitten did look like a ball.

All Ball was the first kitten Koko had, but he was not her first pet; she had played with a rabbit and a bird among other small animals.

"Koko love Ball. Soft good cat cat," she signed.

Then one morning All Ball was hit and instantly killed by a car. I had to tell Koko what happened. At first Koko acted as if she didn't hear me, but when I left the trailer I heard her cry. It was her distress call—a loud, long series of high-pitched hoots. I cried too. Three days later, she told me how she felt.

"Cry, sad, frown," Koko signed.

"What happened to All Ball?" I asked her.

"Blind, sleep cat," she answered. She had seemed to have grasped the concept of death.

Koko finally chose another kitten, a soft gray one.

"Have you thought of a name yet?" I asked her.

"That smoke. Smoke smoke," she answered.

The kitten was a smoky gray, so we named her Smoky.

Many days when Koko has her reading lessons, she sees the written word for cat and then forms the sign for that word. We can't show her too many pictures of cats, though. She still gets sad when she sees any cat that looks at all like All Ball, her adored first kitten.

My language project with Koko, which I began in 1972, has become my life's work. Over the years, I have watched Koko grow up. As a scientist, I have documented every phase of her development. As a "parent," I have cared about and for her and have been proud of her every accomplishment. Koko has surprised, enlightened and inspired me. Although raised by humans and now part of a family of humans and gorillas, Koko has no illusions that she is a human. When asked who she is, she always signs, "Fine animal gorilla."

Francine (Penny) Patterson, D.V.M.

7

SAYING GOOD-BYE

. . . love knows not its own depth
until the hour of separation.

Kahlil Gibran

DAD, DID YOU CHECK ON THE LITTLE RACCOON THIS MORNING?
YES, CALVIN. ...I'M AFRAID HE DIED.

WAAHHHH!!
I'M SORRY TOO, KIDDO. BUT HE DIDN'T HAVE MUCH OF A CHANCE.

WAHH AAHH!
AT LEAST HE DIED WARM AND SAFE, CALVIN. WE DID ALL WE COULD, BUT NOW HE'S GONE.

SNIFF ...I KNOW. I'M CRYING BECAUSE OUT THERE HE'S GONE, BUT HE'S NOT GONE INSIDE ME.
WATTERSON

The Price of Love

If only I can keep the kids from naming him. That would be the trick.

"No family needs two dogs," I began dogmatically. And so I invoked the Bauer Anonymity Rule (BAR), which prohibits the naming of any animal not on the endangered-species list. That includes anything that walks or squawks, sings or swims, hops, crawls, flies or yodels, because at our place a pet named is a pet claimed.

"But we gotta call him something," our four children protested.

"All right, then, call him Dog X," I suggested. They frowned, but I thought it the perfect handle for something I hoped would float away like a generic soap powder.

My no-name strategy proved a dismal failure, however. Long before the pup was weaned, the kids secretly began calling him Scampy, and before I knew it he had become as much a fixture as the fireplace. And just as immovable.

All of this could have been avoided, I fumed, if Andy, a neighborhood mutt, had only stayed on his side of the street. But at age fourteen, this scruffy, arthritic mongrel hobbled into our yard for a tête-à-tête with our blue-blooded schnauzer, Baroness Heidi of Princeton on her AKC papers, who was a ten-year Old Maid. Before one could say "safe sex," we had a miracle of Sarah and Abraham proportions.

We were unaware that Andy had left his calling card until the middle of one night during our spring vacation in Florida. I thought the moaning noise was the ocean. But investigation revealed it was coming from Heidi, whom Shirley, my wife, pronounced in labor. "I *thought* she was getting fat," I mumbled sleepily.

When morning brought no relief or delivery, we found a vet who informed us that a big pup was blocking the birth canal, which could be fatal to Heidi. We wrung our hands for the rest of the day, phoning every couple of hours for an update. Not until evening was our dog pronounced out of danger.

"She was carrying three," the doctor reported, "but only one survived." The kids took one look at the male pup, a ragamuffin ball of string—red string, brown string, black string, tan string, gray string—and exclaimed, "Andy! He looks just like Andy." And there was no mistaking the father. Heidi's only genetic contribution seemed to be his schnauzer beard. Otherwise, he was an eclectic mix of terrier, collie, beagle, setter and Studebaker.

"Have you ever seen anything so homely?" I asked Shirley.

"He's adorable," she answered admiringly. Too admiringly.

"I only hope someone else thinks so. His days with us are numbered." But I might as well have saved my breath. By the time Dog X reached ten weeks, our kids were more attached to him than barnacles to a boat's bottom. I tried to ignore him.

"Look at how good he is catching a ball, Dad," Christopher pointed out. I grunted noncommittally. And when Andy's folly performed his tricks—sit, fetch, roll over, play dead—and the kids touted his smarts, I hid behind a newspaper.

One thing I could not deny: he had the ears of a watchdog, detecting every sound that came from the driveway or yard. Heidi, his aging mother, heard nothing but his barking, which interrupted her frequent naps. He, on the other hand, was in perpetual motion. When the kids went off on their bikes or I put on my jogging shoes, he wanted to go along. If left behind, he chased squirrels. Occasionally, by now, I slipped and called him Scampy.

Then in the fall, after six months of family nurture and adoration, Scampy suffered a setback. Squealing brakes announced he had chased one too many squirrels into the street. The accident fractured his left hind leg, which the vet put in a splint. We were all relieved to hear his prognosis: complete recovery. But then a week later the second shoe dropped.

"Gangrene," Shirley told me one evening. "The vet says amputate or he'll have to be put to sleep." I slumped down in a chair.

"There's little choice," I said. "It's not fair to make an active dog like Scampy struggle around on three legs the rest of his life." Suddenly the kids, who had been eavesdropping, flew into the room.

"They don't kill a person who has a bad leg," Steve and Laraine argued.

Buying time, I told them, "We'll decide tomorrow." After the kids were in bed, Shirley and I talked.

"It will be hard for them to give up Scampy," she sympathized.

"Especially Christopher," I replied. "I was about his age when I lost Queenie." Then I told her about my favorite dog, a statuesque white spitz whose fluffy coat rolled like ocean waves when she ran. But Queenie developed a crippling problem with her back legs, and finally my dad said she would have to be put down.

"But she can get well," I pleaded. I prayed with all my might that God would help her walk again. But she got worse.

One night after dinner I went to the basement, where she slept beside the furnace. At the bottom of the stairs, I met Dad. His face was drained of color, and he carried a strange, strong-smelling rag in his hand.

"I'm sorry, but Queenie's dead," he told me gently. I broke into tears and threw myself into his arms. I don't know how long I sobbed, but after a while I became aware that he was crying too. I remember how pleased I was to learn he felt the same way.

Between eye-wiping and nose-blowing, I told him, "I don't ever want another dog. It hurts too much when they die."

"You're right about the hurt, son," he answered, "but that's the price of love."

The next day, after conferring with the vet and the family, I reluctantly agreed to have Scampy's leg amputated. "If a child's faith can make him well," I remarked to Shirley, "then he'll recover four times over." And he did. Miraculously.

If I needed any proof that he was his old self, it came a short time after his operation. Watching from the kitchen window, I saw a fat gray squirrel creep toward the bird feeder. Slowly the sunning dog pulled himself into attack position. When the squirrel got to within a dozen feet, Scampy launched himself. Using his hind leg like a pogo stick, he rocketed into the yard and gave one bushy-tail the scare of its life.

Soon Scampy was back catching balls, tagging along with the kids, running with me as I jogged. The remarkable thing was the way he compensated for his missing

Reader/Customer Care Survey

If you are enjoying this book, please help us serve you better and meet your changing needs by taking a few minutes to complete this survey. **Please fold it and drop it in the mail.**

Please Print

____
NAME

____
ADDRESS

____

____
TELEPHONE NUMBER

1) Gender

1 ___ Female 2 ___ Male

2) Age

1 ___ 12 or younger 3 ___ 17-21 5 ___ 31-49
2 ___ 13-16 4 ___ 22-30 6 ___ 50+

3) Tell us a little about yourself. Are you . . .

Please check all that apply

3 ___ A parent 6 ___ Married
4 ___ A grandparent 7 ___ Single
5 ___ A student 8 ___ Divorced

9) Do you have pets?

1 ___ Yes 2 ___ No

10) Was this book

1 ___ Purchased for yourself? 2 ___ Received as a gift?

11) How did you find out about this book?

1 ___ Pet Store 5 ___ Print Ad
2 ___ Department Store 6 ___ Friend
3 ___ Veterinarian 7 ___ Website
4 ___ Television Ad 8 ___ Bookstore

CODE CP2

12) Where do you purchase books?

Please rank in order of frequency of purchase:

12 ___ Bookstore
13 ___ Other Retail Store
14 ___ Website
15 ___ Bookclub
16 ___ Catalog/Mail Order
17 ___ Warehouse/Price Club

As a special **"Thank You"** we'll send you news about interesting books and a valuable Gift Certificate. *It's Our Pleasure to Serve You!*

18) Did you enjoy the stories in this book?

1 ___ Almost All 2 ___ Some 3 ___ Few

19) What subject areas do you enjoy reading?

Please rank in order of preference:

19 ___ Spirituality/Inspiration 23 ___ Self-help
20 ___ New Age/Alternative Healing 24 ___ Recovery
21 ___ Religious 25 ___ Business
22 ___ Family/Relationships 26 ___ Nutrition/Health

27) What do you look for when choosing a book?

Please rank in order of importance:

27 ___ Subject 29 ___ Author 31 ___ Price
28 ___ Title 30 ___ Cover Design 32 ___ In-store location

Do you have your own Chicken Soup story you would like to send us?

Please submit separately to:

Chicken Soup for the Soul
P.O. Box 30880, Santa Barbara, CA 93130

Additional comments you would like to make to help us serve you better.

____

____

____

B382-RI

FOLD HERE

NO POSTAGE
NECESSARY
IF MAILED
IN THE
UNITED STATES

BUSINESS REPLY MAIL

FIRST-CLASS MAIL PERMIT NO 45 DEERFIELD BEACH, FL

POSTAGE WILL BE PAID BY ADDRESSEE

CHICKEN SOUP FOR THE PET LOVER'S SOUL
IA-CP2
HEALTH COMMUNICATIONS, INC.
3201 SW 15TH STREET
DEERFIELD BEACH, FL 33442-9875

appendage. He invented a new stroke for his lone rear leg, moving it piston-like from side to side to achieve both power and stability.

His enthusiasm and energy suffered no loss. "The best thing about Scampy," a neighbor said, "is that he doesn't know he's got a handicap. Either that or he ignores it, which is the best way for all of us to deal with such things."

Not that everyone saw him in a positive light. On the playground, some youngsters reacted as if he were a candidate for a Stephen King horror flick. "Look out," shouted one boy, "here comes Monster Dog!" Tripod and Hopalong were other tags. Our kids laughed off his detractors and introduced him as "Scampy, the greatest three-legged dog in the world."

For better than five years, Scampy gave us an object lesson in courage, demonstrating what it means to do your best with what you've got. On our daily runs, I often carried on conversations with him as if he understood every word. "I almost shipped you out as a pup," I'd recount to him, "but the kids wouldn't let me. They knew how wonderful you were." It was obvious from the way he studied my face and wagged his tail that he liked to hear how special he was.

He probably would have continued to strut his stuff for a lot longer had he been less combative. In scraps in which he was clearly over-matched, he lacked two essentials for longevity—discretion and, partly because of his surgery, an effective reverse gear.

One warm August night he didn't return at his normal time, and the next morning he showed up, gasping for air and bloody around the neck. He obviously had been in a fight, and I suspected a badly damaged windpipe or lung.

"Scampy, when will you learn?" I asked as I petted his head. He looked up at me with those trusting eyes and licked my hand, but he was too weak to wag his tail. Christopher and Daniel helped me sponge him down and get him to the vet, but my diagnosis proved too accurate. By midday "the greatest three-legged dog in the world" was gone.

That evening Christopher and I drove to the vet's office, gathered up Scampy and headed home. Scampy's mother, Heidi, had died at fifteen, just a few months before; now we would bury him next to her in the woods by the garden.

As we drove, I tried to engage Christopher in conversation, but he was silent, apparently sorting through his feelings. "I've seen lots of dogs, Christopher," I said, "but Scampy was something special."

"Yep," he answered, staring into the darkness.

"He was certainly one of the smartest." Christopher didn't answer. From flashes of light that passed through the car I could see him dabbing his eyes. Finally he looked at me and spoke.

"There's only one thing I'm sure of, Dad," he choked out through tears. "I don't want another dog. It feels so bad to lose them."

"Yes, I know," I said. Then drawing on a voice and words that were not my own, I added, "But that's the price of love."

Now his sobs were audible, and I was having trouble seeing the road myself. I pulled off at a service station and stopped the car. There, I put my arms around him and with my tears let him know—just as my father had shown me—that his loss was my loss too.

Fred Bauer

Forever Rocky

One gray morning I took the day off from work, knowing that today was the day *it* had to be done. Our dog, Rocky, had to be put to sleep. Sickness had ravaged his once-strong body, and despite every effort to heal our beloved boxer, his illness was intensifying.

I remember calling him into the car . . . how he loved car rides! But he seemed to sense that this time was going to be different. I drove around for hours, looking for any errand or excuse not to go to the vet's office, but I could no longer put off the inevitable. As I wrote the check to the vet for Rocky to be "put down," my eyes welled with tears and stained the check so it was almost unreadable.

We had gotten Rocky four years earlier, just before my first son, Robert, was born. We all loved him dearly, especially little Robert.

My heart ached as I drove home. I already missed Rocky. Robert greeted me as I got out of the car. When he asked me where our dog was, I explained that Rocky was in heaven now. I told him Rocky had been so sick, but now he would be happy and be able to run and play all the time. My little four-year-old paused, then looking at me with his clear blue eyes and an innocent smile on his face, he pointed to the sky and said, "He's up there, right, Dad?" I managed to nod yes, and walked into the house. My wife took one look at my face and started weeping softly herself. Then she asked me where Robert was, and I went back out to the yard to find him.

In the yard, Robert was running back and forth, tossing a large stick into the air, waiting for it to return to the ground and then picking it up and throwing it higher and higher each time. When I asked what he was doing, he simply turned and smiled.

"I'm playing with Rocky, Dad . . ."

S. C. Edwards

"So you're little Bobbie; well, Rex here has been going on and on about you for the last 50 years."

The Lone Duck

Early every morning I'd stand gazing out the window at my husband, Gene, as he left for his walk in his gray running suit. I always felt as though my love for him ran down the driveway and padded along beside him. We'd been married four years. He walked rapidly. Sometimes it looked as though he were trying to hurry away from something or someone. *Silly me,* I'd think, *friendly Gene would never try to avoid anyone.* Why, then, did I stand at the window each day and watch him with a gnawing apprehension? Was I reading something into his body language that simply wasn't there? My husband has often told me I have an overactive imagination.

When we first met I thought I might be imagining that we were falling in love. But it wasn't my imagination at all. It *was* love! Gene was fifty-five when we became acquainted, and I was fifty. We'd both lost our mates of twenty-five years. I'd been a widow for four years when we married and had struggled through my own horrendous process of grieving. For some people, grief takes longer to heal than it does for others.

Gene's wife, Phyllis, had been dead only six months

when we married. Sometimes when Gene came in from walking, he looked . . . pained, sad. But he'd give me a quick smile. I'd search his handsome face, wondering what might be beneath the sometimes not believable smile.

After walking, Gene liked to tell me about a pair of ducks on the pond located five houses down from ours. "The ducks know me, honey, and they talk to me," Gene said one day. "I've been feeding them cracked corn. Even when I don't have corn, they come out of the water to greet me. I want you to come and see them." So I went. At the sound of his voice, they came quacking from way across the lake. He bent down to them as they waddled out of the water. And each day after that I'd ask, "What did the ducks say today?" as Gene came in from his walks. Once he told me, "They said, 'Don't you dare leave the bank before we get there. See how fast we are swimming to you!'"

One crisp fall day I heard Gene calling my name over and over as he came in. Something was drastically wrong. I ran from the back of the house to the living room. He sat in his recliner, bent over, his head in his hands. He was crying. He didn't make any effort to hide his tears. That's one of the things I love about my husband. He doesn't run into the bathroom or pretend he has sinus trouble when he cries. I knelt before him, waiting.

"He's dead!"

Who? I wondered. *Who is dead? A neighbor? Talk to me, Gene.*

Finally, he looked directly into my eyes and spoke softly, haltingly. "One of the ducks . . . is dead." I looked into a face filled with fresh grief unleashed without restraint. "He's lying there in a pile of feathers. The mate is swimming around in circles by the bank, hollering."

I wasn't sure what to do, so I waited. After a few moments Gene stood up and said, "I must bury the duck. The survivor doesn't understand why her mate can't get up."

I stood up, too, and watched him walk to the garage. He picked up a shovel. Suddenly our garage seemed like another world. A world I wasn't certain I should enter. Without my shoes and without any knowledge of how to comfort my husband, I followed him, feeling almost like an intruder. I touched his shoulder so gently he could have easily ignored it. "Would it be okay if I go along?" *Why am I whispering?*

"Yes, I want you to go," he said immediately.

Lord, I don't know how to help him, or even why I'm going. Please help me. I ran to get my shoes and threw on a jacket. Together we set out for the grim task.

We heard the survivor's screams before we reached the water. As Gene dug silently in the red Georgia clay, I sat close to him on the ground, my arms encircling my knees. Rather than look at Gene or the dead duck, I stared at the stunning reflection of the bright red-and-yellow trees in the clear lake. I tried very hard to concentrate on the beauty of fall—but the duck's panicky calls disturbed any attempts at serenity. The lone duck swam near where Gene dug. *"Quack! Quack! Quack!"* she wailed. I guess she thought that Gene could somehow make everything okay again. This was the spot where Gene visited with the ducks on the bank. The duck continued to honk.

I felt like saying, "Look, Duck, it's over. You must accept death and pain. I know because I've lived through it. All this hollering isn't going to help." But the duck had never "talked" to me, so I remained quiet, still uncertain of my role in this unusual drama. Then I saw that Gene had brought a plastic sack. We made brief eye contact and he nodded. I gently lifted the still-warm body of the duck and slipped it into the sack.

Gene kept his eyes on the grave as he dug and started talking to the surviving duck, softly, without ever looking up. She appeared to listen intently as she treaded water inches away. "I know it hurts, Girl. I understand. Really, I do. Life isn't fair. I'm so sorry, Girl."

"Quack. Quack. Quack. Quack. Quack . . ."

I tightened my arms about my knees and looked up at the incredibly blue sky, thinking, *You have to stand it, Duck. You have no choice when you are . . . left.* Something akin to agony stirred within me briefly, and tears suddenly stung my eyes.

To be left—the horror of being left! Gene placed an enormous rock on the grave and we stood looking down at it for what seemed like a long time.

As we turned and walked away, the lone duck shrieked at us. Then she swam slowly, without purpose, back across the lake. I turned to look at her and was immediately sorry. I'd never seen her swimming across the lake alone before. The picture stuck in my mind. *She thinks she has no real reason to live.*

The next morning Gene went walking before I was awake. I was sitting on the sofa when the doorbell rang. An attractive, energetic woman dressed in walking clothes stood there. "Hi. I'm Mary Jo Bailey. I live down the street. Is your husband at home?"

"No. But please come in. Gene's walking."

Mary Jo got right to the point as we sat down. "I walk too. I discovered the dead duck just before your husband found him. I was back in my house and I saw from the window. I could tell that your husband was deeply upset from the way he walked—fast, but sad."

Yes, I knew that walk well.

"Anyway," Mary Jo continued, "I have a friend with forty pet ducks, and tomorrow I'm going to get three." She had an idea that Gene might want to be there when she released them in the lake.

"I'm sure he would," I said.

The next morning Mary Jo came by in her Jeep and we

drove to the lake. Gene lifted the large wire cage and set it down gently on the green bank beside the water. The male mallard inside was especially handsome, with lots of green. The two other ducks looked like the lone survivor, except they were much larger. The grieving duck was nowhere in sight, but we heard her lonesome wails. Gene cupped his hands to his mouth and called, "Here, Girl!"

She came quacking desperately, leaving a large, graceful V trail in the water. It still shocked me to see her alone. She heard the excited quacks of the new arrivals and swam so fast that she looked somewhat like a speeded-up movie. Her calls changed unmistakably to ones of possible hope. *"Quack? Quack? Quack?"*

She approached the bank excitedly as Gene released the three eager ducks. They blended together and quickly went through some kind of get-acquainted ceremony: touching their bills together lightly, again and again, almost as though they were kissing.

The larger, new ducks swam in big circles back and forth in front of Mary Jo, Gene and me, as though to communicate: "Yes. This will work nicely." They, being more mature, were sophisticated enough to glide over the water silently. However, the younger duck kept quacking loudly: "Oh, happy day! I was so terrified! I thought I'd be alone forever in this big lake." Amazingly, I was learning to understand duck talk!

Mary Jo drove off, waving. Gene and I waved back, and then Gene reached out and pulled me to him. Tight and close. In fact, I'd never felt quite so close to him, or so needed.

"Let's go home," he said. We walked past the grave with the large stone marker and up the hill with our arms around each other.

Marion Bond West

With These Hands

With my bare hands, I finished mounding the dirt over Pepsi's grave. Then I sat back, reflecting on the past and absorbing all that had happened.

As I stared at my dirt-stained hands, tears instantly welled in my eyes. These were the same hands that, as a veterinarian, had pulled Pepsi, a little miniature schnauzer, wiggling from his mother. Born the runt and only half-alive, I had literally breathed life into the dog that was destined to become my father's closest friend on earth. I didn't know then just how close.

Pepsi was my gift to Dad. My father always had big dogs on our farm in southern Idaho, but instantly, Pepsi and Dad formed an inseparable bond. For ten years, they shared the same food, the same chair, the same bed, the same everything. Wherever Dad was, Pepsi was. In town, on the farm or on the run . . . they were always side-by-side. My mom accepted that Dad and the little dog had a marriage of sorts.

Now Pepsi was gone. And less than three months earlier, we had buried my dad.

Dad had been depressed for a number of years. And one afternoon, just days after his eightieth birthday, Dad decided to take his own life in the basement of our old farmhouse. We were all shocked and devastated.

Family and friends gathered at the house that evening to comfort my mother and me. Later, after the police and all the others had left, I finally noticed Pepsi's frantic barking and let him into the house. I realized then that the little dog had been barking for hours. He had been the only one home that day when Dad decided to end his life. Like a lightning bolt, Pepsi immediately ran down to the basement.

Earlier that evening, I had promised myself that I would never go back into that basement again. It was just too painful. But now, filled with fear and dread, I found myself heading down the basement stairs in hot pursuit of Pepsi.

When I got to the bottom of the stairs, I found Pepsi standing rigid as a statue, staring at the spot where Dad had lain dying just hours before. He was trembling and agitated. I picked him up gently and started back up the stairs. Once we reached the top, Pepsi went from rigid to limp in my arms and emitted an anguished moan. I placed him tenderly in Dad's bed, and he immediately closed his eyes and went to sleep.

When I told my mom what had happened, she was amazed. In the ten years Pepsi had lived in that house, the little dog had never once been in the basement. Mom reminded me that Pepsi was scared to death of stairs and always had to be carried up even the lowest and broadest of steps.

Why, then, had Pepsi charged down those narrow, steep basement steps? Had Dad cried out for help earlier that day? Had he called good-bye to his beloved companion? Or had Pepsi simply sensed that Dad was in trouble? What had called out to him so strongly that Pepsi was compelled to go down to the basement, despite his fears?

The next morning when Pepsi awoke, he searched for my father. Distraught, the little dog continued looking for Dad for weeks.

Pepsi never recovered from my father's death. He became withdrawn and progressively weaker. Dozens of tests and a second opinion confirmed the diagnosis I knew to be true—Pepsi was dying of a broken heart. Now, despite my years of training, I felt helpless to prevent the death of my father's cherished dog.

Sitting by Pepsi's freshly mounded grave, suddenly things became clear. Over the years, I'd marveled at the acute senses dogs possess. Their hearing, sight and smell are all superior to humans. Sadly, their life span is short in comparison, and I had counseled and comforted thousands of people grieving over the loss of their adored pets.

Never before, though, had I considered how it was for pets to say good-bye to their human companions. Having watched Pepsi's unflagging devotion to Dad and the dog's rapid decline after Dad's death, I realized that our pets' sense of loss was at least equal to our own.

I am grateful for the love Pepsi lavished on my father. And for his gift to me—a deeper compassion and understanding of pets, which has made me a better veterinarian. Pepsi's search for Dad is over now; together again, my father and his loyal little dog have finally found peace.

Marty Becker, D.V.M.

I WENT BACK DOWN TO THE RIVER, AND I WRAPPED HIM IN A BLANKET.

ELIZABETH AND I PUT HIM IN THE CAR, AND DROVE INTO TOWN.

THE VETERINARIAN SAID IT WAS HIS HEART. HE SAID THAT THE COLD AND THE STRESS WERE TOO MUCH FOR HIM.
FARLEY WAS AN OLD DOG, JOHN.
I KNOW.

... BUT I DIDN'T THINK THAT A HEART SO BIG WOULD EVER STOP BEATING.
Lynn

Soul to Soul

I work at the Colorado State University Veterinary Teaching Hospital as a counselor in The Changes Program. We help people deal with the experience of losing a pet, whether through illness, accident or euthanasia.

One time, I had a client named Bonnie, a woman in her mid-fifties. Bonnie had driven an hour and a half from Laramie, Wyoming, to see if the doctors at the hospital could do anything to help her fourteen-year-old black standard poodle, Cassandra, affectionately called Cassie. The dog had been lethargic for a week or so and seemed to be confused at times. The local veterinarian had not been able to diagnose any underlying medical problem, so Bonnie had decided to head to CSU for a second opinion.

Unfortunately, Bonnie hadn't gotten the answer she had hoped for. She had been told earlier that morning by neurologist Dr. Jane Bush that Cassie had a brain tumor that could take Cassie's life at any time.

Bonnie was devastated to learn that her companion animal was so ill. She had been given detailed information about all the treatment options that were available to her.

They all would only buy Cassie a few weeks. There was, they emphasized, no hope for a cure.

That was when Bonnie was introduced to me. The Changes Program often helps people while they wrestle with the difficult decision of whether to euthanize a pet or let nature take its course.

Bonnie had graying, light-brown wavy hair that she pulled back into a large barrette. The day I met her she was wearing jeans, tennis shoes and a white blouse with pink stripes. She had sparkling light blue eyes that immediately drew my attention, and there was a calmness about her that told me she was a person who thought things through, a woman who did not make hasty decisions. She seemed familiar and down to earth, like the kind of people I grew up with in Nebraska.

I began by telling her I realized how tough it was to be in her situation. Then I explained that the doctor had asked me to become involved in her case because there were many difficult decisions she needed to make. When I finished, she commented quite matter-of-factly, "I know about grief and I know that sometimes we need help to get through it."

For twenty years, Bonnie had been married to a man who mistreated her. He was abusive and neglectful in all ways possible. He was an alcoholic, so it was often impossible to predict what would happen from one day to the next. Bonnie had tried many, many times to leave him, but she just couldn't do it. Finally, when she turned forty-five years old, she found the courage to walk away. She and Cassie, who was four years old at the time, moved to Laramie, Wyoming, to heal the old hurts and begin a new life. Cassie loved her and needed her and, for Bonnie, the feeling was mutual. There were many rough times ahead, but Bonnie and Cassie got through them together.

Six years later, Bonnie met Hank, a man who loved her in a way that she had never been loved. They met through her church and soon learned they had a great deal in common. They were married one year later. Their marriage was ripe with discussion, affection, simple routines and happiness. Bonnie was living the life for which she had always hoped.

One morning, Hank was preparing to leave for work at his tree-trimming service. As always, he and Bonnie embraced one another in the doorway of their home and acknowledged out loud how blessed they were to have each other. It was not unusual for them to say these things. They both were very aware of the "specialness" of the other.

Bonnie worked at home that day rather than going into her office, where she held a position as an office assistant. Late in the afternoon, her phone rang. When she picked it up, she heard the voice of the team leader who headed the search-and-rescue service for which Bonnie was a volunteer. Bonnie was often one of the first volunteers called when someone was in trouble.

That day, Margie told her a man had been electrocuted on a power line just two blocks from Bonnie's house. Bonnie dropped everything, flew out of her house and jumped into her truck.

When Bonnie arrived at the house, she saw an image that would be engraved in her mind for the rest of her life. Her beloved Hank hung lifelessly from the branches of a tall cottonwood tree.

All of the training that Bonnie had received about safely helping someone who has been electrocuted left her. She wasn't concerned about her own safety. She had to do everything she could to save Hank. She just had to get him down. She grabbed the ladder stowed in her truck, threw it up against the house and began climbing. Bonnie crawled onto the top of the roof and pulled Hank's body out of the tree toward her. Miraculously, even though she touched his body, which was touching the power line, she was not electrocuted herself. She pulled Hank onto the brown shingles of the roof and cradled his head in the crook of her arm. She wailed as she looked at his ashen face. His eyes stared out into the bright blue Wyoming sky. He was dead. Gone. He could not be brought back to life. She knew to the core of her being that the life they shared was over.

In the four years that followed Hank's death, Bonnie tried to put her life back together. She was up and down, but mostly down. She learned a lot about grief—the accompanying depression, anger, sense of betrayal and the endless questions about why Hank had been taken from her in such a violent and unpredictable way. She lived with the frustration of not having said good-bye, of not having the opportunity to say all of the things she wanted to say, of not being able to comfort him, soothe him, help him leave this life and move into the next. She wasn't prepared for this kind of ending. It was not the way she wanted her best friend, her lover, her partner to die.

When Bonnie finished talking, we both sat in silence for a while. Finally I said, "Would you like Cassie's death to be different from Hank's? By that, I mean would you like to plan and prepare for her death? That way, you won't have any surprises, and although you may shorten her life by a few days, you will ensure that you are with her to the very end. I'm talking now, Bonnie, about euthanasia. With euthanasia, you won't have to worry about coming home from work and finding Cassie dead, and you can ensure that she won't die in pain. If we help Cassie die by euthanasia, you can be with her, hold her, talk to her and comfort her. You can peacefully send her on to the next life. The choice is up to you."

Bonnie's eyes opened wide. Her shoulders relaxed and her face softened in relief.

"I just need control this time," she said. "I want this death to be different from Hank's—for my girl."

The decision was made to euthanize Cassie that afternoon. I left the two of them alone, and Bonnie and Cassie spent the next few hours lying outside under the maple tree. Bonnie talked to Cassie, stroked her curly black fur and helped her get comfortable when she seemed unable to do so on her own. A soft breeze moved through the trees, adding a gentle rustling to the peaceful scene.

When it was time, Bonnie brought Cassie into the client comfort room, an area that those of us associated with The Changes Program had adapted to be more conducive to humane animal death and client grief. I encouraged Bonnie to tell me if there was anything she wanted to do for Cassie before she died. She laughed and said, "She likes to eat Kleenex. I'd like to give her some."

I laughed, too. "In this business we have plenty of that on hand," I said.

The dog was lying down by Bonnie, who was on the floor on a soft pad. Bonnie began to pet and talk to her. "There you are, girl. You're right here by Mom. Everything is okay."

Over the next half-hour, Bonnie and Cassie "talked" to one another and "finished business." Everything that needed to be said was said.

The time for euthanasia arrived and Cassie was sleeping peacefully, her head resting on Bonnie's stomach. She looked comfortable, very much at ease. Dr. Bush whispered, "May we begin the procedure?" and Bonnie nodded in affirmation.

"But first," she said softly, "I would like to say a prayer."

She reached out to take our hands and we all reached out our hands to one another. Within this sacred circle, Bonnie softly prayed, "Dear Lord, thank you for giving me this beautiful dog for the past fourteen years. I know she was a gift from you. Today, as painful as it is, I know it is time to give her back. And, dear Lord, thank you for bringing these women to me. They have helped me beyond measure. I attribute their presence to you. Amen."

Through our tears, we whispered our own "amens," all squeezing one another's hands in support of the rightfulness of the moment.

And then, while Cassie continued to sleep peacefully on her caretaker's belly, the doctor gave the dog the final injection. Cassie did not wake up. Through it all, she did not move. She just slipped out of this life into the next. It was quick, peaceful and painless, just as we had predicted. Immediately following Cassie's passing, I made a clay impression of her front paw. I handed the paw print to Bonnie and she held it tenderly against her cheek. We all sat quietly until Bonnie broke the silence, saying, "If my husband had to die, I wish he could have died this way."

So do I, Bonnie, I thought. *So do I.*

Six weeks later, I received a letter from Bonnie. She had scattered Cassie's remains on the same mountain where Hank's were scattered. Now her two best friends were together again. She said somehow Cassie's death, and especially the way in which she had died, had helped her resolve the death of her husband.

"Cassie's death was a bridge to Hank for me," she wrote. "Through her death, I let him know that if I had had the choice when he died, I would have had the courage and the dedication necessary to be with him when he died, too. I needed him to know that and I hadn't been able to find a way. Cassie provided the way. I think that is the reason for and the meaning of her death. Somehow, she knew she could reconnect us, soul to soul."

Eight months later, Bonnie traveled once again from Wyoming to the Veterinary Teaching Hospital. This time, she brought her new, healthy puppy Clyde—a nine-month-old Lab mix, full of life and love. Bonnie was beginning again.

Carolyn Butler with Laurel Lagoni

The Rainbow Bridge

TIME is
Too slow for those who wait,
Too swift for those who fear,
Too long for those who grieve,
Too short for those who rejoice.
But for those who love,
Time is not.

Henry van Dyke

There is a bridge connecting heaven and Earth.

It is called the Rainbow Bridge because of its many colors. Just this side of the Rainbow Bridge is a land of meadows, hills and valleys, all of it covered with lush green grass.

When a beloved pet dies, the pet goes to this lovely land. There is always food and water and warm spring weather. There, the old and frail animals are young again. Those who are maimed are made whole once more. They play all day with each other, content and comfortable.

There is only one thing missing. They are not with the special person who loved them on Earth. So each day they run and play until the day comes when one suddenly stops playing and looks up! Then, the nose twitches! The ears are up! The eyes are staring! You have been seen, and that one suddenly runs from the group!

You take him or her in your arms and embrace. Your face is kissed again and again and again, and you look once more into the eyes of your trusting pet.

Then, together, you cross the Rainbow Bridge, never again to be separated.

Author Unknown

That Dog Disguise Isn't Fooling Anyone

Give them beauty for ashes, the oil of joy for mourning, and the garment of praise for the spirit of heaviness.

Isa. 61:3

On Christmas morning of 1958, my father had come to church with us, and I was to sing my first solo. I was eleven years old. After the service, in the parking lot, he leaned down, took my hand and confided to me how proud he was to be my dad. I dearly loved him, and it was one of the more perfect moments of my childhood.

The next day, when Daddy returned from a quick trip to the hardware store, he walked through the front door and, apparently feeling unwell, went to the bedroom, where he lay down on the bed and suffered a massive heart attack. Our family watched in helpless disbelief as the man who held our lives together fought bravely to hold onto his own. The ambulance arrived too late, for the tragedy that determined our family's future was over in less than twenty minutes.

The American Indians have a phrase they use to describe children who have an intimate knowledge of sorrow. They say the child has developed *sky-eyes*. I have little memory of the painful years immediately following my father's death, but photos of me from that period show a detached look, a distance in my gaze, as though my vision included a portion of the sky.

When I was twenty-four, I became engaged to a beautiful and charismatic European boy. In the enchantment of love, the numbing impact of my father's death was put aside. I began to dream of the wonderful possibilities ahead of us. Until the morning I received the phone call informing me that my fiancé had been robbed, shot and killed in south-central Los Angeles. The abruptness of it took my breath away.

This second tragedy was as sudden and devastating as the first, and it cemented my belief that life was brutally precarious. I closed my heart and I fell into a diminished living, unable to feel deep joy and worse yet, unable to pray.

I functioned as though two people lived inside of me—the public me and the private me. Publicly, my singing career flourished—I won a Grammy for the song "Up Where We Belong," which I sang with Joe Cocker. I rejoiced in my music—singing had always been a "free zone" for me. But the private me withered; I felt strangled by resentment and deeply betrayed by God.

I survived seven years like this until a perceptive friend gave me a puppy—a badly bred golden retriever and a most unwelcome imposition on my life. Reluctantly, I decided to keep her.

I named her Emma and like every other puppy owner, I began telling her what to do, or more frequently what not to do.

"Don't chew that, walk this way, eat here, poop there, sit up, get off the bed, stop barking . . ." Armed with a stack of training manuals, I became the puppy police, imposing the usual ridiculous rules and inane tricks upon this little creature. While Emma executed these performances well, she stared at me flatly, as if to say, "This is completely unnecessary." Her boldness made me laugh out loud. Now I realize she was simply biding her time, waiting for me to understand.

Around Emma's fourth birthday, our roles began to reverse. Something in me opened up to her and I found that she was often "telling" me what to do, such as "leave the desk now, sit here with me and watch the butterflies, go home and go to sleep, listen to the wild birds singing . . ." I began observing her natural patterns and impulses and noticing the grace with which she greeted the passing of the days. She showed me a view of the world that made mine appear silly by comparison.

I started bringing Emma with me on short trips. I sensed that she *knew something* and I was determined to find out what it was. We drove up the California coast, and I would stop and let her explore whenever she became especially interested in the surroundings. I let her take the lead and followed her as she trotted along old redwood paths and discovered hidden coves. We pawed around with starfish in the moonlight and barked joyfully back at the seals. We raced up and down the shoreline until we were exhausted. I began noticing the smell of it all—fresh clover, seaweed, sage. My hearing, overburdened by the recording studio, began refining and I heard the smaller sounds of nature, like mouse feet or a lizard on a twig.

The dog was my teacher. I watched as she greeted each stranger with curiosity and warmth, graciously prompting me to introduce myself to these often fascinating individuals. I grew to love her frank and friendly nature. The seemingly irreparable scars from my abrupt losses were slowly dissolving as I learned to appreciate the impossibly simple joys of a dog's life.

Emma's influence extended into my music career as well. We were inseparable in the recording studio during the making of two of my most successful CDs. Recording sessions went more smoothly when she was present. Whether sleeping at my feet or being the tireless greeter and relaxer of people, Emma brought musicians together. We laughed more when she was around, and that laughter found its way into the music. There is a photo of us on a stretch of open road in the booklet for one of my CDs and it captures the two of us accurately: wandering in the big world, satisfied just being together.

Some years later, when Emma was eight, she became sick. Exploratory surgery revealed that she had advanced cancer and her vet, a wonderful man named Dr. Martin Schwartz, told me that it was possible she had no more than a month remaining.

The following week was heavy with silence. Evenings, we sat together on the porch, waiting for the stars to come out. Like the many peaceful moments we had shared before, we sat shoulder to shoulder, listening for bits of news whispering down the leaves, watching the fall of light and savoring each other's company. It was useless to talk, but sometimes I sang to her and she appeared to smile.

When I realized she didn't intend to eat any more, I brought her to the vet's for a day of IV feeding to bring back her strength. That whole day, all I could think about was picking Emma up and taking our walk on the beach at sunset. On my way out the door, I happened to look in a drawer and found an old tie tack of Daddy's. I slipped it into the pocket of my jeans as a sort of talisman against the inevitable. I must have known we were near the end.

When I arrived at the vet's and asked for Emma, the nurse said softly, "The doctor wants to speak with you." I felt her gentle words slam into me as I sank into a chair, and the tears came up from an ancient river of defeat.

Dr. Schwartz told me that Emma wasn't strong enough to leave the clinic. He took me back to where my best friend was lying on a blanket on the floor and left us alone together. I lay down beside her.

She had been dying all day, but she wasn't going to go until I was ready. Filled with a deep gratitude that she had waited to share this with me, I rested my cheek on her neck, and with my hand laid softly over her heart, I began to sing.

Without any effort, a simple melody came to me. It was a love song, long ago forgotten, about a love as big as the world itself.

We had so little left, but I needed her to know, or somehow to feel, the steadfast loyalty of my heart. A song can go places unreachable by word or gesture, and despite her weakness, her eyes almost smiled.

Then her body began to strain and I knew that this was it. From my past experience with sudden death, I expected a struggle, a violent resistance to life's end. Holding her with my eyes closed, I braced myself. Instead, I felt a sudden wave of ease and comfort wash over us. My fear vanished, and I marveled at how peaceful it was. She died right there next to me in the gentleness of that moment.

I opened my eyes to find just a body, still and empty. The joy, the spark that had taught me so much, had vanished. Emma was gone.

In my earlier, bitter years, I had angrily asked God to show me his face. But this evening, I had no argument with heaven. His answer, more perfect than I could have ever imagined, had come through this little dog. For it was

Emma's gentle dying that released me from the persistent pain of my early tragedies. And it was her surprisingly wise way of living that gave me back my life.

Jennifer Warnes with Shawnacy Kiker

Rites of Passage

Some of the most poignant moments I spend as a veterinarian are those spent with my clients assisting the transition of my animal patients from this world to the next. When living becomes a burden, whether from pain or loss of normal functions, I can help a family by ensuring that their beloved pet has an easy passing. Making this final decision is painful, and I have often felt powerless to comfort the grieving owners.

That was before I met Shane.

I had been called to examine a ten-year-old blue heeler named Belker who had developed a serious health problem. The dog's owners—Ron, his wife, Lisa, and their little boy, Shane—were all very attached to Belker and they were hoping for a miracle. I examined Belker and found he was dying of cancer.

I told the family there were no miracles left for Belker, and offered to perform the euthanasia procedure for the old dog in their home. As we made the arrangements, Ron and Lisa told me they thought it would be good for the four-year-old Shane to observe the procedure. They felt Shane could learn something from the experience.

The next day, I felt the familiar catch in my throat as Belker's family surrounded him. Shane seemed so calm, petting the old dog for the last time, that I wondered if he understood what was going on.

Within a few minutes, Belker slipped peacefully away. The little boy seemed to accept Belker's transition without any difficulty or confusion. We sat together for a while after Belker's death, wondering aloud about the sad fact that animal lives are shorter than human lives.

Shane, who had been listening quietly, piped up, "I know why."

Startled, we all turned to him. What came out of his mouth next stunned me—I'd never heard a more comforting explanation.

He said, "Everybody is born so they can learn how to live a good life—like loving everybody and being nice, right?" The four-year-old continued, "Well, animals already know how to do that, so they don't have to stay as long."

Robin Downing, D.V.M.

Saying Good-Bye

What troubled me most was the recurring thought: *I didn't get to say good-bye.*

I was away from home for the weekend. The door was left open and my two white shepherd-mix dogs, Lucy and Hannah, had gotten out. My husband called me on Saturday night to tell me that Lucy had been hit by a car. She was alive, but her back legs were severely injured. The vets were observing her and would decide what to do on Monday. He told me not to come home since there was nothing I could do.

I started driving home on Monday morning, calling every few hours en route to get a progress report. With my first call I learned they had decided to amputate one of her hind legs. Many anxious calls later, the vet's office told me the operation had gone smoothly and Lucy was resting comfortably. I knew I wouldn't arrive home in time to see her that day, but they told me I could come as soon as they opened on Tuesday.

Tuesday morning, I was getting ready to leave when the phone rang. It was the vet.

"I'm sorry, but we lost her during the night," he told me.

"Last night, I went to the clinic for an emergency call around two in the morning, and I went in to check on your dog. She was laboring for breath, so I gave her some medicine. Then I sat with her—I was holding her when she died."

My breath wouldn't come and I felt hollow inside. I hung up the phone and my husband took me in his arms. While he tried to comfort me, I thought: *Oh, Lucy, I'm glad you didn't die alone. Did you think I'd abandoned you? Now you're gone and I'll never see you again*. What I also thought was: *Not again.*

Only two weeks earlier, one of my best friends, Sandie, had been killed in a car accident. I received an equally shocking phone call and then, grief. She was gone and I'd never see her again. Too much for me to take in, it hadn't seemed real. And now, neither did Lucy's sudden but permanent absence from my life.

My other dog, Hannah, had seen Lucy get hit. She still seemed confused and upset, searching frantically for Lucy whenever she went outside. I decided that we both needed a strong dose of reality. I called the vet back and asked him not to do anything with Lucy's body—I was coming over and I wanted to see her.

While I felt it was the right thing to do, I still felt apprehensive. I had never seen a dead body in my life—much less the dead body of anyone I had known and loved. Could I handle it?

Hannah and I drove to the vet's office. I had Hannah on a leash as we walked into the room where Lucy lay. I don't know what I was expecting, but the still white form lying on the table was devastatingly beautiful to me. Hannah, distracted by all the interesting smells of the vet's office, had her large nose to the ground and wasn't aware of Lucy until I gently pulled her over to the little waist-high table where Lucy lay. Lucy's tail, her three remaining paws and the tip of her nose stuck out over the table's edge. The instant Hannah's nose scented Lucy's tail, her eyes actually widened. She walked slowly around the table, sniffing every inch of Lucy that she could reach. When she was done, she lay down at my feet, rested her head on her paws and sighed loudly.

I stroked Lucy and felt the texture of her upright ears, her soft fur and the denseness of her muscular body. She looked the same but she felt different, cold and somehow more solid. It was certainly her body, but Lucy was gone. I startled myself by leaning over and kissing Lucy on the head. There were tears running down my face as Hannah and I left.

Hannah was subdued for the rest of the day, her agitation completely gone. For the next few weeks we babied her, taking her for more walks, giving her extra treats and letting her sleep on the couch—a previously forbidden zone. She seemed to be adjusting and perhaps even enjoying her new "only-dog" status.

For me, losing Sandie and then, so immediately, Lucy had been hard. Yet it was actually seeing Lucy's body that finally made the concept of death real. After that, the way I experienced my losses—Lucy, Sandie, even my father, who'd died twenty years earlier—shifted, and as time passed, I could feel that I was steadily healing and moving beyond the pain. It helped to have Hannah to comfort and be comforted by, and I was moved by the unwavering support and love my husband and close friends offered me.

It has been three years since Sandie and Lucy died. I am amazed at how often I still think of them. But now it is always with wistful fondness and a smile, the pain long gone. I am glad that I had the courage to go and see Lucy one last time. For she taught me how to say good-bye.

Carol Kline

Toto's Last Christmas

Snow fell softly on Christmas Eve as I made my final patient rounds. The old cat, fragile in his downy white coat, was sleeping. Days before, his owner had dropped him off to spend the holidays with us. Sadly, she had worried he might not make it to greet her in the New Year. Indeed, the day after she dropped off the cat, I called to warn her that he was failing. Her tear-choked voice let me know she understood. "No heroics, please, Dr. Foley, but let him rest easy and make him as comfortable as you can."

Soft blankets along with a heating pad were wrapped around his frail body to keep him warm. Puréed chicken and tuna had been offered and declined, and now he slept in the deepest of sleeps. Not wanting Toto to be alone in his condition on this holiday night, I wrapped him in a large wicker basket and carried him home.

A gust of wind blew the door from my hand as I entered the house. My cat, Aloysius, greeted us while my other cat, Daphne, peeked timidly from the corner of the room, sniffing appreciatively at the cold winter air. They both knew what a wicker basket with an electric cord hanging from it meant. Aloysius retreated haughtily across the room.

Rescued as an abandoned cat from a clinic I worked at previously, Aloysius has been with me for twelve years—through vet school, my first job and my first home. Other people see him as just a cat, but for me his presence has become a constant in my life. Aloysius is the one who listens to all my tales of woe. On the down side, he is possessive and has a low opinion of anyone, feline or other, who infringes on his territory.

Daphne had come to me a timid and yet ferocious feral tabby kitten that no one could tame. Ten years of love, patience and roast beef tidbits had paid off. Now a round and sassy butterball of a cat, her heart was mine. To keep the peace in the house, however, she usually agreed with Aloysius on the subject of uninvited guests. Sensing his disdain for the fellow in the basket, she politely hissed from the corner.

"Now, now, you big bullies," I said. "This fellow is old and may be leaving us soon. We wouldn't want him to be alone on Christmas Eve, would we?"

Unmoved, they glowered from beneath the Christmas tree.

Old Toto slept on in his basket. I placed him by the table in the kitchen and plugged the cord for his heating pad into the wall. My husband, Jordan, and I prepared our Christmas Eve dinner while Toto slept, and I checked on him every once in a while to be sure he was comfortable. Daphne and Aloysius, still resentful of our guest but moved by the smell of grilling steaks, crept into the room. I warned them that Toto was old and frail and to be good hosts, they must let him be.

Toto still slept.

Dinner was ready, and Jordan and I sat at the table. Relaxing after the long work day, soon we started teasing each other about what surprises were hidden in the gleaming packages beneath the tree. Then Jordan silently nodded toward Toto in his basket, and I turned my head slowly to look at the cats.

Aloysius first, and then Daphne behind him, slowly and cautiously approached the basket. While Toto rested, Aloysius sat up on his haunches, peered into the basket and gave a long, deep sniff. Gently, he lowered himself and walked to the corner of the old cat's basket. Then he rubbed his cheek against it, softly purring. Daphne followed, leaned into the basket and, sniffing Toto's face, placed a gentle paw on his soft blanketed body. Then she, too, lowered herself and purred as she rubbed his basket. Jordan and I watched in amazed silence. These cats had never welcomed any other cat into our home before.

Leaving my chair, I walked over and looked at Toto. With the cats still positioned at each corner of the basket, Toto looked up at me, breathed once and then relaxed. Reaching my hand beneath his blankets, I felt his heart slowly stop beating. Tears in my eyes, I turned to Jordan to let him know that Toto was gone.

Later that night, I called Toto's owner to let her know that he had died comfortably and quietly at our home, with two cats beside him, wishing him a fond farewell and Godspeed on his last Christmas Eve.

Janet Foley, D.V.M.

8

PETCETERA

. . . a morning kiss, a discreet touch
of his nose landing somewhere
on the middle of my face. Because
his long white whiskers tickled,
I began every day laughing.

Janet F. Faure

"Kids today have everything. When I was your age and wanted entertainment, I chased my tail."

Good Neighbors

The old house behind ours was deserted now. My neighbors, the elderly couple who had lived there for many years, had died within a year of each other. Their children and grandchildren had gathered, grieved and gone.

But looking out my kitchen window one morning, I saw we still had "neighbors." Two white cats had made their way up the back steps of the old house to sit in the sun on the back porch. Their favorite overstuffed chair was gone. Everything was gone. Even from my kitchen window I could see they were pitifully thin. *So,* I thought, *no one is going to claim the cats. They've been left to starve. They'll never leave that old place. They're as shy as their owners were.*

I knew they'd never even been inside a house. Even during bitter cold winters, they lived outside. Once, when the female cat had kittens, a dog had killed them. After that the mama cat had her kittens in the attic of the 100-year-old house, entering through a hole in the tin roof. Several times the kittens fell down into the small space between the walls. Once my neighbor told me, "We worked most all afternoon, but we finally got the kittens out. They would have starved to death."

I sighed, looking at the hungry cats sitting on the back porch. A familiar battle began inside me. Part of me wanted desperately to run to the cats. Another part of me wanted to turn away and never look at the starving cats again. It was frustrating to be a forty-year-old mother and still want to pick up stray animals. When I reached twenty-five, then thirty, then surely by thirty-five, I had assumed I would outgrow my obsession with abandoned animals. Now I knew that it was only becoming worse with the years.

Sighing again, I wiped my hands on my apron, grabbed two packages of cat food and headed for the old house. The cats darted beneath the porch as I approached. I crawled part of the way under the house, which sat on concrete blocks, and called, "Here, kitties." I saw four slanted, bright eyes gleaming at me. I could see it would be a long time before I would be able to become friendly with *these* neighbors.

For several months, I fed the cats this way. One day the mother cat came cautiously toward me and rubbed her face against my hand for a brief moment; then fear sprang into her eyes and she darted away. But after that she met me at the fence at five each day. The other cat would scamper away and hide in the bushes, waiting for me to leave. I decided the white male was probably the female cat's son. I always talked to them as I put out their food, calling them by the names I had given them—Mama and Brother.

One day as Mama rubbed slowly against my leg with her eyes almost shut in contentment, she purred for the first time. My hand didn't reach out, not yet, but my heart did. After that she often rubbed against me and allowed me to stroke her—even before she touched the food. Brother, reluctantly and stiff-necked, allowed me to touch him occasionally; but he always endured my affection, never fully receiving it.

The cats grew fat. One day, I saw Mama kitty on my patio. "Mama kitty," I whispered. She had never come into my yard before. My own cats would never permit that—and yet, here she was. "Good for you, Mama," I said to myself. Suddenly she leaped up into the air, and I thought for a moment that she was choking. Then she seemed to be chasing an object rapidly across the patio. For perhaps the first time in her life, Mama kitty was playing. I watched her toss an acorn into the air and leap after it. My cats came lurking toward the patio door to try to hiss Mama kitty away. She only looked at them and continued playing with the acorn in the sun. Brother sat on the fence, as usual, waiting for supper.

That summer Mama kitty had kittens again—in the attic. She came to my back door to get me. The Realtor had given me the keys to the empty house in case of emergency. I went to the house with the cat and crawled somewhat reluctantly into the dark attic, ignoring the spiders, dust, heat and rattling sounds that I suspected were mice. Finally, I located the three kittens. Brother stood guard over them. I brought the kittens down and fixed a box for them in the empty front bedroom of the old house. Mama kitty wasn't too content with my moving her kittens, but she let them stay—for a while, anyway.

A week later, human neighbors showed up! Unexpectedly, another family moved into the house. Their moving frightened Mama kitty and she returned her kittens to the only safety she knew—the dark, terribly hot attic.

I quickly went over to introduce myself and explained to the family who had moved in about Mama kitty. They gave me permission to go into their attic and rescue the kittens. But I discovered Mama kitty had moved them to another spot. The old attic was a maze of hiding places, and I couldn't find them.

Three times I went back to look, apologizing to the new tenants each time. Three times I was unsuccessful. Back at home, I would look out my window at the tin roof of the house. I could see the heat rising off it. The outside temperature stood in the upper nineties. The kittens couldn't possibly survive.

I couldn't let it go; I felt it was my duty to watch over those cats. One morning as I lay in bed, I prayed, "Lord, I'm asking you to get me those kittens out of that attic. I can't find them. I don't see how you can get them out. But just please do it. If you don't, they're going to die." Silly, maybe, but it didn't feel silly to an animal lover like myself. I hopped from my bed and ran to the back door, half expecting to find the kittens there. They weren't there—no sign of Mama or Brother either. Nevertheless, I expected to get the kittens.

I was worried that I was wearing out my welcome with my new neighbors, but I wanted to go over one last time to look for them. When the wife answered the door to find it was me with the same request yet again, she said, without enthusiasm, that I could go up in the attic. Once I got up there, I heard them meowing!

"I'm coming. I'm coming!" I called out, my heart pounding with joy.

The next moment I couldn't figure out what had happened. I seemed to be falling. Plaster broke loose. I wasn't in the dark, hot attic any more, but dangling into the kitchen. I had forgotten to stay on the rafters and had crashed through the ceiling. I climbed back up onto a rafter, only to fall through again in another place.

Thoroughly shaken, I climbed back down. In the kitchen my neighbor and I looked at the damage. I was horrified, and it was clear that I wasn't making the best impression on this woman. Not knowing what else to do, I grabbed her broom and began sweeping. More plaster fell on us and we coughed in the dust. I apologized over and over, babbling that we would have the ceiling fixed. I assured her I would be back over to talk with her husband.

She nodded, silently, with her arms folded, and stared at me with seeming disbelief. I hurried home, humiliated.

That night at supper, when I told my family what had happened, they all stared at me silently, the way my new neighbor had. I was close to tears, partly because of the plight of the kittens and also because of my own stupidity.

The next day I went back to the neighbors' to speak to them about the ceiling. I arrived during a meal. The couple's children were eating with them. They all stared at me as they continued eating. I was introduced as "that woman who goes up in the attic all the time and fell through yesterday." I smiled at them all.

The husband looked up at me, still chewing, and said solemnly, "Get my gun, Ma."

For one horrible moment, my heart froze. Then he broke into a little-boy grin. "Forget it. I'm a carpenter and the ceiling needed repairing, anyway."

I smiled back at him and added, "I came to tell you that I won't be going in your attic any more—ever."

"Okay," he grinned, and I thought I heard his wife sigh.

The next afternoon, our family sat in the living room reading the Sunday paper. Only I wasn't reading, I was praying behind my part of the paper.

"Lord, it seems more hopeless than ever now. But I have no intention of giving up on this request. Give me the kittens, please."

As I prayed, I imagined the kittens in a dark, obscure corner of the attic. I knew almost for certain that Mama kitty had moved them again. Then I imagined a large, gentle hand lifting them up and bringing them down into light and cooler air. I saw it in my mind, over and over, as I prayed. Suddenly, I thought I could actually hear the kittens' tiny, helpless mews.

Silly, I told myself. *Your imagination goes wild when you pray.*

Jerry put down the sports page; the children looked up from the comics. We all listened quietly, almost without breathing. "Mew, mew, mew." It was real!

The doorbell rang and we all ran for it. I got there first and there stood my neighbor, cobwebs in his hair, dust on his overalls, and the impish little-boy grin on his lean face. We all looked down and there, cradled in his hands, were the kittens.

"Lady, you won't have to look any more for 'em. I found 'em for you."

This time Mama kitty let her brood stay where I put them, in our small storeroom, just off the carport. We found excellent, cat-loving homes for the fat, playful kittens. And I found a permanent solution to the attic/kitten problem. I had Mama kitty spayed.

That was over a year ago. Brother still sits cautiously on my backyard fence, cold and often hungry. I keep trying with him, but he's obviously still skeptical about my neighborly good will.

Not Mama kitty. Now she comes right into the kitchen to eat from my other cats' dishes! She rubs against my leg when I let her in. On cold nights she sleeps curled up in a kitchen chair. And often she sits and watches me type. At first, my cats hissed, growled and fumed. Eventually, they just gave up and accepted Mama kitty.

Now when I look out my window at that old house, I have to smile. It's good to see lights on in the kitchen and children's toys in the yard. The new occupants and I have become pretty close. It's not hard to break the ice—once you've broken the ceiling.

Marion Bond West

The Cat and the Cat Burglar

I lived in New York City for many years. As a professional dancer and dance instructor, it was the logical place to pursue my career. The city had its many good points—fine museums, great theater, wonderful food and terrific shopping, but it also had its downside—high prices, crowding, noise and crime. The crime bothered me the most. As a single woman, I felt particularly vulnerable. I considered getting a dog for protection; I had grown up with German shepherds and loved them. But the idea of cramming a big dog in a tiny apartment didn't feel right. So, like every other single woman in New York, I had a few deadbolts on my door, and in the streets, I watched my back.

One day, I huddled under an awning on St. Mark's Place with a group of other people who had been surprised without an umbrella by a sudden cloudburst. A scruffy-looking guy, a street person standing in the small crowd, held up a tiny kitten and said, "Anybody give me ten bucks for this cat?"

The kitten was beautiful. She had a fawn underbelly with a chocolate tail and back, and a deeper cocoa mask with pure white whiskers. I was immediately intrigued. But a kitten didn't fit in my watch-dog scenario. I wrestled with myself internally for a few moments before digging into my purse and scooping out all the cash I had on me—seven dollars and a few coins. I needed a dollar for the subway home, so I said, "Will you take six dollars for her?"

He must have realized that this was his best offer, or else he was so desperate that he just took whatever he could get, because we made the exchange and he left.

I named my new roommate Seal because her whiskers looked like a seal's. She seemed happy in my small apartment, and I enjoyed her company immensely.

One night, after I'd had Seal for about two years, I woke up in the middle of the night to a loud noise. Loud noises are not unusual in New York, even at 2:00 A.M., so I settled back down and attempted to sleep again. Immediately, Seal jumped on my chest and started stomping on me with all four feet. This was not kneading or playful swatting, and I realized Seal was trying to alert me to something. She jumped off the bed and I followed her. We both crept in the dark toward the kitchen. I watched Seal and when she stopped at the doorway to the kitchen, I stopped too. Keeping her body hidden, she poked her head around the corner of the doorway, and I did the same.

There we saw the figure of a man outlined against the frame of the broken window.

He was in my kitchen.

I refrained from emitting the high-pitched and therefore obviously female scream that was welling in my chest. I made myself inhale an enormous breath. Exhaling, I imagined the opera star, Luciano Pavarotti, and a sound like "WHAAAA" blasted out of me. I think I was planning on saying, "What do you think you are doing?" But I didn't need to. Even to myself, I sounded like a linebacker, and that guy was out the window and crawling like the human fly along the brick wall of the airshaft outside my kitchen as fast as his burglar legs could carry him.

After that night, I felt more confident about living in New York City. I kept a bat near my bed and practiced grabbing it and using it from every angle I thought might be necessary.

Seal and I became a team. I found myself trusting her more and more. If I heard a noise, I'd look at Seal. If she seemed curious or concerned, I'd investigate it. If not, I'd ignore it too. She became a source of security for me.

Seal is still around. She's eighteen years old and still spry. I have a bigger place now and I'm toying with getting a German shepherd, but not for protection. Seal and I have that one handled.

Laya Schaetzel-Hawthorne

The Auction

Not Carnegie, Vanderbilt and Astor together could have raised money enough to buy a quarter share in my little dog . . .

Ernest Thompson Seton

A man and woman I know fell into BIG LOVE somewhat later in life than usual. She was forty. He was fifty. Neither had been married before. But they knew about marriage. They had seen the realities of that sacred state up close among their friends. They determined to overcome as many potential difficulties as possible by working things out in advance.

Prenuptial agreements over money and property were prepared by lawyers. Preemptive counseling over perceived tensions was provided by a psychologist, who helped them commit all practical promises to paper, with full reciprocal tolerance for irrational idiosyncrasies.

"Get married once, do it right, and live at least agreeably, if not happily, ever after." So they hoped.

One item in their agreement concerned pets and kids. Item number 7:

"We agree to have either children or pets, but not both."

The man was not enthusiastic about dependent relationships. Kids, dogs, cats, hamsters, goldfish, snakes or any other living thing that had to be fed or watered had never had a place in his life. Not even houseplants. And especially not dogs. She, on the other hand, liked taking care of living things. Especially children and dogs.

Okay. But she had to choose. She chose children. He obliged. Two daughters in three years. Marriage and family life went along quite well for all. Their friends were impressed. So far, so good.

The children reached school age. The mother leapt eagerly into the bottomless pool of educational volunteerism. The school needed funds for art and music. The mother organized a major-league auction to raise much money. Every family agreed to provide an item of substantial value for the event.

The mother knew a lot about dogs. She had raised dogs all her life—the pedigreed champion kind. She planned to use her expertise to shop the various local puppy pounds to find an unnoticed bargain pooch and shape it up for the auction as her contribution. With a small investment, she would make a tenfold profit for the school. And for a couple of days, at least, there would be a dog in the house.

After a month of looking, she found the wonder dog—the dog of great promise. A female, four months old, dark gray, blue eyes, tall, strong, confident and very, very, *very* friendly.

To her practiced eye, our mother could see that classy genes had been accidentally mixed here. Two purebred dogs of the highest caliber had combined to produce this exceptional animal. Most likely a black Labrador and a Weimaraner, she thought. Perfect, just perfect.

To those of us of untutored eye, this mutt looked more like the results of a bad blind date between a Mexican burro and a miniature musk ox.

The fairy dogmother went to work. Dog is inspected and given shots by a vet. Fitted with an elegant leather collar and leash. Equipped with a handsome bowl, a ball and a rawhide bone. Expenses: $50 to the pound, $50 to the vet, $50 to the beauty parlor, $60 for tack and equipment, and $50 for food. A total of $260 on a dog that is going to stay forty-eight hours before auction time.

The father took one look and paled. He smelled smoke. He wouldn't give ten bucks to keep it an hour. "DOG," as the father named it, has a long, thick, rubber club of a tail, legs and feet that remind him of hairy toilet plungers, and is already big enough at four months to bowl over the girls and their mother with its unrestrained enthusiasm.

The father knows this is going to be ONE BIG DOG. Something a zoo might display. Omnivorous, it has eaten all its food in one day and has left permanent teeth marks on a chair leg, a leather ottoman and the father's favorite golf shoes.

The father is patient about all of this.

After all, it is only a temporary arrangement, and for a good cause.

He remembers item number 7 in the prenuptial agreement.

He is safe.

On Thursday night, the school affair gets off to a winning start. Big crowd of parents, and many guests who look flush with money. Arty decorations, fine potluck food, a cornucopia of auction items. The mother basks in her triumph.

"DOG" comes on the auction block much earlier than planned. Because the father went out to the car to check on "DOG" and found it methodically eating the leather off the car's steering wheel, after having crunched holes in the padded dashboard.

After a little wrestling match getting "DOG" into the mother's arms and up onto the stage, the mother sits in a folding chair, cradling "DOG" with the solemn tenderness reserved for a corpse at a wake, while the auctioneer describes the pedigree of the animal and all the fine effort and neat equipment thrown in with the deal.

"What am I bid for this wonderful animal?"

"A hundred dollars over here; two hundred dollars on the right; two hundred and fifty dollars in the middle."

There is a sniffle from the mother.

Tears are running down her face.

"DOG" is licking the tears off her cheeks.

In a whisper not really meant for public notice, the mother calls to her husband: *"Jack, Jack, I can't sell this dog—I want this dog—this is my dog—she loves me—I love her—oh, Jack."*

Every eye in the room is on this soapy drama.

The father feels ill, realizing that the great bowling ball of fate is headed down his alley.

"Please, Jack, please, please," she whispers.

At that moment, everybody in the room knows who is going to buy the pooch. "DOG" is going home with Jack.

Having no fear now of being stuck themselves, several relieved men set the bidding on fire. "DOG" is going to set an auction record. The repeated hundred-dollar rise in price is matched by the soft *"Please, Jack"* from the stage and Jack's almost inaudible raise in the bidding, five dollars at a time.

There is a long pause at "Fifteen hundred dollars—going once, going twice . . ."

A sob from the stage.

And for $1,505 Jack has bought himself a dog. Add in the up-front costs, and he's $1,765 into "DOG."

The noble father is applauded as his wife rushes from the stage to throw her arms around his neck, while "DOG" wraps the leash around both their legs and down they go into the first row of chairs. A memorable night for the PTA.

I see Jack out being walked by the dog late at night. He's the only one strong enough to control it, and he hates to have the neighbors see him being dragged along by this, the most expensive damned dog for a hundred miles.

"DOG" has become "Marilyn." She is big enough to plow with now. Marilyn may be the world's dumbest dog, having been to obedience school twice with no apparent effect.

Jack is still stunned. He can't believe this has happened to him.

He had it down on paper. Number 7. Kids or pets, not both.

But the complicating clauses in the fine print of the marriage contract are always unreadable. And always open to revision by forces stronger than a man's ego. The loveboat always leaks. And marriage is never a done deal.

I say he got off light. It could have been ponies or llamas or potbellied pigs. It would have been something. It always is.

Robert Fulghum

"The bidding will start at eleven million dollars."

Sing We Noel

Happiness is a warm puppy.

Charles Schulz

The year of my tenth birthday marked the first time that our entire family had jobs. Dad had been laid off from his regular employment, but found painting and carpentry work all around town. Mom sewed fancy dresses and baked pies for folks of means, and I worked after school and weekends for Mrs. Brenner, a neighbor who raised cocker spaniels. I loved my job, especially the care and feeding of her frisky litters of puppies. Proudly, I gave my earnings to Mom to help out, but the job was such fun, I would have worked for no pay at all.

I was content during these "hard times" to wear thrift-shop dresses and faded jeans. I waved good-bye to puppies going to fancy homes with no remorse. But all that changed when the Christmas litter arrived in the puppy house. These six would be the last available pups until after Christmas.

As I stepped into the house for their first feeding, my

heart flip-flopped. One shiny red puppy with sad brown eyes wagged her tail and bounced forward to greet me.

"Looks as if you have a friend already," Mrs. Brenner chuckled. "You'll be in charge of her feedings."

"Noel," I whispered, holding the pup close to my heart, sensing instantly that she was special. Each day that followed forged an inexplicable bond between us.

Christmas was approaching, and one night at dinner, I was bubbling over about all of Noel's special qualities for about the hundredth time.

"Listen, Kiddo." Dad put down his fork. "Perhaps someday you can have a puppy of your own, but now times are very hard. You know I've been laid off at the plant. If it wasn't for the job I've had this month remodeling Mrs. Brenner's kitchen, I don't know what we'd do."

"I know, Dad, I know," I whispered. I couldn't bear the pained expression on his face.

"We'll have to brave it out this year," he sighed.

By Christmas Eve, only Noel and a large male remained. "They're being picked up later," Mrs. Brenner explained. "I know the family taking Noel," she continued. "She'll be raised with tons of love."

No one could love her as much as I do, I thought. *No one.*

"Can you come tomorrow morning? I'll be weaning new pups the day after Christmas. Mop the floor with pine, and spread fresh bedding for the new litter. Would you be a dear and feed the kennel dogs, too? I'll have a house full of guests. Oh, and ask your dad to stop over with you. One of the kitchen cabinet doors needs a little adjustment. He did such a beautiful job that I'll enjoy showing it off!"

I nodded my head, barely focusing on her words. The new puppies would be cute, but there'd never be another Noel. Never. The thought of someone else raising my puppy was almost too much to bear.

Christmas morning, after church, we opened our meager gifts. Mom modeled the apron I made her in home economics with a flair befitting a Paris gown. Dad raved about the watchband I gave him. It wasn't even real leather, but he replaced his frayed band and admired it as if it were golden. He handed me the book *Beautiful Joe*, and I hugged them both. They had no gifts for each other. What a sad Christmas, with all of us pretending that it wasn't.

After breakfast, Dad and I changed clothes to go to Mrs. Brenner's. On our short walk, we chatted and waved to passing neighbors, each of us deliberately avoiding the subjects of Christmas and puppies.

Dad waved good-bye as he headed toward the Brenners' kitchen door. I walked directly to the puppy house in the backyard. It was strangely silent, no puppy growls, tiny barks or rustling paper. It felt as sad and dreary as I did. My head gave the order to begin cleaning, but in my heart I wanted to sit down on the lonely floor and bawl.

It's funny looking back at childhood days. Some events are fuzzy, the details sketchy and faces indistinct. But I remember returning home that Christmas afternoon so clearly; entering the kitchen with the aroma of pot roast simmering on the stove, Mom clearing her throat and calling to Dad, who suddenly appeared in the dining room doorway.

With an odd huskiness in his voice, he whispered, "Merry Christmas, Kiddo," and smiling, he gently placed Noel, clad in a red bow, into my arms. My parents' love for me merged with my overwhelming love for Noel and sprang from my heart, like a sparkling fountain of joy. At that moment it became, without a doubt, absolutely the most wonderful Christmas I have ever had.

Toni Fulco

Taking the Zip Out of Zippy

This adventure began when Zippy went through puberty, a biological process that a small dog goes through in less time than it takes you to throw away your Third Class mail. One minute Zippy was a cute little-boy puppy, scampering about the house playfully causing permanent damage to furniture that is not yet fully paid for, and the next minute he was: A Man. When the new, mature version of Zippy sauntered into a room, you could almost hear the great blues musician Muddy Waters in the background, growling:

I'm a MAN
(harmonica part)
Yes I AM
(harmonica part)
A FULL-GROWN man.

Of course in Zippy's case, "full-grown" means "the size of a Hostess Sno-Ball, yet somehow less impressive." But in his own mind, Zippy was a major stud muffin, a hunk of burnin' love, a small-caliber but high-velocity Projectile of Passion fired from the Saturday Night Special of Sex. And his target was: Earnest.

Earnest is my female dog, but she was not the ideal choice for Zippy because all of her remotely suspicious organs had been surgically removed several years ago. Since that time she has not appeared to be even dimly aware of sex, or much of anything else. Her lone hobby, besides eating, is barking violently at nothing. Also she is quite large; when she is standing up, Zippy can run directly under her with an easy six inches of clearance. So at first I was highly amused when he started putting The Moves on her. It was like watching Tommy Tadpole hit on the *Queen Mary.*

But shortly the novelty wore off and I started feeling sorry for Earnest, who spent the entire day staring glumly off into dog hyperspace while this tireless yarn-ball-sized Passion Machine kept leaping up on her, sometimes getting as high as mid-shin, and emitting these presumably seductive high-pitched yips ("What's your sign? What's your sign?"). So I decided it was time to have the veterinarian turn the volume knob of desire way down on the stereo system of Zippy's manhood. If you get my drift.

The next morning Earnest was limping, so I decided to take both dogs to the vet. They bounded enthusiastically into the car, of course; dogs feel very strongly that they should always go with you in the car, in case the need should arise for them to bark violently at nothing right in your ear. When I got to the veterinarian's office they realized they had been tricked and went into Full Reverse Thrust, but fortunately the floor material there is slippery enough to luge on. So when I last saw Zippy and Earnest that morning, they were being towed, all eight legs scrabbling in a wild, backward, futile blur into: the Back Room.

When I picked them up that night, they were a pair of hurtin' cowpokes. Earnest, who had a growth removed, was limping badly, plus we had to put a plastic bag on her leg so she wouldn't lick her stitches off. And Zippy, to keep him from getting at *his* stitches, was wearing a large and very comical round plastic collar that looked like a satellite dish with Zippy's head sticking out in the middle. He had a lot of trouble getting around because his collar kept hitting things, such as the ground.

For the next week, if you came to my front door, here's what happened: You heard the loud barking of two dogs going into Red Alert mode, but you did not see any immediate dogs. Instead, you heard a lot of bumping and clunking, which turned out to be the sound of a large dog limping frantically toward you but suffering a major traction loss on every fourth step because of a plastic bag, combined with the sound of a very small dog trying desperately to keep up but bonking his collar into furniture, doorways, etc. And then, finally, skidding around the corner, still barking, there appeared the dynamite duo: Bagfoot and Satellite Head.

During this week I was not the least bit worried about burglars because if anyone had tried to break into my house, I would have found him the next morning, lying on the floor. Dead from laughter.

Dave Barry

Marty Had a Little Lamb

It was lambing season. The neighbors' phone call brought my dad and me rushing to their barn to help with a difficult delivery. We found a lamb whose mother had died while giving birth. The orphan was weak, cold, still shrouded with the placenta, and walking on impossibly tall and wobbly legs. I bundled him up in my coat and put him in the pickup truck for the short ride back to our small family farm in rural Idaho.

We drove through our barnyard, passing cows, pigs, chickens, dogs and cats, but Dad headed straight for the house. I didn't know it yet, but that lamb was destined to become more than an ordinary sheep, just as I was destined to be more than an ordinary seven-year-old boy—I was about to become a mommy!

Cradling the lamb in my arms, I brought him into the kitchen. While Mom and I wiped the lamb down with dry towels, Dad stoked the furnace with coal so that the newborn would have warming heat to drive away the cold. As I petted his curly little head, the tiny creature tried sucking on my fingers. He was hungry! We slipped a nipple over a pop bottle full of warm milk and stuck it into his mouth. He latched on, and instantly his jaws pumped like a machine, sending the nourishing milk to his stomach.

As soon as he started eating, his tail started wagging furiously. Then suddenly his eyes popped open for the first time, and he looked me right in the eye. He gave me that miraculous moment-of-birth look that every mother knows. The look that says, unmistakably, "Hello Mommy! I'm yours, you're mine, ain't life fine!"

A young boy with tousled blond hair and thick black glasses doesn't look much like a sheep. But this little lamb didn't care in the least. The important thing was that he had a mom—me!

I named him Henry and, just like the nursery rhyme, everywhere that Marty went, the lamb was sure to go. The instant bond we shared that first day turned into the same deep kind of connection that develops between mother and child. We were always together. I'd feed, exercise and bathe Henry. I'd scold him sternly when he got out in the road. Imagine the amazement and delight of my classmates when I had a couple of dogs *and* a sheep run to meet me at the school bus! Every day after school, Henry and I played games together until we both fell asleep, side by side, in the tall cool grass of the pasture.

As I grew up, Henry grew older. Never once, however, did he forgot that I was his mom. Even as a full-grown ram, he nuzzled me fondly, rubbing his big woolly head against my leg whenever he saw me. Functioning as a four-legged lawn mower and wool-covered dog at the Becker farm, Henry had a happy, healthy, full life for the rest of his days.

People sometimes ask me why I became a veterinarian. The answer is: Henry. At seven years old, my love for animals was still just a spark. But it ignited into a flame at that magical moment when I became a mother to a hungry little lamb.

Marty Becker, D.V.M.

The Ice Breaker

It was the perfect setting—a beautiful log house on forty acres of land. We had a solid marriage; we even had the loyal family dog. All that was missing was kids. We had tried for many years to have children, but it just never happened. So my husband, Al, and I applied to be foster parents. We decided we should start with an older child for a number of good reasons. Since we both worked, child care might be a problem. Corby, our springer spaniel—and our only "child" thus far—might be a bit too energetic for a young child to handle. And frankly, we novices were a little nervous about taking on an infant. We sat back to wait the few months they thought it might take to get a school-age child—which was why we were floored when the agency called us within weeks, just before Christmas, and asked if we would take Kaleb, a two-and-a-half-year-old boy, for a few months. It was an emergency, and he needed a home right away.

This wasn't what we had discussed so rationally a few weeks before. There were so many difficulties—it was such short notice, we had made holiday plans and most of all, the boy was a toddler! We went back and forth, and in the end, we just couldn't say no.

"It's only for a couple of months," my husband assured me. It would all work out, we told each other, but privately I was full of doubts.

The day was set for Kaleb to arrive. The car pulled up to our house and I saw Kaleb through the car window. The reality of the situation hit me and I felt my stomach tighten. *What were we doing? This child we didn't know anything about was coming to live with us. Were we really ready to take this on?* Glancing at my husband, I knew the same thoughts were going through his mind.

We went outside to greet our little guest. But before we could even reach the child, I heard a noise from behind me. Turning, I saw Corby tearing down the steps and heading straight for the little boy. In our hurry, we must not have closed the door completely. I gasped. Corby, in all her excitement, would frighten Kaleb—probably even knock him down. *Oh no,* I thought, *what a way to start our first meeting! Kaleb will be so terrified he won't even want to go into the house with us. This whole thing's just not going to work out!*

Corby reached Kaleb before either of us could grab her. She bounded up to the boy and immediately began licking his face in a frenzy of joy. In response, this darling little boy threw his arms around the dog's neck and turned toward us. His face alight with ecstasy, he cried, "Can this be my dog?"

My eyes met my husband's and we stood there, smiling at each other. In that moment, our nervousness disappeared, and we knew everything would be just fine.

Kaleb came to stay those few months. Eight-and-a-half years later, he is still with us. Yes, we adopted Kaleb. He became our son, and Corby . . . well, she couldn't have been happier. She turned out to be Kaleb's dog, after all.

Diane Williamson

Kids Say The Darndest Things— About Dogs

I believe all kids should have pets. It's an essential part of growing up. There's a mystic kinship between a boy and his dog, a sharing of love and trust that's unique. A boy's dog is a pal, a companion, a comforter when tears come, and the best listener to whispered secrets. At the price of a dog tag and a bowl of food each day, a pup's probably the biggest bargain in any kid's life.

Children love to talk about their pets, and with characteristic freedom, they weave many a fanciful tale of improbable goings on:

There was the girl who was befuddled about the sweet mysteries of life:

"Do you have any pets?" I asked her.

"Yes—we have a dog that just laid six puppies."

"Do you have a pet?" I asked one youngster.

"A dog."

"Does he have a pedigree?"

"Sure, lots of them."

"How do you know?"

"Because he bites himself all the time."

Perhaps the answer that brought the biggest laugh from our listeners on the fateful pedigree question was this exchange:

"Do you have any pets?"

"Yes—a cat and a dog."

"Do they have pedigrees?"

"No, we took them out."

One Link in my own family chain loves dogs, so when he saw a magnificent Saint Bernard on the leash, he rushed up, hugged him and then began to stroke his long, bushy tail. Moments later, his mother came along and was horrified to see her child clutching the tail of the tremendous animal.

"Get away from that beast!" she shouted. "He'll bite you!"

"Oh no, Mommy," he reassured her. "This end never bites!"

On the other hand, one little four-year-old cried bitterly when a large friendly dog bounded up to him and licked his hands and face.

"What is it, darling?" cried his mother. "Did he bite you?"

"No," came the reply. "But he tasted me."

Then there was little Susan, who was inclined to exaggeration. Her stories always seemed so full of adventures, and she could never be talked into admitting the complete truth. One day she was playing in the front yard when a fox terrier belonging to a neighbor darted at her playfully. With a shriek of fright, Susan fled to her mother and yelled:

"Mama, a great big lion ran down the street, jumped over the fence and almost ate me up."

"Susan," said her mother sternly, "aren't you ashamed

of yourself? I was sitting here at the window and saw the whole thing. Now you go in your room and get down on your knees and confess that it was just a little pet dog and you lied to your mother. Ask the Lord to forgive you for this sin."

Susan reluctantly went to her room and shut the door. In less than a minute she opened the door and poked her head out.

"It's all right, Mother," she said. "I told God all about it and he says he could hardly blame me. He thought it was a lion, too, when he first saw it."

And while we're on the subject of children and animals, I love this quickie:

"Hurry, Mother, and come look," said little James when he saw his first snake. "Here's a tail wagging without any dog on it!"

Art Linkletter

DENNIS the MENACE

"That's funny . . . my dad can tell if it's a boy or a girl just by lookin' at the bottom of its feet."

Let Sleeping Dogs Lie

One afternoon, I was in the backyard hanging the laundry when an old, tired-looking dog wandered into the yard. I could tell from his collar and well-fed belly that he had a home. But when I walked into the house, he followed me, sauntered down the hall and fell asleep in a corner. An hour later, he went to the door, and I let him out. The next day he was back. He resumed his position in the hallway and slept for an hour.

This continued for several weeks. Curious, I pinned a note to his collar: "Every afternoon your dog comes to my house for a nap."

The next day he arrived with a different note pinned to his collar: "He lives in a home with ten children—he's trying to catch up on his sleep."

Susan F. Roman

"He's very good at down boy!"

The Legacy

When I was growing up, we always had boxers. One time my dad, who was a macho kind of guy, fell in love with a magnificent, black-and-tan Doberman who had just come from the show circuit. Dad had to have this beautiful animal, so he purchased him and brought him home. His name was Baron. He was a young, non-neutered male, about eleven months old. Having been raised for the show ring, Baron had no experience with children. I was five at the time, the second of four kids. Like most homes with young children, there was usually a lot of noise and activity at our house. My parents figured since Baron was relatively young, he would adapt quickly to his new life.

One day, not long after Dad brought Baron home, I came running inside the house, all bundled up from playing in the snow. Not seeing Baron sleeping on the floor, I accidentally stepped on him. Dobermans are highly reactive dogs—this is one of the reasons they make such good guard and police dogs. But in this circumstance, it spelled disaster. Baron leaped up and in his fright grabbed me by the face. His top teeth penetrated my left cheek and my upper lip, just below my nose, while his bottom teeth tore right through my chin. My parents rushed me to the emergency room, where I had immediate reconstructive surgery. When they brought me home, all stitched and bandaged, they put me straight to bed.

When Dad came up to check on me a little while later, he stopped in the doorway to my room, startled by the scene in front of him. Baron had crept into my room. The dog had nudged my elbow with his nose, and by continuing his nudging, had managed to work his head under my arm so that my arm lay across his shoulders. He rested his great black head on my sleeping chest and sat there, still as a statue. Watching and guarding, he conducted a vigil of apology and love. My father said that Baron never moved, but held the same position through the long hours of the night.

Amazingly enough, I have no physical disfigurement from my encounter with Baron. And no lasting fear of dogs, as so often happens in these cases. When I think of Baron, I hardly remember his fierceness; instead, I recall the weight of his head on my chest and the concern in his expressive eyes. I had talked about wanting to be a veterinarian even before this incident, and my love for animals actually grew stronger after experiencing Baron's true display of sorrow. Even now, I still chuckle a little inside every time I treat a Dobie.

Baron's story has become a family legend. My mom rescued an adult Dobie and kept him until he died. Of course, she named him Baron. My younger sister has two Dobermans and, yes, one is named Baron.

Baron was a great dog in the wrong situation. We found him a home where there were no children, and he lived the rest of his life there, happy and loved.

Jeff Werber, D.V.M.

The Truth About Annie

Taco, an orange-winged Amazon, came to us as a rescue bird. Taco had started to pluck. He tore at his back with such a vengeance that he made himself ill. The cost of treating him was beyond his owner's financial capability, so we agreed to take him. We picked him up at the veterinarian's office after he and his owner had said their good-byes.

The essential elements for beautiful feathers and a healthy bird are sound nutrition and a lot of love. We introduced Taco to the diet that our birds thrive on, and within just a few days he lost interest in his back and began playing with the wooden toys in his cage.

By the end of the first week, he was fully acclimated to the food, his cage and his neighbors, Gideon, a double-yellow-headed Amazon, and Tutt, a Mexican red-headed Amazon. Taco accepted the constant handling, bathing and talking going on around him without any hesitation.

Two weeks passed and Taco began acting like a normal Amazon, with one exception. He wasn't talking. In fact, he wasn't making any sounds. This is highly unusual for an Amazon. Most parrots will mimic what they hear in their own environment: a cat's meow, a creaky door and, depending on the parrot, even an entire sentence. Taco didn't whistle or squeak. He was completely silent. I decided to give him one more week and then take him back to the vet for a more thorough checkup.

Friday mornings are bath- and cage-cleaning day at our house. This particular Friday, I decided Taco was ready for his first community bath. I opened his cage and put my hand in, and he stepped onto my finger. I held him at eye level and said, "Taco, aren't you ever going to talk?"

He cocked his head to one side, fluffed his feathers and said, "Annie died. Poor Annie. Annie is bleeding."

The shock was immense. I think my mouth was hanging open. I know the goose bumps were visible on my arms.

Hurrying through the baths and the cleaning of the cages, I was finally able to call our vet and ask for Taco's previous owner's telephone number. I had to know who Annie was. Had Taco witnessed a crime? Had a member of his household died? Maybe he was talking about another animal that lived in one of his previous homes.

I called Taco's most recent owner and told her what Taco had said. She said she had never heard him say that or anything else during the four years she had owned him. She definitely didn't know anyone named Annie. She gave me the name and telephone number of the person from whom she had bought Taco.

After a short conversation with this owner, it was clear he had never heard Taco say a word the entire time he had owned him, either. That was one of the reasons he had sold Taco. He wanted a bird that talked, and Taco never did. He had purchased Taco from a breeder near Chico, California, but he couldn't remember the breeder's name. It seemed I was at a dead end.

In the meantime, Taco was becoming more vocal and was adding to his tale about Annie. His new version was,

"Annie died. Annie died. Poor Annie, she is bleeding. Oh, poor Annie."

The president of our bird club gave me some names and numbers of breeders in the area where Taco came from originally. Each phone call led to another dead end, but I wouldn't give up. I was determined to get to the bottom of this!

My husband suggested that I call the library in Chico and check the local newspaper obituaries going back to the time that Taco might have lived there. The reference librarian was intrigued with the story that Taco was telling and was very helpful. She said she would call her brother, who worked for the police department, and ask him to check their records as well.

Two days passed and the librarian hadn't called. Taco repeated his story so many times that our Congo grays, Jack and Jill, started saying "Poor Annie," too.

Spurred on by the growing chorus of "Poor Annie's," I decided to check on the librarian's progress. She answered on the first ring. "Have you found anything?" I asked.

"No, I'm sorry," she said. "My brother went back fifteen years in their records and he couldn't find anything either." She took a deep breath and asked, "Are you sure the bird is saying 'Annie'?"

I told her that at this point that was the only thing of which I was sure. I thanked her for her help and hung up.

There was one more thing I was certain of—Taco had heard about Annie somewhere. Birds do not make things up. Somehow Annie's plight had stuck in his memory. It was time to accept the fact that I might never find out who Annie was or what had happened to her.

Two months passed. Taco continued gaining weight and was becoming more and more affectionate. He feathered out to a brilliant green and his eyes were clear. His back was completely healed. And he continued talking about Annie. He talked about Annie from morning to evening. We didn't get goose bumps anymore. We just accepted what had happened to poor Annie.

One evening, it was my turn to host our bird club meeting. The coffee and cookies were set out as everyone arrived. We gathered in the living room, which is next to our bird room, to discuss the fund-raiser that was coming up.

Suddenly, a voice sounded loud and clear.

"Poor Annie. Annie died. Annie is bleeding. Poor Annie."

Startled, everyone stopped talking and listened. One of the club members turned to me and said, "I thought you didn't like to watch soap operas!"

"I don't. What are you talking about?" I asked.

"Annie," she said. "She died. I think Robert killed her."

"No," another breeder chimed in. "It wasn't Robert. It was James. Don't you remember? He was having an affair with Annie's sister's neighbor . . ."

I left my fellow bird lovers while they discussed their favorite soap opera and walked to Taco's cage. Now it was clear that one of his owners had watched that same soap opera, and Taco had heard it, too. He cocked his head to one side, looked at me and said clearly, "Is Taco hungry? Do you want me to scratch your head?" The mystery of Annie finally solved, he was ready to discuss something else.

Today, Taco has a mate, another orange-winged Amazon, named Bell. When they had their first baby, we had to name her . . . Annie.

Judy Doyle

A Vet's Wages

As a practicing veterinarian, one of the things you learn to accept is that most of your patients cannot comprehend what you are doing for them. Whether it be routine vaccinations or emergency treatment, most of them associate a visit to the vet with some feelings of apprehension or discomfort. In retrospect, I can think of numerous animals both large and small whose lives I have saved or at least relieved of a serious illness or painful injury. Most of them would not hesitate to bite, kick or gore their benefactor should the opportunity arise. To be sure, some seem to understand that you are helping them. But rarely does an animal come along showing complete trust and obvious gratitude for your efforts.

Several years ago on a warm autumn afternoon, an elderly farmer brought his injured black Labrador to our clinic. The farmer had been mowing weeds with a tractor mower and his dog had jumped in front of the sickle bar. Before he could stop the machine, the dog became entangled in the sickle and one hind leg was badly injured.

We carried him from the back of his owner's pickup into the clinic and laid him on the examination table. He was already weakened from shock and loss of blood, but he placidly licked his hurt leg. A brief examination showed the limb could not be saved. I explained to the owner that we would have to amputate the leg to save the dog's life. He agreed we should do whatever was necessary. I gave the animal a blood transfusion, plus injections for pain and shock, and scheduled him for surgery the next morning. He accepted these procedures calmly, without the slightest whimper or display of emotion.

He came through the surgery in good shape, and by the following morning was hopping about on three legs. For the next few mornings, I took him for brief walks on the clinic lawn and helped him balance himself when he needed it. He was an ideal patient and always seemed to appreciate my help. Later, when I removed the stitches from his leg, he watched undisturbed, with no whimpers and no need for a muzzle.

I had only thought of him as being a very good patient and not really different from other dogs I had treated, until the day he was scheduled to go home. After we put him into the back of his owner's pickup, the farmer and I visited for a few minutes about the dog's condition. As I turned to go back into the clinic, Blackie began whining and attempted to jump from the truck and follow me. His owner, Mr. Burson, remarked, "You know, I believe he's taken up with you and wants to stay here." I was surprised, but all I said was, "Yes, it seems he has, but he'll soon forget me when he gets home." I knew the dog would be treated well, as Mr. Burson was a kindly man who took good care of his animals.

It was nearly a year later when I was called to the Burson farm to deliver a calf. I parked my truck and was busy getting out equipment, when around the corner of the barn bounded a large black dog. He barked loudly and the hair bristled on the back of his neck and shoulders. It was Blackie. As he came running up on his three legs, he suddenly stopped dead still, about six or eight feet away.

Gazing directly at me, Blackie slowly moved forward, wagging his tail. Then he took one of my hands gently in his mouth and just held it, all the while looking up into my face. As he did this, he made little whimpering noises.

I was overwhelmed and felt a lump rise in my throat. Patting him on the head, I talked to him briefly in soothing tones. He gave me a final warm-eyed look and a parting bark, then went brusquely about his business of inspecting the tires of my truck.

In the long line of animals that a vet treats in the course of his career, there are a few who distinctly stand out. To me, Blackie will always be "the one that remembered."

George Baker, D.V.M.

More Chicken Soup?

Many of the stories and poems you have read in this book were submitted by readers like you who had read earlier *Chicken Soup for the Soul* books. We are planning to publish five or six *Chicken Soup for the Soul* books every year. We invite you to contribute a story to one of these future volumes.

Stories may be up to 1,200 words and must uplift or inspire. You may submit an original piece or something you clip out of the local newspaper, a magazine, a church bulletin or a company newsletter. It could also be your favorite quotation you've put on your refrigerator door or a personal experience that has touched you deeply.

In addition to future servings of *Chicken Soup for the Soul,* some of the future books we have planned are *A 2nd Helping of Chicken Soup for the Pet Lover's Soul, the Woman's Soul, the Christian Soul* and *the Teenage Soul,* as well as *Chicken Soup for the Teacher's Soul, Jewish Soul, Kid's Soul, Country Soul, Laughing Soul, Grieving Soul, Unsinkable Soul, Divorced Soul* and *Loving Couple's Soul.*

Send a copy of your stories and other pieces, indicating which edition they are for, to the following address:

Chicken Soup for the *(Specify Which Edition)* Soul
P.O. Box 30880 • Santa Barbara, CA 93130
phone: 805-563-2935 • fax: 805-563-2945
To e-mail or visit our Web site:
http://www.chickensoup.com

We will be sure that both you and the author are credited for your submission.

For information about speaking engagements, other books, audiotapes, workshops and training programs, please contact any of the authors directly.

Who Is The Iams Company?

The Iams Company was built on a simple mission: to enhance the well-being of dogs and cats by providing world-class quality foods. This privately held company is the seventh-largest pet food enterprise in the United States, and is one of the fastest-growing pet food companies in the world. The company's two brands—Eukanuba and Iams Dog and Cat Foods—are distributed worldwide to more than seventy countries.

Paul Iams, an animal nutritionist from Dayton, Ohio, and founder of The Iams Company, put his knowledge to work and began to develop premium dry dog food shortly after World War II. He discovered that family dogs benefited from high-protein, high-fat diets. This revelation led to the development of Iams Plus Dog Food, the most complete dog food of its time. During the 1960s, news about this new product spread among breeders, kennel operators, and veterinarians.

In 1973, after lawmakers in Washington, D.C., imposed nationwide wage and price controls, Iams Company officials had to decide whether they should switch to a lesser quality protein source in their dog food and continue to show a profit, or maintain existing formulas and face financial loss. They agreed not to cheapen the formula and stayed with the high quality protein ingredients, even when the cost of making a bag of Iams Dog Food was fifty cents more than the company made selling the bag. When competitors cut corners, breeders who used the competition's products ran into problems as their dogs suffered skin and coat problems due to inferior diets.

The Iams Company soon outgrew its Dayton production facility, and built a larger plant in nearby Lewisburg, Ohio. In 1982, Paul Iams retired. Clay Mathile, the Iams executive who developed the super-premium dog food

Eukanuba, purchased the business. Clay embarked on a growth campaign that led to the construction of a second manufacturing facility in Aurora, Nebraska, and a third plant in Henderson, North Carolina. In 1992, The Iams Company made its first major acquisition, Heartland Quality Foods, Inc. of North Sioux City, South Dakota, a manufacturer of canned pet food products.

As part of its expansion, The Iams Company built the Paul F. Iams Technical Center in Lewisburg. Completed in 1987, the center includes a state-of-the-art research laboratory, pilot plant and animal care center where nutritionists, process engineers, chemists, veterinarians, and technicians test new products and formula enhancements.

The Animal Care Center is home to a group of dogs and cats that help researchers understand the physical and emotional needs of companion animals. Staff members observe how the animals live, note their likes and dislikes, and examine their interaction with humans and other pets. The center was designed with the "four-footed research associates'" comfort and enjoyment in mind. Pet kennels and cages are large and allow the animals to enjoy maximum mobility as well as regular grooming and daily playtime. In addition, thermostats are installed at pet-height to regulate cooling and heating to dog and cat comfort levels. The animals also enjoy piped-in music.

The Iams Company underwrites studies of companion animal growth and development, geriatric nutrition, renal and gastrointestinal health, and other areas of innovative research in dog and cat nutrition. In addition to examining the needs of house pets, the company studies the nutritional requirements of hunting and working dogs, as well as show dogs and cats, to ensure that its products meet the demanding needs of those animals.

Iams showed its commitment to animals in its 1995 decision to name a dog as its new v.p.: Kersee, a four-year-old golden retriever, was named Vice President of Canine

Communications. Her duties at headquarters include sampling Eukanuba and Iams products, and greeting Iams employees and guests with a firm paw shake. Kersee has her own office, but prefers to spend most of her time in the busy Iams reception area where she can oversee company comings and goings.

The company makes frequent and generous donations to animal shelters, disaster relief organizations and other groups dedicated to dogs and cats in need. Iams has donated thousands of pounds of dog and cat food to canine and feline flood victims, animals rescued from the volcanic eruption on Montserrat and countless other needy pets. In November 1997, The Iams Company was recognized by talk-show host Rosie O'Donnell for its meaningful contributions to local animal shelters and to one dog in particular, a kitten-saving "hero dog" named Sammy. In all its efforts, The Iams Company never loses sight of its primary customers—dogs and cats worldwide—and its mission of enhancing their well-being.

Iams also looks out for people, especially in the communities where it operates. In 1997, when the small town of Aurora, Nebraska, discovered it owed The Iams Company a $92,285 tax refund, Iams knew the local schools (which received 73 percent of the money) and other community organizations would suffer if the county had to pay the money back. Iams officials passed up the tax rebate in order to protect the community and be a good corporate neighbor. In the words of an Iams customer who wrote to the company after hearing about the decision, "This act showed the true heart of The Iams Company."

For more information about Iams, or to talk to one of the company's pet professionals, call Iams Customer Service at 800-525-4267. You can also visit The Iams Company's Internet site at www.iams.com.

Who Is Jack Canfield?

Jack Canfield grew up surrounded by animals of every kind. There was always at least one dog—mostly collies and German shepherds, along with an occasional mutt—and two or three cats, plus hamsters, gerbils, rabbits, parakeets, white mice, box turtles, tropical fish, raccoons, a horse, a cow, a goat, and eventually a kennel full of rambunctious Afghan hounds. This love of animals led to an adult life filled with a series of wonderful dogs—a Samoyed, an English sheepdog and a golden retriever—as well as too many cats to keep track of, all of which have always become members of the family with full run of the house. Currently Jack is the proud owner of Daisy, a golden retriever, and three cats (Bodhi, Ashleigh and Rocky), as well as a pond full of magnificent koi and goldfish.

Jack Canfield is one of America's leading experts in the development of human potential and personal effectiveness. He is both a dynamic, entertaining speaker and a highly sought-after trainer. Jack has a wonderful ability to inform and inspire audiences toward increased levels of self-esteem and peak performance.

He is the author and narrator of several bestselling audio- and videocassette programs, including *Self-Esteem and Peak Performance, How to Build High Self-Esteem, Self-Esteem in the Classroom* and *Chicken Soup for the Soul—Live.* He is regularly seen on television shows such as *Good Morning America, 20/20* and *NBC Nightly News.* Jack has coauthored numerous books, including the *Chicken Soup for the Soul* series, *Dare to Win* and *The Aladdin Factor* (all with Mark Victor Hansen), *100 Ways to Build Self-Concept in the Classroom* (with Harold C. Wells) and *Heart at Work* (with Jacqueline Miller).

Jack is a regularly featured speaker for professional associations, school districts, government agencies, churches, hospitals, sales organizations and corporations.

For further information about Jack's books, tapes and training programs, or to schedule him for a presentation, please contact:

The Canfield Training Group
P.O. Box 30880 • Santa Barbara, CA 93130
phone: 805-563-2935 • fax: 805-563-2945
To e-mail or visit our Web site: http://www.chickensoup.com

Who Is Mark Victor Hansen?

Mark Victor Hansen is a professional speaker who, in the last twenty years, has made over 4,000 presentations to more than 2 million people in thirty-two countries. His presentations cover sales excellence and strategies; personal empowerment and development; and how to triple your income and double your time off.

Mark has spent a lifetime dedicated to his mission of making a profound and positive difference in people's lives. Throughout his career, he has inspired hundreds of thousands of people to create a more powerful and purposeful future for themselves while stimulating the sale of billions of dollars worth of goods and services.

Mark is a prolific writer and has authored *Future Diary, How to Achieve Total Prosperity* and *The Miracle of Tithing.* He is coauthor of the *Chicken Soup for the Soul* series, *Dare to Win* and *The Aladdin Factor* (all with Jack Canfield) and *The Master Motivator* (with Joe Batten).

Mark has also produced a complete library of personal empowerment audio- and videocassette programs that have enabled his listeners to recognize and use their innate abilities in their business and personal lives. His message has made him a popular television and radio personality, with appearances on ABC, NBC, CBS, HBO, PBS and CNN. He has also appeared on the cover of numerous magazines, including *Success, Entrepreneur* and *Changes.*

When Mark was a child, he only had one family dog. He was not then aware that his heart and home would eventually expand to include the forty-six animals that currently inhabit the Hansen compound, including four cats, three dogs, two birds, two horses, several goldfish, one bunny, one duck who thinks he is a chicken, and twenty-five chickens, all of which have names.

Mark is a big man with a heart and spirit to match—an inspiration to all who seek to better themselves.

For further information about Mark write:

P.O. Box 7665
Newport Beach, CA 92658
phone: 714-759-9304 or 800-433-2314
fax: 714-722-6912
Web site: http://www.chickensoup.com

Who Is Marty Becker?

What Jacques Cousteau did for the oceans, what Carl Sagan did for space, Dr. Marty Becker is doing for pets.

As a veterinarian, noted author, university educator, media personality, industry spokesperson, professional speaker and pet lover, Dr. Becker is one of the most widely recognized family doctors for pets in the world. He is one of the most visible and vocal proponents of the family-pet bond (The Bond)—he coined the term. Dr. Becker has demonstrated an uncanny ability to create bonds that transcend geography, culture and species.

In his multifaceted eighteen-year career, Dr. Becker has been at the forefront of changing the way we interact with and take responsibility for our pets. Dr. Becker is the author of a bestselling book, *Becoming Your Dog's Best Friend.* Dr. Becker is also the practice leadership editor for *Veterinary Economics Magazine,* a featured columnist for *PetLife* magazine, and a national spokesperson for Hallmark's Pet Love greetings. In addition, he teaches at most of the veterinary schools in North America.

Dr. Becker is an inspiring, entertaining and dynamic communicator. He has relentlessly and enthusiastically promoted the benefits of pets and people living in harmony and interdependence, as life-enhancing not only for each other, but for society as well. Dr. Becker has proved to be a hit at meetings around the world where he delivers custom-tailored keynote presentations, seminars, and training courses for civic organizations, health care groups, universities and businesses on topics including optimal health, self-esteem, personal empowerment, team building and leadership issues.

For further information about Dr. Becker, contact:

Marty Becker, D.V.M.
250 2nd Ave. South, Ste. B2 • Twin Falls, ID 83301
phone: 888-4BowWow • fax: 208-733-5405
e-mail: TheBond@aol.com
Web site: http://www.bondworks.com

Who Is Carol Kline?

Carol Kline has been a pet lover her entire life. She is the codirector of the Noah's Ark Animal Foundation Dog Rescue Program, in Fairfield, Iowa, a volunteer effort that saves lost, stray and abandoned dogs.

Carol spends many hours a week monitoring the fate of animals that are brought into the city pound. She also walks, feeds and "socializes" the dogs at the Noah's Ark facility, a cageless shelter for cats and dogs. "The gratitude and love I receive from these animals are more fulfilling than any paycheck I could ever receive. Volunteering time with the dogs fills my heart, and brings great joy to my life."

Coauthoring *Chicken Soup for the Pet Lover's Soul* has strengthened her existing appreciation for all animals and deepened her commitment to animal-rescue work.

A freelance writer for ten years, Carol, who has a B.A. in literature, has written for newspapers, newsletters and other publications. Recently she has contributed stories and her editing talents to other *Chicken Soup for the Soul* books.

In addition to her writing and animal work, Carol is also a speaker, self-esteem facilitator and certified instructor of the parenting skills program, *Redirecting Children's Behavior* (RCB). The first RCB instructor in Iowa, Carol presents workshops and in-service programs for childcare providers, and teaches a five-week program for parents. She has also been a counselor at a self-esteem camp in Missouri for teens and kids. Since 1975, Carol has taught stress-management programs to the general public. In 1990, she studied with Jack Canfield, and since then has assisted as a facilitator in his annual Train the Trainers program. Her dynamic and engaging style has won her enthusiastic receptions from the various audiences she addresses.

Carol has the good fortune to be married to Larry Kline, and is stepmother to Lorin and McKenna. Besides her "main" dog, Hannah, Carol houses foster dogs until they find permanent homes.

You may contact Carol at:

P.O. Box 1262 • Fairfield, IA 52556
phone: 515-469-3889 • fax: 515-472-3720
e-mail: lkline@lisco.com

Contributors

Many of the stories in this book were taken from books we have read which are acknowledged in the Permissions section. If you would like to contact authors for information on their books, tapes or seminars, you can reach them at the addresses and phone numbers provided.

Many of the stories were also contributed by readers like yourself, who responded to our request for stories. We have also included information about them.

Vickie Lynne Agee earned her bachelor's degree in English and psychology from Brigham Young University in 1982. She has taught in these two fields for the past fourteen years. Currently, she teaches seventh-grade English at Columbiana Middle School, near Birmingham, Alabama. She enjoys freelance writing in her spare time.

George Baker, D.V.M., has been in a general rural veterinary practice for thirty-four years. His primary area of expertise is with horses. He is currently accumulating material for a book he plans to write about his years of practice, particularly special patients he has come to know.

Fred Bauer, author of many bestselling books, is one of the country's favorite inspirational writers. Former executive editor of *Guideposts* magazine, he is the founder and president of Littlebrook Publishing, Inc., Princeton, New Jersey.

Jan K. Stewart Bass is a freelance writer, newspaper columnist and author of the award-winning book, *At Home in the Heartland: Seasons of Serenity.* She is a member of the National Federation of Press Women and founder of Stillmeadow Society of Iowa. You may contact her at 119 Upland Dr., Council Bluffs, IA 51503.

Gregg Bassett is the founder and president of The Squirrel Lover's Club as well as the editor of the club's newsletter, *In a Nutshell.* The international club serves the interests of squirrels and squirrel lovers and can be reached at 318 W. Fremont Ave., Elmhurst, IL 60126, or by calling 630-833-1117.

Christine E. Belleris is the editorial director at Health Communications, Inc. (HCI), the publisher of the *Chicken Soup for the Soul* series. A native of Denver, Colorado, she now lives in Boca Raton, Florida, with her husband, Jeff, and their animal family: Wilma, a loving mixed-breed dog; Rufus, a spirited gray tabby cat; and Isis, a snow-white 21-year-old kitty. A devoted animal lover, Christine spends her spare time feeding and finding homes for the parade of stray animals that seem to find their way to the HCI offices.

Jean Brody is a national magazine columnist, Kentucky newspaper columnist, creative writing teacher and a public motivational/inspirational speaker. She lives with her husband, a Newfoundland dog, three cats and a pet Nubian goat on their Thoroughbred horse farm, Jean & Gene Farm. Jean has published dozens of short stories, articles and *Braille Me,* a compilation of her published work.

Carolyn Butler directs Changes: The Support for People and Pets Program at Colorado State University's Veterinary Teaching Hospital. She coauthored *The Human-Animal Bond and Grief* and *Friends for Life: Loving and Losing Your Animal Companion* and owns World by the Tail, Inc., the producers of ClayPaws, the original paw print kit.

Leona Campbell has written for the *Idaho Outdoors* magazine, *Valley News, Country Woman* magazine, *Idaho Statesman Newspaper* and *Poet Voices* magazine. Leona is a 1994 graduate of the Christian Writer's Institute. She is presently writing a book entitled *Talk to God: He Listens 24 Hours a Day.*

Jo Coudert is a freelance writer, a frequent contributor to *Woman's Day* and *Reader's Digest,* and the author of seven books, among them the bestselling *Advice from a Failure.* Her most recent works are *Seven Cats and the Art of Living, The Ditchdigger's Daughters* and the forthcoming *The Good Shepherd.*

Cerie L. Couture, D.V.M., is a veterinarian in Norwich, Vermont. She enjoys running with her Shetland sheepdog, Mollie, and hiking in the Green Mountains with her family. She can be reached at 253 River Rd., Norwich, VT 05055.

Angel Di Benedetto is an internationally recognized Guild Certified Feldenkrais Trainer originally from Manhattan. Through The Feldenkrais Method, her teaching focuses on developing creativity to enhance artistic expression, self-confidence, personal awareness and one's quality of life. She can be reached in South Florida at 305-661-5227, or by fax at 305-669-4350, or via e-mail at adiben@aol.com.

Karen Del Tufo was born in Brooklyn, New York. She attended John Adams High School and Brookdale Community College, and graduated from the Long Ridge Writers Group. She has published poems in the *Selected Works of Our Worlds Best Poets, Great Poems of Our Times, The Hale House Newsletter, The International Society of Authors and Artists* and local newspapers.

Robin Downing, D.V.M., is owner of Windsor Veterinary Clinic, PC, in Windsor, Colorado, a progressive veterinary practice accredited by the American Animal Hospital Association. She is a well-known speaker and trainer who was named the Up and Coming Veterinarian of the Year for the state of Colorado in 1995, and who in 1996 was named the Outstanding Woman Veterinarian of the Year in North America. Dr. Downing shares her home and clinic with an assortment of animals, including ten cats, three dogs, several birds, a rabbit, a guinea pig, a hedgehog and a gray squirrel.

Judy Doyle has been adopting and rescuing parrots and educating the public about them for over ten years. She visits elementary schools with her feathered friends and writes for local bird club publications on care and nutrition for healthier and happier parrots.

S. C. Edwards, born into the world as "Robert," credits his two sons and their wonderment with this earth as his driving force. Edwards believes that everyone needs to surround themselves with kindred in order to touch the soul of humankind. A Harley-riding jack-of-all-trades, he is now a middle manager for corporate America.

Janet Foley, D.V.M., is a small-animal practitioner in Northern Virginia. She shares her home with her husband and three cats. In her spare time, she writes stories about her adventures in small-animal practice and about her pets.

Toni Fulco has authored over 150 articles, stories and poems in national magazines and anthologies. She raises cockatiels at home and is known locally as "the bird lady" for her affectionate, talkative, hand-fed babies. Toni can be reached at 89 Penn Estates, E. Stroudsburg, PA 18301, or by calling 717-421-3417.

David Giannelli has been a New York City fireman since 1975 and has been involved in numerous human and animal rescues. David has always been an animal lover and worked in a veterinary hospital when he was a teenager, when he first learned about animal behavior. He can be reached at Ladder Co. 175, Engine 332, 165 Bradford St., Brooklyn, NY 11207.

Bill Goss is a highly sought-after professional speaker and author of *The Luckiest Unlucky Man Alive.* Bill's inspiring and hilarious true story about a garbage man who becomes a Navy pilot has been featured internationally on radio and television shows such as *Extra, The 700 Club* and KIIS 102.7. Contact him at P.O. Box 7060, Orange Park, FL 32073, or by calling 904-278-8900. His Web site is www.bookworld.com/luckiest.

Bonnie Compton Hanson, writer/speaker, is coauthor of three books plus hundreds of published poems and articles. Her family includes husband Don, sons, grandsons, cats, birds and possums! You can reach Bonnie at 3330 S. Lowell St., Santa Ana, CA 92707; phone 714-751-7824; e-mail bonnieh1@ix.netcom.com.

Earl Holliman is the president of Actors and Others for Animals. If you would like further information please write him at 11523 Burbank Blvd., North Hollywood, CA 91601-2309.

Bill Holton is graciously allowed to share his home with three demanding yet adorable Siamese cats and his demanding yet adorable wife, Tara. Bill is a freelance writer from Richmond, Virginia. When not feverishly begging magazine editors for assignments, he actually dreams of retiring to the Florida Keys, where he will concentrate his boundless energy on fishing. He can be reached at bholton@reporters.net.

Roma Ihnatowycz is a journalist who worked four years as a correspondent in Kiev, initially for United Press International and then for the Associated Press. Roma is currently writing a book on Ukrainian cuisine and can be reached at 72 Sunnylea Ave. E, Toronto, Ontario, Canada M8Y 2K6.

Pam Johnson is a feline behavior consultant and author of *Cat Love* (Storey Publishing), *Twisted Whiskers* (The Crossing Press), and *Hiss and Tell: True Stories from the Files of a Cat Shrink.* Her house calls cover everything from routine training problems to the most eccentric feline behavior. She has made numerous TV and radio appearances, and her techniques have also been featured in magazines and newspapers.

Lynn A. Kerman is a homegrown urban mystic who spends as much time frolicking and communing in the wilderness as possible. She is available for writing, speaking, and holding classes and individual sessions on spiritual awakening. This is her effortless work and joy. You may contact her at 310-301-6559 or 818-777-2860, or e-mail her at rmarons@unistudios.com.

Henry (Hank) Ketcham created DENNIS THE MENACE in October 1950 and it was syndicated the following March. Today DENNIS THE MENACE is distributed by North America Syndicate to more than 1,200 newspapers in 48 countries and is translated into 19 languages.

Shawnacy Kiker is a nineteen-year-old Christian college student with a passion for words and for the God who created them. Contact Shawnacy at 310-397-0161, or by writing her at 2532 Lincoln Blvd., Suite 500, Marina Del Rey, CA 90291 with your story. She would love to help you write it!

Paul H. King, D.V.M., is director of Veterinary Technical and Professional Support for Ralston Purina Company. Paul has spoken at hundreds of U.S. and international veterinary meetings. He developed the Purina "Caring For Pets" program and is the editor of *Dietary Management in Small Animal Practice.*

Joe Kirkup's essays have appeared in weekly magazines throughout the U.S. He is the recipient of two Sigma Delta Chi awards for feature writing. An anthology, *Life Sentences,* can be purchased from Xpress, P.O. Box 63, Colchester, CT 06415. Call 860-572-0079 or e-mail at kirkup@compuserve.com.

Larry Paul Kline is a pilot, sailor, inventor and real estate developer who currently lives in Fairfield, Iowa. He has a wife, Carol, and children, Lorin and McKenna. Although it's been a long time since his "mountain man" days, he still enjoys adventure, animals and the wilderness. Some of his goals include: designing living systems for complete self-sufficiency, living on a sailboat while exploring the world, and experiencing inner joy and peace in every moment. Larry can be reached at P.O. Box 1262, Fairfield, IA 52556.

Laurel Lagoni directs Changes: the Support for People and Pets Program at Colorado State University's Veterinary Teaching Hospital. She coauthored *The Human-Animal Bond and Grief* and *Friends for Life: Loving and Losing Your Animal*

Companion and owns World by the Tail, Inc., the producers of ClayPaws, the original paw print kit.

Art Linkletter is the originator of *Kids Say the Darndest Things* and star of *CBS House Party* for 26 years and NBC's *People Are Funny* for 19 years.

Mary Marcdante is an inspiring and compassionate professional speaker, trainer and author whose programs on personal change, stress management, and communication bring insights, solutions and fun to conventions, businesses, communities and health care conferences around the world. She helps people make healthier choices, push personal boundaries and live a more creative, inspired and fulfilling life. She is the author of *Inspiring Words for Inspiring People* and the upcoming *Questions for My Mother*. She can be reached at 619-792-6786. Write P.O. Box 2417, Del Mar, CA 92014, or e-mail mmarcdante@aol.com.

Sara L. (Robinson) Mark, D.V.M., owns a small-animal practice and has interest in animal-assisted therapy programs and zoonotic disease control. In The Children's Hospital Prescription Pet Program since 1985, Sara authored the program's original protocol and advocates setting up similar hospital-based programs. She can be reached at Southwest Veterinary Hospital, 250 E. Dry Creek Rd., Littleton, CO 80122.

Yvonne A. Martell is a sixty-nine-year-old retired person who lives with her beloved pet in a lovely small town in California. She has never before written anything for publication, but couldn't resist the opportunity to share her "pet" true story with other pet lovers.

Jane Martin (Jana to friends), the author and editor of many books, including *Cats in Love* and *Scarlett Saves Her Family,* has appeared on *Geraldo Rivera* and Fox News and in *Cosmopolitan* and *People* magazines. Now completing a novel, she shares a Brooklyn warehouse with her boyfriend and a dog.

Dennis McIntosh, D.V.M., veterinary practitioner for thirty years, has been published in *Veterinary Economics, Veterinary Forum, D.V.M. Management* and others. Active in veterinary associations and youth groups, he teaches veterinary technicians and also provides grief counseling. He can be reached at 13039 Nacogdoches, San Antonio, TX 78217 or by calling 210-656-1444.

Faith McNulty's career as an observer and advocate for wildlife began with the story of Mousie, first published in 1964. Since then her writing on whooping cranes, whales, blackfooted ferrets and other endangered species has appeared in *Audubon Magazine* and *The New Yorker,* and in book form. You can contact Faith by e-mail at faithsaddress@compuserve.com.

W. W. Meade started writing at the age of fourteen. His first story was published in *Collier* magazine at the age of twenty-two. He wrote short fiction stories for the *Saturday Evening Post, Gentlemen's Quarterly* and several others. He then turned to writing nonfiction for magazines such as *Cosmopolitan, Redbook* and the *Reader's Digest.* Later he took a position in the publishing world and became the managing editor of *Cosmopolitan* and then the managing editor of the *Reader's Digest Book Club*. His last position in publishing was president and editor in chief of Avon Books, which he continued to do for ten years. Today, Walter is retired and writing short stories for *Reader's Digest* as well as many other magazines and periodicals. He can be reached at 4561 NW 67 Terrace, Lauderhill, FL 33319.

Cathy Miller is a Canadian teacher and freelance writer. *Delayed Delivery* first won a short story contest in her hometown of Sudbury, Ontario, in 1992. The following year it was published in *Christmas in My Heart 2*, edited by Joe Wheeler, Review & Herald Publishing, Hagerstown, Maryland. It has since been reprinted in several anthologies and magazines.

Lori S. Mohr is a freelance writer who dedicates her craft to enlightening humanity to the ways of responsible pet parenting. Her versatile and seasoned writing style lends itself to a variety of subject matter, including vegetarianism and celebrity profiles. She also publishes newsletters. You can reach Lori at poochsaver@aol.com, or by calling 1-888-4EZ-CAMP.

Kathleen M. Muldoon is a freelance writer who lives in San Antonio, Texas. She is the author of *Princess Pooh*, a picture book, as well as many other children's stories and articles. The original Ralph died in August of 1996, but she continues to babble to Prissy, a four-year-old black-and-white stray who came to stay last year.

Kathe Neyer has been a Registered Nurse for the past thirty-two years and a longtime volunteer at the Arizona Humane Society. She has been involved with the Samaritan Health Systems in Phoenix and in dog therapy programs since 1993. She is firmly convinced that the power of an animal's unconditional love can benefit the health, mind and spirit of those whose lives they touch.

Dr. Francine (Penny) Patterson is president and director of research of the Gorilla Foundation. She is conducting the longest ongoing interspecies communication project using sign language to communicate with two Western lowland gorillas, Koko and Michael. Reach her at: P.O. Box 620-640, Woodside, CA 94062, or by calling: 800-ME GO APE. E-mail: penny@gorilla.org; www.gorilla.org.

Penny Porter is a former teacher and school administrator. She is one of the most successful freelancers to ever hit *Reader's Digest*. She has published in a wide range of national-circulation magazines, including *Arizona* magazine, *Catholic Digest, Guideposts, Honda* and *Arizona Farmer and Rancher*. Penny is the author of *The Keymaker: Born to Steal* and *Howard's Monster* as well as the biography, *Eugene Gifford Grace*. She lives in Tucson, Arizona, with her husband and continues to write and provide reading and writing workshops for students and adults.

Susan Race, whose family consists of four dogs and two cats, spends most of her free time helping unloved animals through a variety of organizations in the Pittsburgh area. Susan is currently trying to help start a new organization to rehabilitate injured, ill or orphaned wild songbirds. She can be reached at 205 Chan Mowr Dr., Valencia, PA 16059, or by calling 412-898-3275.

Roxanne Willems Snopek Raht is a registered animal health technologist from

Abbotsford, British Columbia. Her life revolves around three daughters, a veterinarian husband, three cats, a cockatiel and a greyhound. She teaches veterinary assistant students, helps manage the couple's animal hospital and writes whenever she can. You can e-mail her at 5alive@bc.sympatico.ca.

Herbert J. (Reb) Rebhan, D.V.M., served in the Peace Corps in Malawi, Central Africa, from July 1984 to October 1986. In addition to his duties as a mixed animal practitioner in Waianae, Hawaii, Herbert is also a marketing consultant and motivational speaker. He can be reached at P.O. Box 493, Waianae, HI 96972.

Monty Roberts was born and raised in Salinas, California. After graduating from high school, he attended college, where he triple majored in biological science, animal husbandry and farm management. He married his wife, Pat, in 1956, and together have three children. They moved to Flag Is Up Farms in the Santa Ynez Valley in 1966, a world-class horse farm that Monty designed, built, landscaped and developed over the past thirty years. Monty's goal in life is "to create a better world for the horse," but he also hopes to have an impact on the human aspect of people relationships.

Honzie L. Rodgers grew up in Texas. He served in World War II with Texas' 36th Infantry Division. He became a Lieutenant Colonel and after the defeat of Germany and Japan, he stayed in the Army, serving in France, Germany, Alaska, Japan, China, Cambodia, Korea, Laos and Thailand. He and his wife lived in Texas until his death on August 15, 1997 at the age of eighty-two.

Susan Roman is a freelance writer and editor living in New York City. She is currently in graduate school for her master's degree. E-mail her at: sroman@mary.fordham.edv.

Roberta Sandler is an award-winning freelance lecturer and travel/lifestyle/features writer. She is the author of *Guide to Florida Historical Walking Tours* (Pineapple Press). She can be reached at 1773 Harborside Circle, Wellington, FL 33414, or by calling 561-795-1106.

Laya Schaetzel-Hawthorne is an artist, choreographer, speaker and healer who has worked throughout Europe and North America. Her hands-on energy healing work and movement-voice teaching have dovetailed into her "SomaSoul" personal and spiritual integration practice. She can be reached at P.O. Box 1366, Fairfield, IA 52556.

Diane M. Smith is an award-winning freelance writer and a certified veterinary technician whose particular interests lie in the fields of feline health and nutrition. Her work has appeared in a number of publications, including *Cats* magazine, *Cat Fancy* and *CATsumer Report*. She is a member of the Cat Writers' Association. Diane lives with her husband, David, and four cats.

Steve Smith is one of America's bestselling outdoor authors. The author of more than a dozen books, he is the editor of *The Retriever Journal* and the managing editor of *The Pointing Dog Journal*.

David E. Sykes is the co-founder and director of the Noah's Ark Animal Foundation. He is also president of a mail-order company affiliated with the Noah's Ark Animal Foundation, that sells healthy and natural pet-care products. He has been rescuing companion animals for ten years and his love for these animals seems to have no limit. For information about the foundation or company write to: P.O. Box 886, Fairfield, IA 52556; or call: 800-501-1100.

Dawn Uittenbogaard works for Village Northwest Unlimited, which is a home for disabled adults, and manages a pet store and kennel. She is married and has two adult children and a house full of pets, of course. This is her first-ever published story. She has lived in rural Iowa her whole life. Dawn can be reached at 3578 Nettle Ave., Sheldon, IA 51201.

Roberta (Rusty) VanSickle, M.S.W., is a certified disability specialist and a published author of disability articles. She has extensive experience in the vocational rehabilitation field. She coordinates an Internet Stroke Support Group for survivors and caregivers. Visit the group's site at rv51@aol.com.

Jennifer Warnes is a two-time Grammy winner and singer of three Oscar-winning film themes who has spent two decades making music for the heart, mind and soul. Contact her at: 2532 Lincoln Blvd., Ste. 500, Marina Del Rey, CA 90291; or at: http://www.jenniferwarnes.com. Her e-mail address is raincoat@jenniferwarnes.com. No song demos are accepted.

Jeff Werber, D.V.M., had been a practicing veterinarian for over fourteen years, during which time he has become one of the nation's foremost media veterinarians. He has served as the on-air pet expert on ABC's *Home Show, Mike and Maty* and *Leeza.* He currently hosts his own show, *Petcetera,* on the Animal Planet Channel. He is also a nationally recognized author and lecturer. He can be reached at 310-559-2530.

Marion Bond West has written for *Guideposts* for over twenty-five years and is a contributing editor. She has authored six books including *The Nevertheless Principle* and is an inspirational speaker. Her pets are a fifteen-year-old "pound cat" and Red Dog who "found her" and, a golden retriever-Lab mix. Marion may be reached at 706-353-6523, or by writing to 1330 DeAndra Dr., Watkinsville, GA 30677.

Diane Williamson grew up in the Midwest and graduated from the University of Iowa. She is an avid reader, journal writer, and lover of gardening and animals. She and her family love life in the country with their many pets. "Camp Williamson" provides pet care for many furry friends when the need arises from their owners.

Richard Wolkomir, in collaboration with his wife, Joyce Rogers Wolkomir, is a contributing writer for the *Smithsonian* magazine and a frequent contributor to other magazines, from *Reader's Digest* to *National Geographic.* The Wolkomirs' book, *Junkyard Bandicoots & Other Tales of the World's Endangered Species,* was published by John Wiley.

Bettie B. Youngs, Ph.D., Ed.D., is a professional speaker and one of the nation's most respected voices in the field of human potential and personal effectiveness. She is the author of fifteen books translated into twenty-nine languages, including the award-winning *Values from the Heartland, Gifts of the Heart: Stories That Celebrate Life's Defining Moments* and *Taste-Berry Tales,* from which her story is adapted.

Rosamond M. Young has written fourteen books in all and is hard at work on another cat tale. The publisher, J.N. Townsend Publishing, specializes in books for animal lovers. For a catalog or information, write to 12 Greenleaf Dr., Exeter, NH 03833, or call 603-778-9883/800-333-9883.

Lynne Layton Zielinski enjoys the friendship of her seven adult children, the magical inspiration of thirteen grandkids and the loving partnership of her husband of forty-one years. Formerly a nurse, now a business owner and always a people-watcher, Lynne believes life is a gift from God, and what we do with it is our gift to God. She tries to write accordingly.

Permissions *(continued from page iv)*

Delayed Delivery. Reprinted by permission of Cathy Miller. ©1997 Cathy Miller.

Frisk. Reprinted by permission of St. Martin's Press, Inc. ©1994 James Herriot, D.V.M. From *James Herriot's Cat Stories* by James Herriot, D.V.M.

Becky and the Wolf and *A Different Kind of Angel.* Reprinted by permission of Penny Porter. ©1997 Penny Porter.

Friends. Reprinted by permission of Karen Del Tufo. ©1997 Karen Del Tufo.

The Puppy Express, An Experiment in Love and *The Deer and the Nursing Home.* Reprinted by permission of The Richard Parks Agency. ©1984 Jo Coudert.

When Snowball Melted. Reprinted by permission of Bonnie Compton Hanson. ©1997 Bonnie Compton Hanson.

Heartstrings. Reprinted by permission of Susan Race. ©1997 Susan Race.

Home and *Dog of War.* Reprinted by permission of Joe Kirkup. ©1997 Joe Kirkup.

Innocent Homeless. Reprinted by permission of Lori. S. Mohr. ©1997 Lori S. Mohr.

Priorities and *The Rescue.* Reprinted with the permission of Simon & Schuster from *Out of Harm's Way* by Terri Crisp and Samantha Glen. ©1996 by Terri Crisp and Samantha Glen.

Pepper's Place. Reprinted by permission of Dawn Uittenbogaard. ©1997 Dawn Uittenbogaard.

Sparkle the Wonder Dog. Reprinted with the permission of Simon & Schuster from *It's Always Something* by Gilda Radner. ©1989 by Gilda Radner; 1990 renewed by The Estate of Gilda Radner.

Pet Love. Reprinted by permission of William Morrow & Company, Inc. ©1983 Betty White and Thomas J. Watson.

Little Lost Dog. "A Long, Long Way" by Donna Chaney, January 1983 appeared in *Positive Living Magazine* as "Little Dog Lost," November/December 1997. Reprinted with permission from *Guideposts* Magazine. ©1982 by *Guideposts,* Carmel, NY 10512.

The Gift of Subira. Reprinted with permission by publisher Health Communications, Inc., Deerfield Beach, Florida, from *Taste-Berry Tales* by Bettie B. Youngs, Ph.D., Ed.D. ©1998 Bettie B. Youngs, Ph.D., Ed. D.

The Dog Next Door. By Jimmy Stewart as told to Richard Schneider, June 1992. Reprinted with permission from *Guideposts* Magazine. ©1992 by *Guideposts,* Carmel, NY 10512.

The Joy of the Run. Reprinted by permission of W. W. Meade. ©1997 W. W. Meade. A version of this story previously appeared in *Reader's Digest* magazine.

Summer of the Raccoons and *The Price of Love.* Reprinted by permission of Fred Bauer in the September and August 1992 *Reader's Digest.* ©1992 Fred Bauer.

Birds, Bees and Guppies. ©Newsday, Inc., 1996. Reprinted with permission.

The Star of the Rodeo. Reprinted by permission of Larry Paul Kline. ©1997 Larry Paul Kline.

Life Lessons from Lovebirds. Reprinted by permission of Vickie Lynne Agee. ©1997 Vickie Lynne Agee.

Cheyenne. "A Pointer Named Cheyenne" by Catherine Moore, October 1995. Reprinted with permission from *Guideposts* Magazine. ©1995 by *Guideposts*, Carmel, NY 10512.

The Gift of Courage. Reprinted by permission of Roxanne Willems Snopek Raht. ©1997 Roxanne Willems Snopek Raht.

Saddle Therapy. Reprinted by permission of Bill Holton. ©1997 Bill Holton. Excerpted from *Woman's World Magazine.*

Kitty Magic. Reprinted by permission of Lynn A. Kerman. ©1997 Lynn A. Kerman.

The Golden Years. Reprinted by permission of Yvonne A. Martell. ©1997 Yvonne A. Martell.

Swimming with Dolphins. Reprinted by permission of Roberta (Rusty) VanSickle. ©1997 Roberta (Rusty) VanSickle, M.S.W.

There's a Squirrel in My Coffee! Reprinted by permission of Bill Goss. ©1997 Bill Goss.

Finders Keepers. Reprinted by permission of Leona Campbell. ©1997 Leona Campbell.

Seeing. Reprinted by permission of Kathe Neyer. ©1997 Kathe Neyer.

Guardian Angels. Reprinted by permission of Richard Wolkomir. ©1997 Richard Wolkomir.

A Real Charmer. Reprinted by permission of Lynne Zielinski. ©1997 Lynne Zielinski.

Socks. Reprinted by permission of Steve Smith. ©1997 Steve Smith.

Jenny and Brucie. Reprinted by permission of Cerie L. Couture, D.V.M. ©1997 Cerie L. Couture, D.V.M.

An Extra Ten Minutes. Reprinted by permission of Mary Marcdante. ©1997 Mary Marcdante.

The Language of Horses. Reprinted by permission of Monty Roberts. ©1997 Monty Roberts.

Lucky to Be Alive. Reprinted by permission of Christine E. Belleris. ©1997 Christine E. Belleris.

Turkeys. Reprinted by permission of Addison Wesley Longman, Inc. ©1993 Bailey White. Excerpted from *Mama Makes Up Her Mind* by Bailey White.

Tiny and the Oak Tree. Reprinted by permission of Dennis K. McIntosh, D.V.M. ©1997 Dennis K. McIntosh, D.V.M.

The Captain. Reprinted by permission of David Sykes. ©1997 David Sykes.

The Woman Who Took Chickens Under Her Wing. Reprinted by permission of Earl Holliman. ©1997 Earl Holliman.

Miracles Do Happen. Reprinted by permission of Paul H. King, D.V.M. ©1997 Paul H. King, D.V.M.

Darlene. Reprinted by permission of Sara (Robinson) Mark, D.V.M. ©1997 Sara (Robinson) Mark, D.V.M.

The Little Dog That Nobody Wanted. Reprinted by permission of Jan K. Stewart Bass. ©1997 Jan K. Stewart Bass.

Buffalo Games. Excerpted from WINTERDANCE: THE FINE MADNESS OF RUNNING THE IDITAROD, ©1994 by Gary Paulsen, reprinted by permission of the publisher.

Doctola. Reprinted by permission of Herbert J. Rebhan, D.V.M. ©1997 Herbert J. Rebhan, D.V.M.

A Mother's Love. Reprinted by permission of David Giannelli. ©1997 David Giannelli.

The Eyes of Tex. Reprinted by permission of Mrs. Honzie L. Rodgers. ©1997 Honzie L. Rodgers.

The Christmas Mouse. Reprinted by permission of Diane M. Smith. ©1997 Diane M. Smith.

Juneau's Official Greeter. Reprinted by permission of Roberta Sandler. ©1997 Roberta Sandler.

Simon. From *Two Perfectly Marvellous Cats: A True Story,* by Rosamond M. Young. Reprinted by permission of J. N. Townsend Publishing. ©1996 by J. N. Townsend Publishing.

The Ugly Pupling. Reprinted by permission of Angel Di Benedetto. ©1997 Angel Di Benedetto.

Babblers Anonymous. Reprinted by permission of Kathleen M. Muldoon. ©1997 Kathleen M. Muldoon.

A Damaged Dog. Reprinted by permission of Roma Ihnatowycz. ©1997 Roma Ihnatowycz.

A French Cat. Reprinted by permission of Jean Brody. ©1997 Jean Brody.

A Lesson in Love. Reprinted by permission of Pam Johnson. ©1997 Pam Johnson.

Tailless Tom. Reprinted with the permission of Simon & Schuster from *All My Patients Are Under the Bed* by Louis J. Camuti. ©1980 Dr. Louis J. Camuti, Marilyn and Haskel Frankel.

The White House Dog. ©1990 by the Barbara Bush Foundation for Literacy. By permission of William Morrow & Company, Inc.

Barney. Reprinted by permission of Gregg Bassett. ©1997 Gregg Bassett.

Mousekeeping. Reprinted by permission of Faith McNulty. ©1997 Faith McNulty.

The Cat and the Grizzly. Reprinted by permission of Dave Siddon and Jane Martin. ©1997 Dave Siddon and Jane Martin.

Fine Animal Gorilla. Reprinted by permission of Francine (Penny) Patterson, D.V.M. ©1997 Francine (Penny) Patterson, D.V.M.

Forever Rocky. Reprinted by permission of S.C. Edwards. ©1997 S.C. Edwards.

The Lone Duck. By Marion Bond West, April 1992. Reprinted with permission from *Guideposts* Magazine. ©1992 *Guideposts,* Carmel, NY 10512.

Soul to Soul. Reprinted by permission of Carolyn Butler, M.S. and Laurel Lagoni, M.S. ©1997 Carolyn Butler, M.S. and Laurel Lagoni, M.S.

That Dog Disguise Isn't Fooling Anyone. Reprinted by permission of Jennifer Warnes and Shawnacy Kiker. ©1997 Jennifer Warnes and Shawnacy Kiker.

Rites of Passage. Reprinted by permission of Robin Downing, D.V.M. ©1997 Robin Downing, D.V.M.

Toto's Last Christmas. Reprinted by permission of Janet Foley, D.V.M. ©1997 Janet Foley, D.V.M.

Good Neighbors. Reprinted by permission of Marion Bond West. ©1997 Marion Bond West.

The Cat and the Cat Burglar. Reprinted by permission of Laya Schaetzel-Hawthorne. ©1997 Laya Schaetzel-Hawthorne.

The Auction. From *MAYBE (MAYBE NOT)* by Robert Fulghum. ©1993 by Robert Fulghum. Reprinted by permission of Villard Books, a division of Random House, Inc.

Sing We Noel. Reprinted by permission of Toni Fulco. ©1997 Toni Fulco.

Taking the Zip Out of Zippy. From DAVE BARRY TALKS BACK by Dave Barry. ©1992 by Dave Barry. Reprinted by permission of Crown Publishers, Inc.

The Ice Breaker. Reprinted by permission of Diane Williamson. ©1997 Diane Williamson.

Kids Say the Darndest Things—About Dogs. Reprinted by permission of Art Linkletter. ©1997 Art Linkletter.

Let Sleeping Dogs Lie. Reprinted by permission of Susan F. Roman. ©1997 Susan F. Roman.

The Legacy. Reprinted by permission of Jeff Werber, D.V.M. ©1997 Jeff Werber, D.V.M.

The Truth About Annie. Reprinted by permission of Judy Doyle. ©1997 Judy Doyle.

A Vet's Wages. Reprinted by permission of George Baker, D.V.M. ©1997 George Baker, D.V.M.

PUPPIES FOR SALE
and Other Inspirational Tales
A "Litter" of Stories & Anecdotes That Hug the Heart & Snuggle the Soul
DAN CLARK
One of the best-loved storytellers from the
#1 New York Times Bestseller
Chicken Soup for the Soul®
with
Michael Gale